T0305472

Roads, Runways and Resistance

Roads, Runways and Resistance

From the Newbury Bypass
to Extinction Rebellion

Steve Melia

First published 2021 by Pluto Press
345 Archway Road, London N6 5AA

www.plutobooks.com

Copyright © Steve Melia 2021

The right of Steve Melia to be identified as the author of this work has been
asserted in accordance with the Copyright Designs and Patents Act 1988

British Library Cataloguing in Publication Data
A catalogue record for this book is available from the British Library

ISBN   978 0 7453 4057 9   Hardback
ISBN   978 0 7453 4059 3   Paperback
ISBN   978 1 7868 0798 4   PDF eBook
ISBN   978 1 7868 0800 4   Kindle eBook
ISBN   978 1 7868 0799 1   EPUB eBook

Typeset by Stanford DTP Services, Northampton, England
Printed and bound by CPI Group (UK) Ltd, Croydon, CR0 4YY

Contents

Preface

This book tells a 30-year story of the most controversial issues in transport in the UK and the protest movements they provoked. Between 2017 and 2020 I interviewed over 50 government ministers, civil servants, political advisers, lobbyists, activists and protest leaders. Their stories and thousands of documents, published and unpublished, have unearthed many surprises. I did not expect to be writing a crime or spy story, but fraud, violence, spying, sexual 'misdemeanours' and ambivalent actions by the police all feature at different points; so does lobbying by interest groups, but not necessarily in the ways you might expect.

For over 30 years I have observed these events, as a would-be politician, a local campaigner and then an academic. I played a minor role in several of the earlier episodes, but I had no idea when I started researching this book that I would eventually become a direct participant.

The story begins when Margaret Thatcher's government announced 'the biggest road-building programme since the Romans', provoking the biggest protests ever seen against road-building in Britain. Twyford Down, the Newbury Bypass and a human mole nicknamed 'Swampy' became part of the history and mythology of a generation, who may have forgotten the politics and the ultimate outcome of that conflict. Chapters 1 and 4 will tell the political story, while Chapters 2 and 3 will tell the story on the ground through the words of the protestors and an under-sheriff tasked with removing them.

Chapter 5 tells the story of a brief interlude when the New Labour government under John Prescott tried, with limited success, to re-orient transport policy away from road-building and car-based travel. Political interests, personal conflicts and bad luck were all hampering Prescott's strategy when a handful of farmers and hauliers brought the nation to a standstill in protest at rising fuel taxes in 2000. That protest was short-lived but its impact has endured in ways which few would have expected at the time. Chapter 6 tells the inside story of the protestors and those in government who set out to foil them by all available means.

Chapter 7 explains how a government which gave local authorities powers to introduce congestion charging, then tried to undermine the first local leader planning to use those powers. Despite their efforts, Ken Livingstone, the first Mayor of London, introduced congestion charging in central London in 2003. London was supposed to be the first of many, until motoring campaigners mobilised to prevent charging in other cities and halt the government's plans for national road pricing. Chapter 7 explains how they did it.

Chapters 8 and 9 tell how campaigners and changing political circumstances halted the seemingly inexorable expansion of Heathrow and other airports in southeast England. They reveal for the first time how protestors unmasked a spy and evaded security to climb onto the roof of the House of Commons as the government launched a sham consultation in 2008.

Previous protests against airport expansion were motivated by purely local concerns, such as aircraft noise and traffic generation but by the mid-2000s climate change was becoming a bigger issue for protestors and transport policy. Chapter 8 describes one such campaign, the Big Ask, which led to the UK Climate Change Act and similar legislation in several other countries. It was one of the most successful environmental campaigns of all time, and yet it has been largely forgotten today, for reasons explained in Chapter 15.

By contrast, the long-running campaigns against high-speed rail, described in Chapters 10 and 11, have made some of the biggest impacts on political debate and public consciousness but have been less successful in achieving their aims. Those chapters explain how governments became locked-in to a project plagued by delays, ballooning budgets, whistle-blowing scandals and conflict with local communities.

The decisions to approve and confirm HS2 reflected a change in official ideology after the recession of 2009; big infrastructure was back. In 2013 the Coalition government trebled the national road-building budget despite ongoing austerity for most public spending. Chapter 12 explains the changing political climate that led to those decisions and also claimed the political scalp of a minister who tried to maintain her party's manifesto commitment not to expand Heathrow Airport.

Chapters 1–12 recount these events in the words of the people involved, keeping my own views and analysis to a minimum. That will change in Chapters 13 and 14, which tell a more personal story. By early 2019 I was becoming increasingly worried about the warnings of climate scientists and frustrated at the lack of action by governments, so I decided to join a newly formed movement called Extinction Rebellion (XR). In April 2019 I took part in actions which brought central London to a standstill, landing me in Westminster Magistrates' Court and on the scrupulously accurate pages of the *Daily Mail*. Along the way I met several of the leaders of this 'leaderless movement'. Chapters 13 and 14 tell how a handful of British activists with a history of false starts ignited an international movement and scored some big early successes, despite internal tensions and some tactical mistakes.

How much difference did the protest movements make, and what tactics are more or less likely to work? Chapter 15 will address both of those questions, using road-building as an example. Alongside this book, I wrote a research article which explains why Conservative governments decided to slash the road-building budget in the late 1990s but treble it during a period of austerity after 2013.[1] Protest (or its absence) acting on public opinion was part of the answer. Other factors included a change in economic ideology and a rational response by governments to past failures.

Governments do occasionally act rationally, but civil disobedience may also be necessary to make them take notice of evidence and act on expert advice. That is particularly true of climate change and the threat of wider ecological collapse. XR has made governments notice but their responses remain inadequate. In most of this book I write as an external observer, but in Chapter 15 I am partly addressing my fellow members of XR. Our tactics have worked well so far, but to compel governments to act we now need a change of strategy. The main conclusion of Chapter 15 is that protest movements rarely, if ever, achieve their aims directly. Public opinion makes the difference between their success and failure; XR now needs new tactics to influence public opinion and increase pressure on decision-makers.

I finished the first draft of this book shortly before COVID-19 confounded transport expectations and forced protest movements, along with the rest of the population, into lockdown. I decided not to change the main text, but will comment on the uncertainties we now face in an afterword.

Chapters 1–12 are interspersed with quotes from my interviews. Many of them reveal sensitive information; some reveal conflicts and dirty tricks at the heart of government. Some people were happy to speak on the record but I have anonymised others and changed a few details to protect identities.

Timeline of Events

Year	Political Events	Transport Policy	Protest Movements
1989	Margaret Thatcher Prime Minister (PM)	Roads for Prosperity	
1990	John Major PM	Trunk Roads England	
1991	Recession begins		
1992			Twyford Down protest begins
1993			Anti-roads protests
1994		Review of transport policy	Anti-roads protests
1995		Newbury Bypass approved	Reclaim the Streets formed
1996		Road programme cut back	Newbury Bypass
1997	Tony Blair PM	Road Traffic Reduction Act	Anti-roads protests end
1998		Integrated Transport White Paper	
1999		Heathrow Terminal 5 approved	
2000	Ken Livingstone Mayor of London	Transport Ten Year Plan Government cuts fuel taxes	Fuel tax protests HACAN Clearskies formed
2001			
2002			
2003		London congestion charge Aviation White Paper	
2004		White Paper encouraging road pricing	

Year	Political Events	Transport Policy	Protest Movements
2005		Edinburgh road pricing referendum	The Big Ask launched
2006			National road pricing Plane Stupid formed
2007	Gordon Brown PM Credit crunch leading to recession	Government abandons road pricing	Manchester Against Road Tolling (MART) formed
2008	Climate Change Act	Manchester road pricing referendum Heathrow third runway approved	
2009			
2010	Coalition government	Plans for HS2 published	Stop HS2 formed
2011			51M formed
2012			
2013		Investing in Britain's Future trebles roads budget	
2014		Parliament passes HS2 Hybrid Bill	51M negotiates compromises
2015	David Cameron PM with a majority	Roads Investment Strategy 1	
2016	Brexit referendum Theresa May PM		Rising Up! formed
2017			
2018		Roads Investment Strategy 2	Extinction Rebellion formed
2019	Net zero legislation Boris Johnson PM	Oakervee Review into HS2	Spring and autumn rebellions
2020		Bristol Airport expansion refused HS2 confirmed Court of Appeal rejects Airports National Policy Statement	

List of Abbreviations

ABD	Association of British Drivers
AGHAST	Action Groups Against HS2
AGMA	Association of Greater Manchester Authorities
ALARM	All London Against the Roadbuilding Menace
ALARM UK	national organisation which grew from ALARM
AONB	Area of Outstanding Natural Beauty
BAA	British Airports Authority (later privatised – the owners of Heathrow)
BAAN	Bristol Airport Action Network
BRF	British Roads Federation
CAT	Centre for Alternative Technology
CBI	Confederation of British Industry
COBRA	Cabinet Office Briefing Room A (where governments hold emergency meetings)
DEFRA	Department of the Environment, Farming and Rural Affairs
DETR	Department of the Environment, Transport and the Regions (1997–2001)
DfT	Department for Transport (2002 onwards)
DTI	Department of Trade and Industry
DTLR	Department of Transport, Local Government and the Regions (2001–2)
DTp	Department of Transport (until 1997)
EDM	Early Day Motion (in parliament)
FoE	Friends of the Earth
GLA	Greater London Assembly (2000 onwards)
GLC	Greater London Council (until 1986)
HACAN	Heathrow Association for the Control of Aircraft Noise (later HACAN Clearskies)
MART	Manchester Against Road Tolls
MP	Member of Parliament
NAO	National Audit Office

NHS	National Health Service
PFL	People's Fuel Lobby
RAC	Royal Automobile Club
RJRF	Rees Jeffreys Road Fund
SACTRA	Standing Committee on Trunk Road Assessment
SRA	Strategic Rail Authority
SSSI	Site of Special Scientific Interest
TIF	Transport Investment Fund
WWF	World Wildlife Fund (later World Wide Fund for Nature)
XR	Extinction Rebellion

Acknowledgements

I would like to extend a big thank you to the many people, named and anonymised, who gave up their time to be interviewed, or who helped me with access to documents. I would like to congratulate the Freedom of Information sections of several public authorities, particularly the Cabinet Office, for the creativity they displayed in their reasons for withholding information.

The research was greatly assisted by a travel grant from the University of the West of England – I did a lot of travelling across Britain during the course of the interviews, all of it by train!

1

The Biggest Road-Building
Programme Since the Romans
(1989–92)

In 1992 a small group of protestors formed a chain, trying to stop contractors on the route of a planned new road. One of them locked himself to the axle of a lifting machine, which the contractors started up, threatening the life of the man below. His supporters, held behind a cordon, surged forward, calling on the police to intervene, which they eventually did.

Those few protestors had struck the first blow in a struggle which would initially last for five years, provoke a backlash from other campaigners, and recur in different ways over the following three decades. Conflict is endemic to transport, conflict between humanity's desire for movement and resistance to the damage caused by attempts to satisfy that desire. This book will tell the story of that conflict over those three decades.

To understand what provoked that group of protestors we must go back to May 1989 when Paul Channon, UK Transport Secretary, stood up in the House of Commons to announce that he was 'more than doubling' the national road-building programme. He spoke with the confidence of political support, a booming economy, a national Treasury in surplus for the first time since the 1970s and a widespread consensus that faster road-building was urgently needed. 'Roads for Prosperity', the title of the new transport White Paper, boldly announced the government's top transport objective and the justification for it. One road lobbyist described it as 'a strategic plan that really looked long-term' but there was little sign of strategic thinking in the White Paper itself. The text was only eight pages long. It stated that traffic had increased by a third since 1980 and forecast that it could more than double again by 2025. It talked of the evils of congestion and explained why expanding the rail network would make little difference to road traffic. Higher taxes on road users might reduce demand but they were already highly taxed; the only solution was a 'step change' in road-building.

A single paragraph mentioned the environment, claiming that bypasses would bring welcome relief to local communities and promising to 'take all reasonable measures to minimise any adverse effects'. An appendix listed 168 proposed road schemes that would create or widen 2,700 miles of motorways or national roads across England (Scotland and Wales would also receive a similar increase in funding for roads). Two of the most controversial schemes, Twyford Down and the Newbury Bypass, had not yet gained ministerial approval and many schemes in London were awaiting the outcome of an assessment study, but several schemes on the list would provoke mass protests and transform the lives of the people I interviewed for Chapters 2 and 3.

All of that lay in a future that would have seemed unimaginable to Paul Channon as he listened to a succession of MPs 'warmly welcoming' the plan that would bring new or wider roads to their constituencies. Channon was fortunate to have as his principal opponent John Prescott, whose response for the Labour opposition was riddled with contradictions. He berated the Conservative government for 'complacency and inactivity' that had caused the growth in congestion, comparing this to European countries that had planned for rising car ownership with 'road improvements', which Labour supported in principle. He claimed that transport users were overtaxed and then posed the following questions:

> Does the Secretary of State accept that 10-lane super-highways speeding traffic into the cities are useless if chronic congestion means that it cannot move in the cities when it arrives there? What effect will the White Paper's plans have on the environment, especially in respect of vehicle emissions?[1]

'It was rather difficult' Channon replied 'to discover whether the hon. Gentleman was in favour' of the plan or not and added that if Prescott didn't like it, he could cancel the two road schemes proposed for Prescott's Hull constituency. The idea that many people might want to cancel road schemes in their areas did not seem to occur to many in the House that day. Several MPs, including Prescott, called for more investment in rail but only the maverick Labour member Tony Banks attacked the principles behind the plan. It was 'motorway madness', he said, and 'a great big transfer of cash from the taxpayer to the British Road Federation lobby, as represented here by Conservative Members'.[2]

A Victory for the British Roads Federation

'Roads for Prosperity' was a major victory for the road lobby and the British Road Federation in particular. The BRF was 'an alliance of interests'; its members were all companies or other organisations. Their board included representatives from the motor industry, motoring organisations, oil companies and aggregate industries that supplied the road-builders. Following cuts to the trunk roads budget in 1987, the BRF's archives describe a 'year-long campaign... at national and local level' to reverse the cuts and achieve a longer-term commitment to road-building and widening. A joint review of roads policy involving the Treasury and the Department for Transport (DTp) offered an opportunity for influence.

Early in 1988 Peter Bottomley, the junior transport minister responsible for roads, invited the Chairman and Director of the BRF for 'an informal discussion in his office'. Bottomley was 'at pains to suggest that delays in the bypass programme were entirely procedural and in no way due to lack of funds', the BRF noted, adding that 'our response was to politely disagree'. In March 1988 they 'entertained to lunch' MPs on the all-party Transport Select Committee, taking the opportunity to 'raise our concerns'.

The hospitality activities of the BRF provoked much criticism. A researcher for a shadow minister of transport recounted how they took him to lunch at the Waldorf Hotel.[3] A Labour Member of Parliament (MP) reported how he was invited to a lunch by Lancashire County Council to discuss the County's road strategy and then discovered that it was organised and funded by the BRF. Richard Diment, who joined the BRF in 1985 and later became its director, believed these criticisms were unfair:

This used to really annoy me – accusations that we were spending millions on expensive functions. Our budget was in six figures [£360,000 in 1989]; we had six to eight staff most of the time I was there. Other lobby groups, including those who were bitterly opposed to the road-building programme, did this kind of thing. If you can persuade a member of parliament to sponsor a meeting, if you are prepared to pick up the catering bill, it's normally just tea, coffee and a slice of cake or a sandwich.

The size of the BRF's budgets may have been exaggerated but they were considerably larger than those of Transport 2000, their main opponent at the time. Transport 2000 was funded by the subscriptions of individuals and the public transport unions. It campaigned for more investment in public transport and against large-scale road-building. Their director Stephen Joseph recalled: 'We were very much "outside track"; we would have a few low-level meetings with officials but no one important in the Department of Transport would talk to us, back then.'

The BRF, on the other hand, were very much on the inside track. An internal report noted that their lunch for the members of the Transport Committee had 'provoked a number of probing parliamentary questions and, with the BRF's subsequent submission to the Committee, provided the basis for the detailed and persistent grilling of DTp officials at a subsequent Committee hearing.' In July 1988, the Committee produced a report, which the BRF noted 'relied extensively on the BRF submission'. The Committee cited the BRF's analysis of traffic flows to support its conclusion that the Government 'should urgently review the case for providing more trunk road capacity'.

The following month Paul Channon invited the Chairman and Director of the BRF for 'a friendly informal chat'. 'Discussion centred on the need for more resources to accelerate the trunk road programme' and Channon asked the BRF for 'more specific examples from individual companies of the benefits of good roads and/or the cost of inadequate ones'. By this stage the usual relationship between lobbyists and ministers had been reversed; Channon was already convinced; he needed more ammunition from the BRF to persuade the Treasury and the Prime Minister to allocate more funds.

The Chancellor of the Exchequer Nigel Lawson was sympathetic to the road lobby but he and most of the Conservative cabinet had an ideological preference for private finance. If ways could be found to build new roads without increasing public spending, then there was no problem but any minister seeking a big increase in their budget would meet resistance from the Treasury. The Adam Smith Institute, a think tank with links to the right wing of the Conservative Party, advocated privatisation of roads and road pricing – charging motorists for the use of roads – an idea endorsed by the Confederation of British Industry (CBI).

The BRF found the CBI's attitude 'particularly disturbing'. The BRF accepted the principle of private finance and even some tolling, of new bridges for example, as long as this was additional to major investment in new public roads, which were free to use. At their private meeting Channon conceded that private finance would make 'only a marginal contribution'. In November 1988 he made a speech to the Adam Smith Institute rejecting the privatisation of existing roads 'tempting as it might seem'. There would be no general policy of tolling new motorways but he would encourage the private sector to look for opportunities where new toll roads or bridges might 'attract road users'.

The success of Channon's negotiations was confirmed a few days before 'Roads for Prosperity' when Treasury Secretary John Major announced that rules restricting private finance for public projects were to be relaxed. Any private schemes would be additional to the publicly funded roads, as the BRF had advocated.

Reactions to 'Roads for Prosperity'

Media reaction to 'Roads for Prosperity' was overwhelmingly positive. Support from the Conservative press was hyperbolic; *The Times* led with Channon's phrase that this would be 'the biggest road-building programme since the Romans'. The *Daily Express* described the White Paper as 'nothing short of a miracle'. More surprising, in retrospect, was the reaction of the non-Conservative papers. The Independent described the plans as 'better late than never'. *The Guardian* also attacked the government for its past inaction and asked 'will this increased level of investment be enough?' Several business and motoring organisations expressed their enthusiastic support. The CBI estimated that congestion was costing the average household £10 a week and said 'two years ago this package would have been beyond our wildest dreams'. The BRF was equally enthusiastic about 'Roads for Prosperity', at first. Its minutes noted that the White Paper included 'virtually every addition to the trunk programme for which the Federation has been campaigning ... either as firm proposals or as part of a study'.

The initial press reports devoted just a few lines to a token statement of dissent from an environmental organisation. Transport 2000 called for more investment in rail instead; Friends of the Earth criticised a 'knee-jerk reaction' and said 'Mr Channon knows that these new roads will be as congested as ever within a few years'. That statement was a rare challenge to the conventional beliefs that building or widening roads would reduce congestion and boost the economy. The White Paper repeated one of those beliefs; it claimed that new roads would 'assist economic growth'; but it was more ambiguous about congestion. It stated that new and wider roads would be 'the main way to deal with' inter-urban congestion; but what did that phrase mean? Would congestion improve, or grow worse more slowly? And what difference would inter-urban road-building make to congestion in towns and cities? The White Paper made no predictions; the reader was left to infer that more roads must be good for congestion. Over the following years both of those beliefs would be more widely challenged.

One future challenge to conventional beliefs about road-building began in 1989 with an offer of funding from an unlikely source. William Rees Jeffreys was a pioneering road engineer, an early advocate of motorways in the UK. In 1950 he set up a charitable trust, the Rees Jeffreys Road Fund (RJRF) to continue his work. The BRF regarded the RJRF as a sympathetic source of research funding. They were alarmed in 1989 when the trustees of the RJRF decided to concentrate their funding on a major research project called 'Transport and Society', to be led by Oxford academic Phil Goodwin. The BRF regarded Goodwin and most of his collaborators as 'anti-road'; the Chairmen of the BRF and the Freight Transport Association met the Chairman of the RJRF to 'express their concern' about this. Whatever they said failed to sway the trustees and Goodwin was allowed to continue his work over the next two years. When the BRF approached the RJRF again, to fund one of its own ideas, they were told that it would have to come within the 'Transport and Society' project, managed by Goodwin.

After the initial rush of enthusiasm for 'Roads for Prosperity', the BRF began to reserve judgement on the government's progress. The White Paper contained little detail; the junior minister for roads promised a 'full roads report' later that year but it was delayed. Although the government was committed to spending more money on roads, public spending was controlled by the Treasury on a year-by-year basis. The plan would depend on decisions made in future budgets and that would leave opportunities for opponents to delay or frustrate it.

The environmental organisations took a few months to coordinate their response to 'Roads for Prosperity'. Nine of them, including Transport 2000, Friends of the Earth, the Council for the Protection of Rural England and the World-Wide Fund for Nature issued a joint statement in September 1989 entitled 'Roads to Ruin'. It condemned the plan for threatening air quality, wildlife and the countryside; it called for more spending on public transport and for a joint committee between the DTp and the Department of the Environment (DoE) to resolve the 'contradiction of policy between the two'.

Conflict between Transport and the Environment under Mrs Thatcher

The environmental organisations wanted to involve the DoE in transport policy because their relations with that department were better than with the DTp; they believed some ministers and civil servants at the DoE shared their concerns. Previous actions of the DoE had not always inspired such confidence. Things began to change after June 1989, when the Green Party achieved its highest ever share of the vote in European elections (15%). The Conservatives dropped behind Labour for the first time in a European election. A month later Prime Minister Mrs Thatcher implemented a wide-ranging ministerial reshuffle. One of her targets was the Environment Secretary Nicholas Ridley, an abrasive right-winger with little sympathy for the green movement. Sir George Young, formerly one of Ridley's junior ministers, publicly called for him to be replaced by someone with 'more conviction and credibility'.

Thatcher replaced Ridley with Chris Patten, a moderate Conservative who was more sympathetic to the environmentalists. In an hour-long meeting she reportedly briefed him to 'see off the Green Party' by strengthening the government's green credentials. One of his junior ministers, David Trippier, signalled a 'U-turn' in the government's attitudes by inviting environmental organisations to come and talk to him.

At the same time Thatcher decided to replace Paul Channon as Transport Secretary. Among her reasons for that decision dissatisfaction with 'Roads for Prosperity' did not appear to feature. Channon's tenure at the DTp had been unlucky. The press cited two rail crashes, the Zeebrugge ferry disaster (which actually occurred just before he took over) and even the Lockerbie air explosion, caused by a bomb planted in Germany, as reasons for his departure from the cabinet. His replacement by Cecil Parkinson, one of Thatcher's closest allies, sent a signal that transport was moving up the political agenda.

Parkinson was the seventh Transport Secretary in ten years of Thatcher's governments, a pattern of rapid turnover which her successors would perpetuate. He took the job 'with some reluctance' and found a department that 'felt under siege waiting nervously for the next disaster and the next round of criticism'.[4] To restore the confidence of his new department Parkinson believed the DTp needed a bigger budget, for 'investment, not subsidy'. He regarded 'Roads for Prosperity' as 'ambitious and necessary', an essential element of the 'balanced transport policy' he would promote, in contrast to Labour's 'unbalanced' plans to 'discriminate against the private motorist'.

With these ministerial changes Thatcher triggered a conflict between the departments responsible for transport and environmental protection, which would recur many times in different ways over the next three decades. The conflicting priorities of the DTp and DoE reflected Thatcher's own divergent views on transport and the environment. On the few occasions when she mentioned transport, she made clear her preference for travel by car and her support for road-building, but she also expressed serious concerns about environmental degradation, and climate change in particular. Her background as a research chemist made her receptive to the evidence emerging from British climate research institutes. Addressing the United Nations Assembly in November 1989 she quoted a letter she had received from a British scientist in the Antarctic Ocean, describing 'a significant thinning of the sea ice' and warning of 'runaway' climate change that might become 'irreversible'. In response she proposed an international agreement with binding targets for each country to reduce its greenhouse gases, a proposal which would eventually form the basis of the Kyoto Protocol nine years later.

Many years later, Nigel Lawson, Thatcher's former Chancellor and a leading climate 'sceptic', questioned whether she really believed what she said in public about climate change.[5] John Selwyn Gummer (now Lord Deben), who wrote some of her earlier speeches and later became Environment Secretary, who I interviewed in 2019, is scathing about these claims: 'She not only "got it" but you could see that she "got it" … There is no argument about what she really meant, except by those for whom it is embarrassing.'

Although Thatcher appreciated the scientific evidence and understood the need for action, she did express concerns, which grew more strident in her later years, that climate change might be used as an excuse to attack multi-national companies and promote 'worldwide supra-national socialism'.[6] If some activities needed to be constrained for environmental reasons, her preference, shared by most of her cabinet colleagues, was to use pricing mechanisms, rather than laws, regulations, or planning at a national level. When asked why Britain did not have a national transport strategy Parkinson said he was 'sceptical about integrated national plans' associating them with the communism that was crumbling in Eastern Europe.[7]

Patten was less averse to planning or regulations but found an alternative strategy closer to Conservative preferences lying in his in-tray at the DoE. His predecessor, Nicholas Ridley, had commissioned a report, from a group of economists led by David Pearce. Its main argument was that the value of the environment could and should be priced in monetary terms; the 'price' of environmental damage should be included when making public decisions, on road-building for example, and added as a tax on products with environmental impacts, such as petrol and diesel. Ridley had quietly filed the report; Patten decided to publicise it and invited Pearce to become his adviser.

Over the next few months Patten and Parkinson clashed in private and occasionally in the media over the future direction of transport policy, and road-building in particular. While Parkinson was lobbying the Treasury for more money to implement 'Roads for Prosperity', Patten announced a review of all government policy affecting the environment. It would consider Pearce's approach but also the need for 'government to regulate on behalf of the community'. Talking to journalists at the CBI conference in November 1989 he challenged the traffic forecasts behind 'Roads for Prosperity': 'Even if you were to deal with emissions while at the same time having an enormous increase in the vehicles on the roads, you would lose many of the gains...so we are obviously going to need to look at the future of transport policy.'[8] When the Transport Select Committee questioned Parkinson about his reported conflict with Patten, he replied: 'He and I will work together to reduce the environmental impact of growth, but we have to accept that growth will occur.'

Although Patten made progress on some issues, he ultimately failed to change the direction of transport policy. In February 1990 Parkinson published 'Trunk Roads England – into the 1990s', updating 'Roads for Prosperity', adding some new schemes and providing more detail on the others. It responded to environmental concerns in three ways, starting by emphasising the benefits of bypasses for towns and villages. The report confirmed that Parkinson had won a big commitment from the Treasury. Over the following three years the budget for new motorways and national roads would increase by 50 per cent, after allowing for inflation. Twenty new schemes were added to the list in 'Roads for Prosperity', including the Newbury Bypass and the missing link in the M3 near Twyford Down in Hampshire. Several schemes in London were listed for the first time, including the M11 Link Road and the East London River Crossing, both of which would spark big protests in the years to come. Maps of each region showed the proposed schemes 'in diagrammatic form', with a note that precise routes were yet to be decided.

The hopes of the environmentalists that Patten might soften the government's road-building plans were disappointed a week later, when he and Parkinson jointly announced a decision about the missing link in the M3; it would pass in a cutting the height of a six-storey building, and four times as wide, through the chalk hill of Twyford Down. This scheme was particularly controversial because it lay within a protected Area of Outstanding Natural Beauty; it would damage several archaeological sites and a protected water meadow (a

Site of Special Scientific Interest), which inspired John Keats to write 'Ode to Autumn'. An embankment, the height of a house, would raise the motorway to meet the cutting, elevating the noise and scarring the landscape over a wide area.

These proposals had already been through two public inquiries; a local group, led by two Conservative councillors and a landscape architect (who later formed the Twyford Down Association) had been fighting the scheme since 1985. They accepted the need for the motorway but were arguing for a tunnel through Twyford Down. Their first response was to seek a judicial review. When the High Court found against them, their next step was to appeal to the European Commission, as opponents of the East London River Crossing had already done. These moves would start another chain of events with far-reaching longer-term consequences.

As local groups formed or expanded to fight a growing number of road schemes, the media, which had welcomed 'Roads for Prosperity', became more critical of individual schemes. An editorial in *The Times* attacked the Twyford Down decision as 'motorway madness' and backed the opponents' call for a tunnel.[9] The Independent dubbed plans for the East London River Crossing, with a road through the ancient Oxleas Wood: 'the Greenwich Chain-saw Massacre'.

Worse still for Parkinson, two of the government's own advisory bodies, the Countryside Commission and English Heritage, attacked the government's plans in public. A report published by English Heritage in October 1990 estimated that road-building would destroy or partially destroy 5,000 archaeological sites. This estimate particularly riled Parkinson who described the report as 'a warped projection ... nothing more than guesswork'.[10]

The First Battleground: London

Although 'Roads for Prosperity' was mainly focussed on inter-urban routes some new roads were planned through urban areas. 'Trunk Roads England' argued that 'the construction and improvement of trunk roads can ... help to restore the vitality of inner city areas by relieving traffic congestion, making them more attractive places for people to live and work'. Residents of urban areas did not always agree. Plans for a network of motorways within London had provoked widespread protests in the early 1970s. They were abandoned after the Conservatives lost control of the Greater London Council in 1973. This history made the Thatcher Government more cautious about road-building in London. The BRF noted that 'the government was reluctant to take any decisions over London. MPs were anxious to look after their individual constituencies without due regard to the overall benefits to the Capital'.[11]

One way for politicians to defuse opposition to controversial proposals is to set up a long-running review process. The London Assessment Studies began in 1984 as a study of traffic problems along four trunk road corridors. A second stage, investigating potential solutions, was awarded to four transport consultancies looking at different sectors of London. The BRF was involved in every stage. In March 1988, before the terms of reference for the second stage study had been made public, three of the consultants approached the BRF 'to make confidential submissions' to them about two of the corridors.[12]

When the second stage of the study was publicly launched in July 1988 it caused outrage. Forty-eight options, mainly involving new roads, would be assessed. In total 5,000 homes were put at risk of demolition, some of them in wealthy Conservative-voting neighbourhoods such as Kensington, Chelsea and Wandsworth. As opponents pointed out, one of the road schemes would route traffic away from the home of Paul Channon; another would demolish the home of the Labour MP Chris Smith.

The announcement of the studies spawned many local protest groups, which came together to form ALARM (All London Against the Roadbuilding Menace). John Stewart, its Chairman, explains:

Eventually there were about 250 groups across London. Each one of them campaigned in their own way, appropriate to their own area. There was just one golden rule in ALARM; every group said: 'no to all the road schemes' ... That was initially quite a hard battle because some groups were keen to put the road somewhere else. For example, I remember an early meeting with a group in Dulwich – a pretty up-market area. Up-market residents there were saying: 'Oh well, we can't have the road scheme here but what about a road scheme through Brixham and Peckham – that would really regen-

erate those areas.' ... But groups began to understand that they were
stronger together than apart.

NIMBYism ('not in my back yard') is a tendency of many local protest
groups that Stewart was keen to avoid. He would apply this principle in several different contexts, as explained in Chapter 9. Another
lesson learned from past experience was that effort spent on public
consultations and public inquiries rarely changed any significant decisions. ALARM's aim was to defeat the proposals before they reached
a public inquiry.

Stewart describes the people who ran the groups in ALARM as
'regular citizens'. There was no suggestion at this stage of law-breaking
direct action. However, some of the older campaigners had learned
that personalising campaigns could produce results (an approach
which unfortunately influenced some of their dealings with fellow
campaigners). Cecil Parkinson became a key target. One protest played
loud music outside his house; another involved a Valentine's cake from
the celebrity brothel madam Cynthia Payne ('Madam Cyn'), whose
own street was threatened by one of the schemes. With a reminder of
the jilted mistress who had caused Parkinson's earlier departure from
the government, this stunt attracted interest from the tabloid press,
who did not normally pay much attention to environmental protests.

Although individual groups lobbied their own MPs, ALARM
never met, nor sought to meet, any government ministers. Their most
effective tactic was probably mass letter-writing to MPs. The mail-
boxes of several London Conservative MPs were swamped; Jeremy
Corbyn, the Labour MP for Islington, reportedly received 17,000
letters. Although the Labour Party had prevaricated on 'Roads for
Prosperity', in London they came down firmly against the 'Tories' disastrous road plans'.

With local elections looming, the leaders of Conservative-led
London boroughs began to fear that opposition to the road schemes
could cause them to lose political control. In March 1990, a few weeks
before the elections, Parkinson announced a climb-down. All of the
schemes proposed in the London Assessment Studies were scrapped.
This decision did not apply to the few London schemes listed in
'Trunk Roads England', including the M11 link road, the East London
River Crossing, and the widening of the M25 (the orbital motorway

around London) to 8 lanes, initially. The East London River Crossing was planned to cut through 72 hectares of ancient woodland, a threat which would continue to mobilise opposition. Nevertheless it was a great victory for ALARM.

This unexpected outcome was noticed by groups fighting road schemes in the rest of the country. Some of them contacted Stewart asking for assistance. He recalls:

After any big protest most of the local residents doing normal jobs go back to being local residents doing normal jobs. It was only sad cases like me who carried on. Four or five of us got together and said: 'What do we do now? We are being contacted by all these people.' We were sitting around a kitchen table and we thought: 'Let's go for an ALARM UK and see what interest is out there.'

A 'Power-Hungry' European Commissioner Intervenes

During 1990 several environmental organisations, local protest groups, Euro MPs and thousands of individuals complained to the European Commission about several of the road schemes. The legal grounds for the complaints were that the UK Government had not conducted environmental impact assessments on these schemes, as required by a European directive, incorporated into UK law in 1988.

The European Commissioner for the Environment, Carlo Ripa di Meana, was a flamboyant Italian socialist with a mission to strengthen environmental protection across Europe. In conflicts with national governments, he believed that public opinion would support stronger measures.

In November 1990 John Major replaced Mrs Thatcher as Prime Minister and leader of a party divided over Britain's place in Europe. Cecil Parkinson, Thatcher's ally, left the government. He was replaced by Malcolm Rifkind, who showed some initial interest in attempts to 'green' transport policy, but then confirmed the new government's intentions to press ahead with the controversial road schemes.

In March 1991 the Commission decided that several complaints relating to Twyford Down, the East London River Crossing and the M11 Link Road were justified, although they did not make this public at the time. Their enforcement powers were slow and cumbersome, only to be used as a last resort. Over the following seven months Di Meana and his staff met with, and spoke by telephone to, Rifkind and UK officials several times, seeking to reach a negotiated settlement.[13] These negotiations were conducted in private; the Twyford Down Association was still awaiting a response to their complaint when they learned in May 1991 that the DTp had published a tender to begin 'preparatory works' on a protected water meadow near the Down.

The Association alerted the Commission, fearing that work would begin before their complaint could be properly considered. Meanwhile, the negotiations between the two parties were leading nowhere; the DTp was determined to press ahead with the road schemes without delay. In October 1991 Di Meana finally wrote to the UK Government commencing infringement proceedings over its failure to follow European environmental procedures. Those legal proceedings would take some time so Di Meana also sent a personal letter to Rifkind, urging him to stop all work on the disputed schemes in the meantime.

Rifkind's decision to release that letter to the media provoked a crisis in UK–European relations. Several anti-European Conservative MPs attacked the 'power hungry' Di Meana in the media.[14] Norman Tebbit said the letter was 'a little preview of what life might be like in a united Europe'. John Major wrote to the European Commission's President Jacques Delors saying that Di Meana's actions made it less likely that the UK would support the draft treaty, due for signature at the Maastricht summit in a few weeks' time. This threat achieved its desired effect; Delors was furious with Di Meana; relations between the two deteriorated, eventually prompting Di Meana to leave the Commission and return to Italy.

'Close contacts of the Prime Minister' told a member of the Twyford Down Association that 'when the European Commission entered the fray so publicly ... Twyford Down's fate was effectively sealed'.[15] In January 1992, with no resolution to the dispute in view, the government took a decision with consequences no one appeared to anticipate; defying the European Commission they authorised the bulldozers to begin their 'preparatory' work on Twyford Down.

2

Direct Action, Arrests and Unexplained Violence

Twyford Down – the First of Many

We created a diversion. Local campaigners were down by a gate making lots of noise. The construction workers went to find out what was going on, leaving the machinery unguarded ... I scrambled under and put a [bicycle] D-lock around the axle of a lifting machine then put my neck inside it, locked it and waited. It was cold in the mud. I was there for three or four hours. The police were there and later cameras came. I could hear lots of commotion. Everyone else was removed from the machinery and I was isolated. When they turned the machinery on I was terrified [at first] but fairly quickly became at peace with the whole thing and I realised at that moment – extraordinary, thinking about it now – it was something I was prepared to die for.

Jason Torrance was 21 years old when the anti-roads movement turned to illegal direct action at Twyford Down. He and a college friend, Jake Burbridge, had recently set up Earth First!, described by *The Times* as 'an offshoot of a militant American organisation ... [raising] concern that violence may be brought into British environmental politics for the first time'. In fact Earth First! was not really an organisation; it called itself a 'disorganisation', a network of autonomous groups committed to 'non-violent direct action', which might involve damage to property. Their willingness to break the law and their rejection of formal structures, posed a challenge to the more established environmental organisations. After taking part in a mass blockade in the Netherlands, Torrance contacted Friends of the Earth (FoE) and Greenpeace with his plans for more active resistance to environmental damage in the UK and was 'given the brush-off'. He viewed them as 'part of a middle-class green elite that was not responding to the catastrophe that we saw unfolding around us, globally and locally'.

Unlike several of the other early activists, who had been to private schools, Torrance was brought up on a council estate. He dropped out of college to campaign full-time. Like many others he sometimes claimed unemployment benefit; at a time of high unemployment the local benefit offices were often sympathetic to people who dedicated their lives to environmental campaigning.

Roger Higman was an anti-roads campaigner based at FoE's head office. He remembers meeting Torrance for the first time early in 1992:

> We had never heard of Earth First! but it was apparently something to do with direct action. I cannot stress enough how little we knew about direct action. We both agreed on the need to do something; the question was whether we could do anything together. Andrew [Lees, FoE's National Campaigns Director] was very nervous and took the view that we couldn't. In February 92, the first thing the Department of Transport wanted to do was to demolish two bridges over the railway. We took one bridge and Jason's group took the other. We were under strict instructions from Andrew that if the police came we were to leave.

Eventually the police did arrive, and the FoE members left, as planned. The other Earth Firsters were quickly removed behind a cordon leaving Torrance locked to the axle of a vehicle, which made several mock attempts to start moving. The protestors cried 'turn it off!' which the police eventually told the driver to do. Torrance had found the idea to use a D-lock around his neck in the journal of Earth First! in the USA. The tactic was new, so he didn't realise that keeping the key on a cord round his neck would make it easy for the police to find, once they had removed his clothes. Torrance and six others who refused to leave the site, including a 15-year-old boy, were arrested, held overnight and charged with breach of the peace. Over the following years Torrance was arrested over 20 times. To begin with, the legal consequences for young people with no financial assets were minimal. That would change as governments began to perceive a growing threat from direct action.

Over the following five years Conservative ministers would repeatedly condemn the activists who obstructed road-building schemes, but the initial appeals for FoE and Earth First! to intervene came from David Croker, the Conservative councillor who chaired the Twyford Down Association. Jason Torrance remembers an 'excitable meeting' at the offices of the Conservative councillors, where the tactics, of people chaining themselves to machinery, were agreed. As Croker explained to *The Times*:

> I have always believed that the Conservatives, being the party of conservation and the countryside, would be our natural allies in this. And it has not turned out like that...It's the logical conclusion of the fight. It's like war. You exhaust all the diplomatic channels and in the end you've got no alternative but to fight.[1]

The following month Croker tipped off FoE that the DTp was planning to begin work on the water meadows, despite the ongoing legal threat from the European Commission. FoE decided to organise a symbolic protest, arguing that they were there to uphold European law. Several FoE volunteers and staff, including Higman, chained themselves across the entrance to the construction site. Their instructions were, as before, to leave when asked to do so by the police. While they were there Higman remembers being approached by members of Earth First! wanting to get involved. He referred them to his manager.

> On the one hand you had a team of people working professionally, used to deferring to authority, in a situation where the authority is incredibly nervous, so they are deferring to authority even more than normal. And then they interface with a group of people who are not used to working with authority at all. [When my manager rebuffed them] they continued trying to influence us. We'd been camping in field for days in icy conditions and were absolutely knackered; we felt very got at.

Legal risks may have been one reason for the nervousness of FoE management but their main concerns were territorial. As Higman explains: 'Andrew [Lees] was always very nervous about people taking publicity from FoE, things that FoE had done.'

The human chain delayed the work by five days until the DTp obtained an injunction – not against the protestors on site but against 'the poor women in the finance office' of FoE.[2] FoE management felt they had no choice but to comply. They instructed all their staff to leave and stay away from the site. No one explained their reasons to the few protestors remaining on the site, who felt abandoned. These events created a rift in the environmental movement, which would last for about three years. Higman acknowledges: 'They were rebuffed and got very bitter about it ... FoE got a lot of bad publicity for walking away from Twyford Down, and understandably so.'

Among the people who tried to join FoE's actions on the water meadows were two young travellers who had arrived in the area by coincidence, looking for somewhere to pitch their tipi. When FoE left they moved their tipi onto the ancient trackway known as the Dongas, on the line of the new road. They were initially joined by about ten other people, some coming specifically to protest, others with troubled pasts looking for somewhere to live for a while. Together, this unlikely group formed the nucleus of the first anti-road protest camp, whose residents became known as the Dongas Tribe.

One of those who joined in the summer of 1992 was Alex Plows. She had finished her degree the year before and had been unemployed 'squatting in a counter-cultural scene' in London, when she heard about 'this amazing place' – the protest camp at Twyford Down. She decided to hitch down with a friend to join the camp.

Our tactics went through a rapid, innovative curve as things progressed. It was all quite low-scale at first, maybe one bulldozer and five or six of us trying to stop them – just being there in front of them. We had the camp on the route of the road and there was a court action, where we said: OK we'll move the camp 20 feet off the route, which still meant we could be right there when they came to clear us off again. There was one official report which said: work stopped by 12 people dressed as a dragon!

In June 1992 FoE and the Twyford Down Association organised a final protest march. Seven hundred people followed a piper along the line of the planned road. Most local objectors now feared that defeat was inevitable; their fears were strengthened a few days later when the

European Commission announced the departure of Carlo Ripa Di Meana. His successor announced that the Commission was dropping four of the seven environmental cases against the UK Government, including Twyford Down and the M11 link, although they still intended to pursue the case against the East London River Crossing. The legal arguments for the dropped cases were flimsy;[3] the decision was a political compromise, 'a rancid, grubby back-room fix' in the words of Liberal Democrat MP Simon Hughes.[4]

Although the Twyford Down Association enjoyed much local support, public opinion in the city was divided; many people wanted a new motorway although opinions varied on the best route. During the 1970s the government had proposed a route closer to the city and to Winchester College (a private boarding school), which had strongly objected. The college supported the new plans for a cutting through Twyford Down because it was further away and because the DTp would pay it £300,000 for its land. In a historical twist which made the college unpopular with many locals, the land on Twyford Down was bequeathed to the college in the 1950s to protect it from development.[5] With the European legal threat removed, in late 1992 they applied for an injunction to remove the protestors from their land.

Alex Plows vividly remembers 'Yellow Wednesday', when 80 security guards arrived to evict them:

> Numbers had been fluctuating; there would be people there at weekends and not during the week and that was when they would try to catch us unawares ... There were maybe 20 people on site that morning. We had this wake-up call ... It was an early morning haze and we could see this yellow shimmer and we thought: 'What the fuck is that?' As it moved towards us across the downs we realised it was yellow machinery and all these guards in yellow jackets ...
>
> There was this face-off where no one was quite sure what would happen. At some point they started to push forward and we tried to get in front of them to stop them and were thrown around by the security guards ... We were breaking free, diving in front of machinery and being dragged back out ... They weren't trained for this. Some of them were in shock as much as we were, and others were just thugs ... I was manhandled, my hair was pulled and I was thrown down again ... Some of the girls said they were groped.

Some of the guys were more heavily taken down. I saw people with blood on their faces. It was assault on a grand scale.

By lunchtime TV cameras had arrived and the use of violence raised the media profile of the protests, and the protestors. The naturalist David Bellamy, who witnessed the evictions, told *The Guardian*: 'I have been in many protests around the world in some very hairy countries and I never seen such unreasonable force used, especially on women.'

It took two days to remove the camp. The Dongas moved to another site 15 miles from Winchester for the rest of the Winter, still supported by local sympathisers, one of whom suggested that they should camp on the lawn of Winchester College. In February the camp was re-established on Plague Pit Valley, near to the College and the tactics of obstruction and locking to machinery recommenced.

The small core of people living at the camp were strengthened by a growing number of occasional visitors. Roger Geffen, who was working as a part-time record producer in London, organised mini-buses to bring part-time protestors to Twyford on Saturday mornings, when the contractors were attempting to work on site. He recalls: 'We would work out where the diggers were and how close we could get to the site before they could see us. It was all very cat-and-mouse or British Bulldogs: can you capture their digger before the security got there?'

In response to these tactics, the DTp employed a detective agency to gather intelligence on the activists to serve them with injunctions. The 'detectives' made no secret of their presence. Jason Torrance remembers them standing with clipboards observing his actions and 'engaging in low-level intimidation, particularly against the women.'

Legal Injunctions and Prison Sentences

In April 1993 the DTp sought injunctions against 74 individuals, whose names were not all known. Some of them had pinned to their clothing the names of species threatened by the road, which the agency used to identify them. After an adjournment, on 2 July a High Court judge eventually granted injunctions against Coot, Ruff, Siskin and Reed Warbler, among others. 'Miss Raspberry' was so named after she blew one at a police security camera. The injunctions were served two days before a planned protest on the cutting, which had now pierced through the chalk of the Down.

Many of those named on the injunction were local residents with houses and jobs, which they stood to lose. Torrance (alias Reed Warbler) said: 'Most of those people were terrified ... they had reached the limits of their willingness to take action so it just whittled down to a few of us who had limited, or in my case no, assets, who were prepared to break the injunction.'

On 4 July around 500 people climbed the hill for a protest with a carnival atmosphere. TV footage, still available online, shows four protestors with injunction numbers pinned to their chests, including Torrance, dancing around a circle of police.[6] Dancing next to Torrance was Emma Must, a children's librarian from Winchester. Must had joined the protestors a year earlier when she saw bulldozers on the water meadows she had known since her childhood.

Three weeks later Torrance, Must and five others were jailed for 28 days. One of the others decided to ignore the summons. (S)he went to live 'off grid' in a remote location, spending several years in and out of protest camps, successfully evading the law. They are now employed in a professional position and would rather remain anonymous.

Although some of the protestors had been arrested several times, prison was a new experience. Torrance's greatest anxiety was 'who I'd be locked in a small room with.' In the event, the four men were kept together in Pentonville prison. The officer in charge of that section of the gaol was sympathetic, because his own home was threatened by another road scheme. Things were tougher for the women in Holloway prison. Must recalls: 'We were strip searched, split up and moved all the time. The thing you don't expect is the noise, from all the radios; it sounds trivial but it's not if it's 24 hours a day and you can't escape from it.'

While protestors kept a vigil outside the DTp's headquarters, the prisoners received a stream of visitors including Chris Smith, the Shadow Environment Secretary and Carlo Ripa Di Meana, no longer a Commissioner, but keen to show 'solidarity, sympathy and admiration.' To the consternation of some anti-European Conservatives he wrote in *The Guardian*: 'The road is a brutal and unneeded monster. I have great sympathy for [the prisoners]. I myself could stand such a reason for going to prison.'

The Protests Spread

The main reason for Di Meana's visit to Britain was to attend a celebration. Three days after the injunction-breaking carnival on Twyford Down the government announced the cancellation of the East London River Crossing through Oxleas Wood. Chapter 4 will tell this story from the government's side, but whatever the reasons for their decision there was no doubt that public protest was a factor. Over 3,000 people and organisations had signed a pledge to take direct action against any attempt to build through Oxleas Wood. The conflict at Twyford Down made the threat seem credible.

Roger Geffen, who had joined the action at Twyford Down, was also active in the campaign to save Oxleas Wood. He recalls a 'mobilisation rally', which unexpectedly became a victory celebration.

> Di Meana gave this wonderful speech about 'all of your efforts – and those of the prisoners who cannot be with us today … Everything that was done at Twyford Down helped save Oxleas Wood. I hadn't seen it before; it's a beautiful place'. And he ended his speech saying: 'Oxleas Wood will be forever etched on my heart'. Many of us were moved to tears.

Six of the prisoners were released after fourteen days (one was released earlier), still vowing to continue their campaign and defy the injunction. Another celebratory rally was held outside the headquarters of the DTp. One of the speakers was John Stewart, whose ALARM UK coalition now boasted 220 local protest groups around the country. At the start of the actions on Twyford Down, Roger Higman noted that the Earth First! activists were purely focussed on stopping that one road; they displayed little awareness of the national situation, until January 1993 when several of them travelled to a national conference organised by ALARM UK. Stewart and his collaborators were planning the conference at the end of 1992 when 'Twyford Down exploded. It took us all by surprise.' They invited the Twyford activists and the people from many local groups, who had contacted Stewart after the media coverage of ALARM's success in London.

Must recalls: 'From that point on we were working with ALARM UK and alongside them. Everyone was perceiving Twyford as a flagship for what could happen to 'the biggest road-building pro-gramme since the Romans' ... From that point on we were aware of that bigger significance.'

Must and some others from Twyford Down went on to form Road Alert!, an umbrella group for the direct action groups, which presented itself as 'the direct-action arm of ALARM UK'. Stewart describes the two as 'sister organisations' sharing similar aims but 'serving different constituencies'. Most of the groups affiliated to ALARM UK were run by local residents with jobs and commitments that would limit their ability to engage in direct action. However, most of them appreciated, and were willing to work with, the direct-action activists, who were smaller in number but achieving a disproportionate impact on media coverage and political awareness.

ALARM UK operated on the same principles as ALARM in London. Groups would act independently, in their own names, using different tactics with just one 'golden rule: don't support road-building anywhere else'. The central office provided some logistic support for groups, organised events and also engaged with NGOs, such as Transport 2000 and academics working on the technical, political and economic case against large-scale road-building.

During late 1993 and early 1994 these two organisations, together with local FoE groups and many others set up two 'Corridor Alliances', which aimed to oppose piecemeal road schemes forming part of a longer-distance plan. One of these concerned the A36/46 road between Southampton and Bristol, the other opposed plans for a highway along the South Coast; these alliances would endure long after the national anti-roads protests had subsided.

Although the different strands of the campaign worked closely together, the initial separation between Road Alert! and ALARM UK created an image of the latter as the law-abiding wing of the anti-roads movement, enabling politicians to start talking to them, eventually – though not in the early years, when direct action began to spread around the country.

Direct Action and Unexplained Violence: The M11 Link Road

Of the road schemes referred to the European Commission, the M11 Link Road (now part of the A12) was the 'Cinderella of the three', receiving less attention from the media and politicians. According to Roger Geffen, who helped to start the direct action there, 'There were no ancient monuments, no Areas of Outstanding Natural Beauty, just 350 homes that had been left to rot by the DTp ever since they had decided this was to be the line of the road.'

Outline plans for the road were first published in the 1960s, as part of the abortive plan for a network of urban motorways in London. Three and a half miles of dual carriageway would mainly run alongside the surface-running Central Line of the London Underground. It was a classic radial route, designed to carry larger volumes of traffic from outside the city towards central London – an approach which had generally fallen from favour. As with many of the other schemes, local residents had fought the plans at several earlier stages but opposition had dwindled by the summer of 1993, when activists from Twyford and elsewhere began moving into some of the derelict houses, which they used as a base to obstruct the early building works.

The road was planned to start in Wanstead, a middle-class suburb, and run through Leytonstone and Leyton, two poorer areas of east London that Geffen describes as 'a community which they thought they could treat like shit and bulldoze out of the way':

A lot of the houses were squats, some had been bought by the DTp and were let out on short-term leases to alternative types ... They had to start building at the leafy affluent end where we thought we wouldn't get any support ... We would have to fight them for a year in unfertile territory, we thought. Actually we were wrong. The residents of Wanstead were motivated specifically by a tree.

The plans for the road included two short stretches of tunnel, one of which would run underneath a small park, George Green, in Wanstead. Instead of a bored tunnel, as the residents were expecting, this would be a shallow 'cut and cover' tunnel, removing a 250-year-old chestnut tree, as the residents belatedly discovered. As at Twyford Down, residents and activists began working together.

A key organiser among the local residents was Jean Gosling, the 'lollipop lady', employed by the Metropolitan Police to help children cross the road to the local primary school. Like many other people drawn into protest movements using direct action, she would pay a high personal price.

In November 1993 contractors erected fences around the chestnut tree in preparation for its felling, reneging on an earlier agreement to allow the local children to participate in a tree-dressing ceremony. A documentary, still available online,[7] shows activists, residents and their children invading the fenced area, confronting the contractors and tearing down the fences. Jean Gosling can be seen in her uniform brandishing her 'lollipop', an act which led to her dismissal, after several weeks where she was forbidden from leaving her home area without police permission.

Some of the protestors built a treehouse and, with the help of a local solicitor, won a case in the High Court to register it as a dwelling, causing the contractors further delay. While the authorities prepared the eviction proceedings, the protestors ensured that the treehouse was continually occupied. Some protestors camped around the tree, while others squatted in the condemned houses. This peaceful stalemate was shattered on the evening of 3 December 1993 when nine hooded men arrived in two cars, armed with crow bars and claw hammers.

They began by smashing cars parked outside some of the squatters' houses, then moved on to the camp around the treehouse. Six of them surrounded the camp, doused the benders in petrol and set fire to them before running off. A couple of the protestors suffered minor burns – it could have been worse.

Two of the attackers were arrested and gaoled a year later. At their trial they told how they were approached at a drinking club in Essex and offered £50 and £100 'to remove some squatters' by men who claimed to have '£12,000 earmarked' for the attack. In sentencing, the judge regretted that 'those responsible for hiring you are not before the court'.[8] The DTp conducted an internal investigation and found 'no evidence to suggest' that its staff or agents were involved. The paymasters behind the attack were never identified.

The eviction of the treehouse four days later involved 200 police and 150 security guards. A planned early start was delayed when the authorities discovered that the hydraulic platform hired to remove protestors from the tree had been sabotaged. The use of covert sabotage was a divisive issue among some of the activists. In 1992, the first gathering of Earth First! in Britain decided to split the movement into two; those willing to use covert sabotage formed the Earth Liberation Front, which the FBI would later classify as an 'eco-terrorist organisation'. Those continuing to use the Earth First! name generally acted openly and caused only limited damage (e.g. tearing down fences), although labels and distinctions became more fluid as the protest movement expanded. The violence aimed at the protestors on this occasion may have hardened some of their attitudes; if it was intended to frighten them off, it did not succeed.

After the felling of the tree the focus of the campaign moved to the condemned houses at different points along the route. Some existing residents, including Dolly, a 92-year-old woman who had lived all her life in one house, were refusing to leave. Another family, evicted in December 1993, moved back in with the squatters, who declared an independent Republic of Wanstonia, sparking several satirical articles in the national press. Geffen recalls: 'We created our own passports and made a nine-year-old kid Education Secretary. The Foreign Office wrote us a wonderfully strait-laced response, explaining why we couldn't secede from the UK under international law!'

During 1994 and early 1995, the squatters were evicted from small groups of occupied houses. Treehouses, towers and bunkers were built, with protestors 'locking on' to fixings in concrete to make the task as difficult as possible. A new tactic of tunnelling would prove useful in future protests. Geffen recounts:

> The security were really puzzled when people they thought had been kicked out kept reappearing. They eventually discovered that we'd built a tunnel [between two of the houses under their gardens]. We'd dug a trench, lined it with oil drums and turfed over it. Eventually they used a metal detector ... it was a fantastic laugh when they finally twigged what was going on!

The eviction of that street, in December 1994, took four and a half days, involving 700 police and 200 bailiffs. The Home Secretary addressing the House of Commons condemned the £2 million cost of the operation. Geffen replied to a *Guardian* journalist: 'The cost of the police operation is the cost to the Government of going over the heads of public opinion. No government would consider building a road like this again.'

Quiet Victories and Noisy Defeats

What motivated the activists and what did they hope to achieve? In a diverse, unstructured, spontaneous movement there were, and are, many answers to those questions.[9] Most were motivated by ecological beliefs of some kind, often with spiritual foundations, sometimes connected to paganism. Many activists defined their beliefs in opposition to 'progress culture', with varying degrees of hostility towards modern technologies and materialist values. Many were angered by specific road schemes; some were drawn towards the lifestyle and identity offered by the protest camps, which others found cold, wet and not always welcoming towards outsiders. There were a few widely shared values, however. Alex Plows, recalling Twyford Down, explains: 'People were horrified at what it was doing to that particular bit of landscape ... It was a very visceral thing – and a very British thing, I think – that sense of connection with the landscape ... There was a sense of ecological citizenship.'

Emma Must, who was brought up in Winchester, talks of a 'visceral inability to sit back and watch that happen ... [Then, later] the motivation became to stop this being repeated at the other places around the country'. She recalls some lively debates with Jason Torrance, who was arguing for climate change as a more explicit campaign theme. Some of Torrance's statements at the time were suffused with anger, peppered with expletives. This is how he describes the motivations of the activists, with hindsight:

> Our earlier aspirations were just around stopping environmental damage ... I don't think we had a sophisticated strategy or plan about providing alternatives ... We were young, angry and possibly one of the vital ingredients for our success is that we were very naïve. [If we had been less naïve] we would have been more cautious; we would have spent too long strategising. We had a dream, not a Gantt chart.

This activist strategy contained a contradiction. To sustain that type of motivation, the activists had to believe – as most of them did at some points in time – that they could stop the schemes they were fighting. This was a necessary delusion, which usually gave way to more realistic aims: to delay construction, increase costs and raise the political price of road-building elsewhere in future. No road scheme was ever stopped by direct action after construction began but past experience did not seem to prevent an upsurge of optimism on each occasion.

Several of the interviewees talked of 'noisy defeats and quiet victories' – a pattern which they only realised in retrospect. Geffen credits John Stewart and ALARM UK for providing a vital link between the small number of roads obstructed by direct action (around 20) and the much larger number (over 200) opposed by local groups at an earlier stage, before construction began. For those groups, the threat of direct action was a useful deterrent.

By mid-1995, the government's commitment to the plan first outlined in 'Roads for Prosperity' appeared to be weakening. In March 1994, 49 of the original schemes were scrapped, followed a year later by the cancellation of plans for further widening of the M25. The government was now talking to (the less radical) environmental opponents of the roads programme. The energy behind the anti-roads movement could have begun to wane, were it not for one explosive decision, announced as the last act of an outgoing Transport Secretary on 5 July 1995.

3

The Newbury Bypass,
Reclaim the Streets and 'Swampy'

The Newbury Bypass

The four-lane A34 running through the market town of Newbury formed part of a longer-distance route from Oxford to Southampton, joining the M3 at the junction before Twyford Down. As with many of the routes targeted by Cecil Parkinson's 'Trunk Roads England', the A34 had been gradually dualled through open countryside, putting greater pressure on the remaining urban and two-lane sections.

As with several of the other schemes, there was a groundswell of support in the town for a bypass but also local groups active against it. After a public inquiry in 1992 approved the DTp's plans local opposition subsided until 1994 when a new group, the Third Battle of Newbury, was formed. Their name referred to the two battles fought in the English Civil War on sites along the route of the new road. As at Twyford Down, the road would cut through several archaeological sites, three Sites of Special Scientific Interest and an Area of Outstanding Natural Beauty.

There were two protest camps along the route by December 1994, when Transport Secretary Brian Mawhinney announced that the scheme would be put on hold for 'at least a year' pending a review of environmental and other concerns. At least one of the protest camps remained on the site, while supporters of the bypass lobbied in parliament and organised meetings in the town. The bypass dropped out of the national news until July 1995 when Mawhinney made a surprise announcement, approving the original scheme. It was his last major decision as Transport Secretary; a cabinet reshuffle was announced on the same day. Why did he make that decision, when he could have left it to his successor? The next chapter will explain.

The announcement, and particularly its timing, surprised and annoyed the national environmental organisations, whose relations with ministers had been improving. A week before the announcement, DTp officials told Charles Secrett, FoE's director, that they were looking forward to receiving a report that FoE had commissioned into alternatives to a bypass. 'Who is ever going to trust this Government again? We will do all we can to stop the bypass' he told *The Guardian*.

One of Secrett's top priorities when he became director of FoE in 1993 was to rebuild relationships with the radical activists. He publicly acknowledged that FoE had made a mistake in abruptly abandoning the action at Twyford Down. Roger Higman recalls them both attending an Earth First! gathering: 'They were impressed with Charles ... We realised we were all on the same side. We had different ways of working. *We* were mainly about organising opposition *before* construction began. *They* were mainly about opposing roads *after* construction had begun.'

This did not mean that FoE had no interest in roads under construction. They had identified Newbury as a 'potential flashpoint' and were keen to find ways of supporting direct action there, providing they could do so without risking legal action or provoking violence. Secrett had instructed staff and local groups not to take part in any direct action under FoE's name that might lead to arrest, but with an unwritten proviso that anyone could act as an individual. FoE also agreed to help in a new way by providing legal observers, staff or volunteers who would take notes and photographs in case of any legal disputes. FoE local groups would also provide material support to the activists, while staff including Higman would spend time on site and talk to the media.

During 1994 and 1995 members of FoE and Road Alert! gradually began to attend meetings of the Third Battle of Newbury. One resident recalled: 'The local residents were rather resentful of the direct-action protestors at first but discovered they were very articulate and resourceful ... We began to realise that their full-time commitment and radical action would be an asset.'[1]

Even traditional conservation groups, the World Wide Fund for Nature and the Council for the Protection of Rural England, agreed to join the activists in legal action against the authorities, while Road Alert!, the umbrella group set up by Emma Must, moved to Newbury in anticipation. For the first time, it seemed that all three elements of the environmental movement: national organisations, local residents and direct-action activists were ready to work together.

The Newbury Bypass triggered the largest anti-road action ever seen in Britain. During late 1995 and early 1996, 38 separate protest camps were set up along its route, involving a 'hard core of some 300 to 400 protestors'[2] assisted by a larger number of local residents and others, who joined the actions from time to time. Protestors and the authorities had learned lessons from earlier protests and both were prepared for a major conflict.

At many of the other road sites action only began after construction was under way. At Newbury the protestors were determined to build their defences in advance and to strike at the early preparations. During the autumn of 1995 protestors began arriving from around the country. They built three new camps with treehouses linked by walkways consisting of two ropes: one to walk on and the other to hold on to. At a central camp on Snelsmore Common they dug a network of narrow tunnels, leading to an underground chamber equipped for a protracted occupation. A national telephone tree was established to spread news and bring in reinforcements when needed. Their first action blocked the coaches of the security company, delaying the start on site.

As at Twyford and the M11, objectors appealed to the European Commission over the absence of an environmental impact assessment, but the Commissioner, Neil Kinnock, declined to intervene. However, European law did impose another constraint on the authorities. Trees could not be felled during the bird nesting season, which would begin at some time in the Spring. Delaying evictions and defending trees until that legal deadline became a key objective for the protestors.

In February, while the DTp applied to the courts to remove the camps, FoE organised a 5,000-strong demonstration along the route of the road. The following day protestors raided the offices of the security company Reliance and Tarmac, the contractors at Twyford Down, who were considering whether to tender for the bypass. Staff tried unsuccessfully to barricade the office against 200 protestors, 80 of whom broke in and occupied the building.

By 1996 covert sabotage – given the friendly name of 'pixieing' – was generally accepted as legitimate, providing it did not cause physical harm to people or animals. However, some pixieing did create risks of injury, despite the attempts made to minimise them. For example, trees were spiked with metal objects to deter cutting by chainsaw, then fixed with warning signs.

Most of the police and security guards seem to have acted with restraint but there were exceptions[3] and some evidence that excessive force might have been coordinated. In January 1996 *Guardian* reporter John Vidal applied to join Reliance as a guard, giving his own name and a bogus reference. The company's operation's manager reportedly told him: 'Anything in a tree, f*** it off. Thwack it with your helmet. Anything. Don't get caught.'[4] A manager was suspended the following day, prompting *The Guardian* to back growing calls from the police and MPs for regulation of the security industry.

The Sheriff Clears the Forest

Nick Blandy is a retired solicitor and former Under-Sherriff of Berkshire. For a few months early in 1996, when he directed the eviction of the Newbury camps, he became a hate-figure for some in the protest movement. Today, in his riverside garden surrounded by birdsong, he talks almost fondly of the Newbury evictions and his dealings with the protestors – or most of them.

In planning the operation with the police Blandy wanted to learn from the mistakes made at Twyford Down: 'The popular wisdom was that Twyford Down effectively financed the protestors at Newbury because the police techniques were not good and there were lots of successful actions for wrongful arrest – huge sums of damages were paid out.'

To avoid such problems at Newbury, officers would be carefully briefed on techniques of arrest and police observers would video the whole process. Ironically, some of their unpublished footage, which I have seen, corroborates some of the protestors' claims, about the treatment of women. In a moment of blokeish banter the climbers make crude or funny gestures towards a cameraman, who then turns to focus on a lone woman exercising in the woods. Then the cameraman, or one of his colleagues, shouts at her: 'D'you mind taking your top off?'

Another change since Twyford Down was the Criminal Justice Act 1994, which created a new offence of 'aggravated trespass' with a maximum penalty of three years imprisonment. These controversial powers were used sparingly against protestors at first but following pressure from ministers the police began using the Act more widely at Newbury. One of the first targets of this new tougher approach was a pantomime cow called Buttercup. The front half pleaded guilty to aggravated trespass while the rear half argued that his vision was obscured when they pranced across a security cordon.

The partiality of the police and legal system was a recurring theme in the bulletins of Earth First! and the writings of sympathetic journalists such as John Vidal. No security guard or official was ever arrested or cautioned for acts against the protestors. Two local men were arrested for throwing petrol bombs at a bus where two protestors (one of them pregnant) and their six-year-old child were sleeping. One of the men pleaded guilty to arson with intent to endanger life. The other man, the son of a local car dealer, admitted making the petrol bombs and travelling with his friends to 'give the travellers a hard time'. His defence lawyer argued that this was a 'drunken prank' and he was acquitted.[5] On that occasion, the controversial decision was taken by a jury but the growing perception of a biased system, turning a blind eye to violence against protestors, strengthened the arguments of the protestors who advocated a more forceful response.

The evictions began in late January 1996, during a particularly cold winter. The first camp to be evicted was Snelsmore Common. Blandy recalls:

> The Police had undercover people [among the protestors]; I never knew who they were... the imperative was to take the tunnel. The strategy, which amused me, was to go in on a Friday morning on the basis that they would all have received their benefits on Thursday; they would have all gone out drinking and would be in a bad state at two o'clock in the morning, which was when we went in. Sure enough ... there was nobody in the tunnel. We took possession of it, filled it in and that was game over as far as tunnelling was concerned.'

To remove protestors from trees and roadside walkways Blandy hired a group of professional climbers and cavers he had seen in action at another protest eviction: 'They had nerves of steel and concentration, all the good skills for getting up there, talking to people and persuading them to come down. They were scrupulous about safety. They were unbelievably good.'

Others were more critical of their techniques. A solicitor acting as Senior Legal Observer for FoE complained that his team had been denied access to some of the flashpoints but from what they had seen he said: 'Arresting people 70 ft in the air and turning them upside down is so reckless as to quite likely constitute a criminal offence. These arrests are highly dangerous.'

The involvement of climbers in protest camp evictions caused dissension within the climbing community. The British Mountain Festival in February 1996 gave an 'anti-award' to Richard Turner Ltd 'for abusing climbing skills'. The Director of the Festival called on other climbers to ostracise 'these mercenaries and renegades'.[6] A few days later one of the Newbury climbers defected to the protestors. Other climbers were already helping the protestors with training and equipment. In March 1996 observers were treated to a spectacle of two teams of top climbers 'grappling and swapping punches'[7] as they swung between trees and aerial walkways. Eventually the climber-protestors were brought down on hydraulic platforms and arrested.

Later that month a group of protestors struck back at Blandy, climbing onto the roof of his home and unfurling a banner. They climbed down and left before the police arrived; then a few days later he received an anonymous letter containing two pages of abuse, including a death threat. He says: 'We had to have a police guard there for 24 hours for the next week. The police started escorting me home; I started taking different routes. I had to repair a few slates on the roof … It could have been worse.'

On 2 April, just within the Environment Agency's bird-nesting deadline, the last two camps were evicted; the following day Blandy formally handed over possession of the site to the contractors, Costain. This marked the end of Blandy's involvement in the project. A framed letter from roads minister John Watts still hangs on his wall, thanking him for 'the manner of evictions', which 'avoided any serious injuries'.

After the evictions the scale of protest at Newbury reduced. Some of the protestors moved to camps along the A30 in Devon. Some continued to harass Costain during construction of the bypass; they also occupied the home of Sir George Young, the new Transport Secretary, digging up his lawn to build a mock motorway.

In January 1997, a year after the start of the evictions, 750 protestors gathered for a rally on the site. Things started peacefully enough as they listened to speeches by Charles Secrett and Tony Benn MP. Then about 300 protestors broke through security fencing, attacked machinery and set fire to a cabin and a dumper truck. These actions strained the new alliance between the activists and FoE; Secrett publicly condemned them at the time[8] and still believes that they were counterproductive.

By the time the bypass opened, in secret, in 1998 over a thousand arrests had been made. Although the protestors failed to significantly delay the project, they did substantially increase its cost; the security arrangements added £23.7 million, around a third of the original tender price.[9]

Reclaim the Streets and Unorthodox Police Methods

In early 1995, after the last protestors were removed from the M11 link road several of the London-based activists were looking for a new challenge. Roger Geffen suggested that they revive Reclaim the Streets, a name and idea pioneered on a small scale in London in the 1970s, when protestors closed off streets without authorisation or warning to hold street parties. Geffen explains: 'The aim was to make a really positive statement of how much nicer, cleaner, safer, how much more freedom children have to play in the street when you haven't got cars there.'

Ironically, the relaunch was helped by the Criminal Justice Act, which had united environmental protestors, squatters, animal rights activists and ravers, whose informal gatherings were also criminalised. Like Earth First! Reclaim the Streets called itself a 'disorganisation' but the threat of police disruption necessitated some organisation. They decided to borrow techniques familiar to the ravers. A small core would make arrangements in secret, with precise locations only revealed at the last moment. For their first action in May 1995, they chose a relatively easy site. Camden High Street in North London was a one-way street (so easier to block); there were many pedestrians and relatively little traffic on a Sunday. Geffen recalls:

It started with a piece of street theatre – which became a bit of a trademark. We bought two clapped-out old cars from a breakers yard; they were driven out of opposite side roads and crashed into one another. No one knew it was deliberate apart from the drivers, who then got out and started sledge-hammering one another's cars so people in the street were thinking: 'what the hell's going on?' Meanwhile the people who'd come for the party had assembled one tube-stop up the road, not knowing where they were going. When they got to Camden Town station they were told: now get out of the tube ... Out came the trestle tables, the food, the sound systems and the space for children to play.

An estimated 500 protestors partied with some local people for several hours, keeping the road blocked. The press reported that some parked cars were sprayed with paint, but no one was arrested. The *Evening Standard* wrote of 'a new breed of eco-warriors who threaten to bring London to a standstill' identifying Geffen as the man 'pulling the strings', while *Auto Express* magazine described the group as 'urban terrorists'.[10]

The second event on another Sunday two months later targeted a much busier street in nearby Islington. At about 2 p.m., around 1,000 people arrived from the tube station while others entered from side streets with an armoured car to block the street. Jimmy Cauty, the KLF guitarist, who achieved notoriety by burning a million pounds, apparently lent the armoured car,[11] as he had done to other anti-roads protests.[12] The police initially moved to divert the traffic until around 8 p.m., when 150 riot police moved in to clear the remaining protestors, provoking scuffles and some minor damage to property. A few protestors were arrested.

The high-profile actions in London sparked interest among activists in many other cities. As Geffen explains: 'Reclaim the Streets became two things: a group in London and a type of action that lots of people were doing elsewhere.' Reclaim the Streets actions took place in: Bristol, Brighton, Cambridge, Birmingham, Manchester, Nottingham and Edinburgh, mostly organised by local Earth First! groups.

Meanwhile, in London, the police were paying more attention to the group. Geffen says: 'We knew we weren't going to get away with a third one as easily. We knew we had to get much bigger and much more sophisticated. The next one took six months' planning.' They decided to target the M41 (now part of the A3220), which connected the Westfield shopping centre to the motorway network in West London. This symbolic choice was a remnant of the unfinished network of motorways cancelled in the 1970s, revived in the London Assessment Studies and cancelled again by Cecil Parkinson.

A date was fixed in July 1996. To keep the police guessing a meeting point was chosen at the opposite side of the city, where 3,000 people boarded the tube, accompanied by a smaller number of police officers. As they neared their destination they discovered that the police had closed the nearest tube station, forcing the group to walk back towards a police line. At the time Geffen believed the police were cleverly anticipating their tactics and rapidly responding. No one suspected a tip-off:

> For a while we were stuck on Shepherd's Bush Green until we had enough people getting off the train two stops earlier at Notting Hill and walking a mile and a half down the hill, then we'd got the police surrounded on both sides and they retreated – the police do not like being in the middle of a crowd; that leaves them very vulnerable.
>
> [To close the motorway] we used people power at one end and two cars and two lorries at the other end. Then we partied for the rest of the day. Inside the lorries we had the sound systems and this amazing enlarged Marie Antoinette skirt, a wooden skirt, dome-shaped 20 feet high, draped with material and a woman on a platform on top. These things were on wheels, so she could move around waving regally to the crowd. The skirt was also cover for a jackhammer, which was digging a trench in the motorway to plant some trees, so they couldn't reopen the motorway that evening until it was repaired.

An estimated 7,000 people took part in the event, of whom only eight were arrested for minor offences. Unbeknown to the organisers, the police were now using less orthodox methods against them.

During 1995 a man calling himself Jim Sutton joined Reclaim the Streets, gradually gained the confidence of the other activists and worked his way into the inner core. Geffen says he was 'quiet and unobtrusive, and I remember little about him'. No one suspected that he was an undercover police officer. From late 1996 onwards, the police began to foil Reclaim the Streets actions. Geffen remembers a plan to occupy an oil tanker arriving at Coryton Refinery in Essex; the protestors were stopped at a motorway service station by a big police presence. 'It clearly wasn't coincidence ... We assumed it was our phones that were being bugged, not our actual face-to-face conversations by someone we knew and trusted.'

Sutton's real name was Jim Boyling. Over five years of involvement with Reclaim the Streets he had sexual relationships with three female activists, marrying one with whom he had two children. She later divorced him, describing their relationship as 'abusive'. His story, exposed by *The Guardian* in 2011,[13] was one of several cases which led to the long-running Public Inquiry into Undercover Policing. In May 2018 the Metropolitan Police dismissed Boyling for 'sexual misconduct', describing his relationships as 'unauthorised'. Boyling responded that: 'The Met does a good line in selective amnesia as indeed they do in selective disclosure.' In a similar case involving another undercover officer exposed in 2011 the Met admitted seven years later that managers knew about his sexual relations and permitted them to continue. The public inquiry is not expected to conclude before 2023.

After the M41 event Reclaim the Streets was contacted by a group of striking dockers in Liverpool seeking their help to raise the profile of a conflict that was slipping out of the media headlines and political attention. The organising core agreed and from the autumn of 1996 the aims of Reclaim the Streets began to broaden. This was part of a general trend, which led many of the anti-roads activists towards broader opposition to capitalism. Geffen says:

> That's when we started over-reaching ourselves, and I felt so at the time. We had a critique of cars as part of an economic system, which I wished we had stuck with for longer ... Having had the confidence boost of getting several thousand people out on the motorway, we felt, 'Well, let's overthrow capitalism.'

The idea of Reclaim the Streets spread to several other countries. By 1998 the London group had fused with a global anti-capitalist protest movement, which organised big demonstrations to coincide with meetings of the G8 heads of government over the following years. Geffen was no longer part of the core. Jason Torrance, who left Britain after Twyford Down, went to Sydney where he helped to set up the only Reclaim the Streets group which still pursues the original aims today.

Swampy and the Media

In the collective memory of the anti-roads protests one name has lingered longest: Swampy. Some of the interviewees associated Swampy (whose real name is Dan Hooper) with the Newbury Bypass and he did spend some time there but the events that triggered a media obsession took place in Devon, along the route of the new A30 near Honiton. This project was managed in a new way, designed, built, financed and operated by a private consortium, who would be reimbursed over 30 years based on traffic volumes. This would save money in the short term but cost more in the long term and create an incentive for the private operator to encourage more traffic – consequences which protestors, including Hooper, were keen to publicise.

During 1996 protestors set up three camps along the route with treehouses and labyrinthine tunnels, designed to make evictions as difficult as possible, using pinch points, blind bends and reinforced steel doors. Hooper explains: 'I used to really enjoy digging … it appealed to my monotonous work ethic, but also I loved inventing defences.'

None of the protestors had any formal training; they were learning by trial and error, running the risk of tunnel collapse, flooding and asphyxiation. Hooper explains that in some tunnels they would use computer fans to pump air from the surface, but funds limited their availability. For lighting: 'We used candles so you'd know if there's no air anymore, because the candle would go out … it happened a couple of times.'

The evictions began in October 1996. By January 1997 just one camp remained, Fairmile, where Hooper and several others had built the most elaborate defences. When the bailiffs arrived, 'we were still digging … the person [nearest the entrance] managed to slam the door shut.' Five protestors reinforced the doors and retreated inside. So began a drama to capture the imagination of a nation brought up with stories of prisoners of war escaping through makeshift tunnels.

'Human Moles Lead Bailiffs Deeper into Treacherous Tunnels', led one story in *The Times*, with a photograph of Hooper and a diagram of the tunnel with arrows leading to 'routes unknown'.[14] The under-sheriff employed cavers and tunnelling experts on lucrative temporary contracts, with unintended consequences:

> They didn't want to do it quickly. They came through the first door … it was a crap door, and they were microphoned up and this guy goes: 'there's another door and it's *just as good* as the *first* one … [and whispers to a colleague] just shine your camera on the metal – don't show that bit …' They were doing all right!

Over the next six days the tunnellers gradually removed the other four protestors, including a 16-year-old girl known as 'Animal', leaving Hooper till last. 'Risk Grows as Swampy Digs Deeper' ran another headline. In fact, 'I didn't have enough room for my legs to sleep and I also needed something to cover my faeces down the bottom of the shaft, so I was still digging, but I wasn't digging away from them.'

With Hooper isolated, the authorities began to increase their psychological pressure. All communication now passed through their intercom. Hooper's brother was at the surface with a few of the other protestors, trying to persuade him to give up. Had part of the tunnel really collapsed, as the media reported? 'Had the protestors been infiltrated by undercover police?' he wonders today.

After a week underground Hooper voluntarily resurfaced, a decision he later regretted. TV images still available online show him dwarfed by policemen in flak jackets, halting just long enough to say to the media scrum, with a gentle lisp, 'I feel this is the only way to get a voice these days. If I wrote a letter to my MP would I have achieved all this? Would you lot be here now? I think not.'

That rhetorical appeal sparked a frenzy of media interest. Following arrest and a court appearance in Newbury, Hooper went to another protest camp, at Manchester airport, pursued by journalists who were now treating him as a celebrity. As usual, the camp needed money for materials, so he began charging for media interviews, paying the money into central funds. With hindsight, the pitfalls were predictable: 'It diverted attention from the protest. You get a bit arrogant about yourself. Your ego is inflated. Most people are there for the right reasons but it felt to me like trying to compete – blokes – not being themselves around me ...'

Among the offers Hooper accepted were a toe-curling appearance on the BBC's *Have I Got News for You* and a weekly column, 'The World According to Swampy', in the *Daily Mirror*, which was heavily edited by another protestor who 'thought he knew what the media wanted ... He would put stupid things in the article about what [I ate or drank], stuff about who was my girlfriend, stuff that I hadn't written; I was trying to stick to the politics ... Then I said I would stop writing it.'

His most notorious appearance was a two-page spread in the *Daily Express* titled 'Look What Emerged from the Swamp', showing him before and after a makeover, wearing an Armani suit. His mother was quoted saying: 'underneath he's a normal lad from a normal family'. He agreed to pose for these images because the £500 offered by the *Express* settled an outstanding fine.

Hooper's collaboration with this type of media coverage was criticised inside and outside the protest movement,[15] but the image created of protestors as part of Middle England almost certainly helped to increase their impact. That lesson would influence future protests, as we shall see in Chapter 9.

The growing resentment among the protestors began to affect some of Hooper's close friends. He heard indirectly that: 'They didn't think that I was handling the media very well, but saying it in a not very nice way. It was very hurtful. I wish they had just phoned me. As soon as I heard that I stepped out of it all.'

He cut his hair, stopped using the 'Swampy' name and tried to avoid the media, though still participating in protest actions. He was now well known to the police, who would often target him when moving against protestors or making arrests. He discovered, like many before and since, that unwanted celebrity can be difficult to shake off. In one incident journalists from the *Daily Mirror* accosted him and his partner at a coach station: 'They were pursuing us with our baby. I remember kicking their car bonnet and I thought I would be arrested but the security guard came and asked 'Are they hassling you?', and kept them out of the station ... I just hated the media. I didn't want anything to do with them.'

The End of the Anti-Roads Movement

The A30 was the last of the big protest camps against road-building in the 1990s. In 1996, in the final months of John Major's Conservative government, the programme was very substantially cut. In May 1997 a Labour government was elected committed to a new 'integrated' transport strategy, with less emphasis on road-building. John Stewart recalls:

> Tony Blair's big tent was very alluring. Labour was making all the right noises and the environmental movement generally, and the transport movement in particular, went into the tent – which is fine; I'm not criticising that – but we felt: we've won; we've made the arguments and we don't need to make them again. But had we made them long enough to change the culture and the thinking?'

With the road programme winding down, FoE shifted their focus towards aviation, climate change and greenfield housing development. The next big protest camp, where Dan Hooper moved during 1997, was against the expansion of Manchester Airport. As the protestors who were not burnt out moved on to other issues, the specific anti-roads organisations were wound up. Stewart says of ALARM UK: 'We felt that by 1997 the bulk of our work had been done. The organisation was there to service local groups; most of those groups had won their schemes ... It was better to end it very decisively, with a good track record of victory behind it.'

How much impact did the protest movement have on that 'victory'? That question exercised many academic studies over the following years, with no clear consensus emerging. Chapter 15 will re-examine it with the benefit of hindsight and comparison with more recent events.

Whatever the protestors did or did not achieve during the 1990s, other factors were also at work. The last two chapters have focussed on the protest movement. The next chapter will return to the political story over the same period, picking up where Chapter 1 left off.

4

The Biggest Hit on the Road
Programme Since the Romans Left
(1992–7)

In the general election of April 1992, the Conservative manifesto made a strong commitment to spend £6.3 billion on trunk roads and motorways, and to speed up procedures for building new roads. Labour's manifesto committed to review the road programme and to subject all new road schemes to environmental impact assessments, naming Twyford Down and Oxleas Wood as two examples of 'proposals for sensitive areas' which would be subject to 'full environmental assessment'. The unexpected Conservative victory dashed the protestors' hopes for a reprieve from those schemes and set off the conflicts that would last for the next five years.

Changing Ideas, but No Change of Policy

John Major appointed John MacGregor as Transport Secretary, a former merchant banker, who had been Chief Secretary to the Treasury under Margaret Thatcher and had aspirations to become Chancellor of the Exchequer. He was a strong supporter of road-building. A civil servant explains: 'His perspective was very much driven by his [rural] constituency. If you live in Norfolk and it takes you ages to get to London by road, and even longer by train in those days, and there's a [congested] roundabout [on the route], you're going to think it's the roundabout that's the problem.'

A few weeks after his appointment he enraged the environmental groups with a speech saying: 'We in Britain have an environmentally conscious approach to our roads programme which is acutely developed ... New roads benefit the environment by relieving the congestion and taking heavy traffic out of unsuitable towns and villages.'[1]

In November 1992 he secured a three-year settlement from the Treasury to spend around £2 billion a year on new roads. This was more favourable than some other departments but as the programme had now grown to around 500 schemes progress was still slower than MacGregor wanted. One partial solution was to invite private companies to design, build, finance and operate new roads, a process which would eventually produce eight new schemes from 1997 onwards, including the A30 in Devon.

The environmentalists' nightmare seemed complete when MacGregor appointed Steven Norris, a former car dealer, as Minister for Transport in London. In fact, over the next four years Norris would confound some of those expectations. John Stewart, who met Norris on various committees in London, contrasts his experience of the two ministers:

> John MacGregor had no time for us whatsoever; he thought we were pointless, we were going nowhere, and his job was to fight us … I saw Steven Norris in action elsewhere and I thought: he's a bit different … He's a bright guy … He began to understand where we were coming from.

Like several ministers, Norris felt the direct-action protestors antagonised traditional Conservative supporters, but he did meet them on occasions as well as more 'respectable' campaigners such as John Stewart and Stephen Joseph, of whom he says: 'I don't think he'd had any previous contact with the department at ministerial level – it sounds incredible these days but it was certainly the case then – because he was regarded as the enemy.'

Norris was not opposed to all road-building; he generally supported bypasses, but he had concerns about the scale and approach to road-building within the DTp:

> The mindset was to get a planning consent [for a new road] and therefore if somebody's in the way, our job is to move them to one side … we had a road programme that was simply undeliverable. It amounted to about £27 billion, of schemes which had been accepted by the DTp with more coming on board every day. But the spend that we had available to us was no more than £2 billion a year … So

it became clear that we were going to have to become more discrim-
inating on what we kept on the list and what we discarded.

Among the first schemes that Norris decided to discard was the East
London River Crossing through Oxleas Wood, a decision which
delighted the anti-roads protestors:

> I visited the site and delved into the detail and really couldn't see
> the justification for a scheme that caused undoubted environmental
> damage in a very sensitive site and delivered very little in strategic
> traffic improvement. My Secretary of State [MacGregor] approved
> because we had huge budgetary pressures ... I could think of a lot
> better ways to spend scarce resources and this cancellation was
> almost universally approved.
>
> When I was asked by a reporter why I had cancelled the scheme
> I told him that my son Edward, then aged nine, had asked me why I
> was intending to plough through a precious piece of woodland and
> I couldn't think of a good answer. It was picked up by the reporter
> and a few weeks later Ed was sent a Blue Peter badge by the BBC
> for services to the environment!

This decision was a rare example where a decision to cancel a road
scheme was directly influenced by environmental concerns. During
the late 1980s and early 1990s UK governments strengthened their
formal position on several environmental issues, particularly climate
change, but this did not appear to have any impact on the road-building programme. In January 1994 the Environment Secretary John
Gummer published a White Paper on Sustainable Development,
which expressed concern at the scale of environmental impacts from
the programme. It suggested that national and local government
should do more to 'influence the rate of traffic growth', stating that
'if it was no longer acceptable to build some roads, prices and physical
management measures would be the best way to ration the limited
resource.' The feasibility of motorway tolling and urban road pricing
would both be investigated. Gummer (now Lord Deben) describes
this as: 'A document which set out my environmental programme ...
These were very consciously, my own views ... It is about man the
steward [of the land], which is a very Conservative concept ...'

In areas where the DoE had direct responsibility, such as the planning system, these ideas did begin to change government policy. New planning policy published in 1994 made it more difficult for developers to build out of town retail parks, for example. The Treasury also saw an opportunity and a new justification to raise revenue; in two budgets in 1993, the Chancellor introduced, and then increased, a 'fuel duty escalator'; henceforth the duties on petrol and diesel would rise by 5 per cent more than inflation each year; but on the issues controlled by the DTp, nothing much was changing, yet. Norris explains:

> The DoE did not stray onto DTp's turf although of course John took a personal interest ... Climate change was only just beginning to be on the agenda ... I'd love to say it was more prominent but it wasn't at the time ... It was long after I left the Department that climate change was taken really seriously.

Although environmental concerns did not make much impact on road-building policy, emerging evidence questioning the effectiveness of road-building in combatting congestion, did. The 'Transport and Society' study mentioned in Chapter 1, led by Professor Phil Goodwin, concluded in 1991 with a report called 'Transport: The New Realism'. This pointed out that even the big road programme in 'Roads for Prosperity' could not keep pace with rising traffic volumes, based on the DTp's own forecasts. So if governments wanted to stop congestion getting worse they would have to use 'demand management', in other words, measures to reduce traffic. The report offered two scenarios for achieving this. Both involved pedestrianisation, traffic calming and more investment in public transport. Their preferred scenario also included road pricing as the most direct way to control traffic volumes and raise revenues. If that was too radical, or too unpopular, an alternative scenario would rely more on parking controls and priority lanes for buses and lorries. Without road pricing, other taxes would be needed to pay for better public transport.

The report drew on the views of many practising transport professionals, reflecting an emerging consensus among many of them. As Goodwin recalls: 'It was the enlightened traffic engineers whose line of argument was: well I've always been a road-builder but now it's not working is it? We've got to do something different. I heard that many times.' A few days later Labour's transport spokesperson, John Prescott, made a speech reflecting these conclusions, using a phrase which would stick in the public and official minds: 'we cannot build our way out of congestion'.

The report made a lasting impression on the transport professions; it influenced some in the Labour Party but made little impression on the DTp or many Conservative ministers at the time. Norris remembers meeting Goodwin, but says that 'Phil only ever had a limited influence with Tory ministers', who mainly regarded him as a 'brown rice and open-toed sandals man'.

Goodwin looked startled at the reference to rice and sandals (and I can't say I have ever seen him wearing or eating either!), but confirmed that he had little direct contact with Ministers after publication of 'Transport: The New Realism'. However he says:

> The report did have an impact on the government through the (mostly Conservative) County Councils in the South East, such as Surrey, who were living with the contradiction between congestion, road-building and demand management. They were the main voices putting pressure on ministers.

Another report from one of the DTp's own advisory committees, which also included Goodwin, helped to change official thinking more directly. In 1992 MacGregor invited an advisory committee of the DTp, SACTRA, the Standing Committee on Trunk Road Assessment, to consider 'whether new or improved trunk roads induce extra traffic'. Goodwin was tasked with gathering evidence from previous studies and drafting the first two chapters. He recalls:

> Most of the meetings were attended by one or two people from the DTp. When it started out, the DTp guy felt it was his duty to be the official spokesperson defending the orthodoxy, whatever it was. After a while that stopped happening. I don't know whether someone had had a word with him and said: it's all right, we can live with what they're saying. Clearly the DTp knew what was going on … The evidence base turned out to be a lot more substantial than anybody thought it was when we started.

The final report came to a strong conclusion: building or widening roads induces more traffic. Its language was studiously technical, making no direct criticism of government policy, but the implications were clear; a big road-building programme was not an effective way to reduce congestion.

SACTRA sent its final report in May 1994 to John MacGregor, a Transport Secretary under pressure. A few months earlier proposals to widen sections of the M25 to 14 lanes using parallel distributor roads had united Conservative MPs in affected constituencies in a campaign against it. A DTp report, leaked to *The Guardian*, identified 103 'highly controversial' schemes, not all officially announced; 90 of them would pass through Conservative-held constituencies. Some of their MPs began to publicly criticise the programme. George Walden, the MP for Buckingham, said: 'You have a philosophy that is danger-ously one-sided … underpinned by a primitive image of freedom of the car and against railways. I've never known my constituents to be so wild about something.'

In March 1994 MacGregor announced the cancellation of 49 road schemes, mainly for budgetary reasons but also reducing the number of unpopular new roads through open countryside. However many controversial schemes, including the widening of the M25, remained in the programme. On 26 April protestors from the M11 occupied the roof of MacGregor's house, helped by one of his neighbours who said he 'believed in free speech and I don't think they are doing anybody any harm'. MacGregor responded that 'I won't be intimidated', but the view was growing among at least some Conservative MPs that he was becoming a liability.

John Major's government was suffering from instability on several fronts at that time. Disagreements over Britain's role in Europe were again dividing the party, prompting one MP to say he would stand as a 'stalking horse' to trigger a leadership contest and open the way for others to stand. In May 1994 another MP speaking anonymously to *The Times* called on Major to sack MacGregor, along with five other ministers, in a cabinet reshuffle to reassert his authority. Shortly after-wards, as Major was considering a reshuffle, MacGregor told him he wanted to leave the government.[2] In July 1994 he returned to the backbenches, leaving the SACTRA report still unpublished in his suc-cessor's in-tray.

Brian Mawhinney and Great Transport Debate

His replacement, Brian Mawhinney, began with a very different agenda. Comparing him to his predecessor Norris says: 'Brian was more political; he would have judged everything that I did against its political acceptability and I suspect that he did get wind of the idea that looking for ways to moderate demand for travel was becoming more popular.' In appointing Mawhinney, John Major told him to '"get a grip" on the DTp and the way it functioned'.[3] As Norris wrote, and several interviewees confirmed, Mawhinney 'has a combative debating style, which could occasionally strike fear and loathing in the hearts of officials.'[4] Mawhinney later wrote:

> The country's road-building programme had been increasingly controversial for some time. As we became more prosperous people bought more cars, businesses moved more goods … which in turn meant more road traffic … The pressure for more roads was huge … Clearly this process could not continue indefinitely. The countryside could not stand it and the Exchequer could not afford it.[5]

One of his early objectives was to engage with environmental organisations, or at least those 'which operated within the law'. He described Norris as an 'honourable exception' within the DTp who already had contacts they could develop. In making a public invitation, he told the media that road-building and the environment would be on the agenda. The main organisations all accepted, though they were not all convinced of Mawhinney's sincerity. Charles Secrett described him as a 'conventional economic growth person'. Others, such as Stephen Joseph of Transport 2000, found the new approach more encouraging:

> I remember that turn from being in outer darkness to being invited in by the DTp … I think John Major told Mawhinney to sort out the DTp, to get the Tory MPs off his back … Steven Norris led a big questioning, saying: look at all these things that the DTp had spent their time ignoring, like green space, quality of life, pollution and so on. Those are legitimate parts of the transport debate. That wasn't the standard DTp view at all; it was all about roads and time savings …

In October 1994 the Royal Commission on Environmental Pollution published a report highlighting multiple threats to public health from growing traffic volumes. One of its recommendations was to halve the road-building budget; another was to increase taxes on fuel, to double its price over the next ten years. These proposals proved useful to the Treasury at a time when pressure was growing on the public finances. The economy was beginning to recover from recession but this had left an overhang of public borrowing and national debt. In the budget of November 1994 the future budgets for road-building were cut back; over the next three years they would fall by 20 per cent, a move described by the British Roads Federation, with a little exaggeration, as 'the biggest hit on the road programme since the Romans left'.

Mawhinney held onto the SACTRA report for seven months, until December 1994 when he published it with an announcement that most of the schemes in the road-building programme, would undergo 'extra assessment to determine their overall impact on traffic'. Although that review did not produce any radical change the view already held by Norris and Gummer that road-building created more traffic began to gain more credence among ministers and civil servants. For Norris, the proposals to build distributor roads around the M25 were an extreme illustration of this problem:

It came with a health warning that said this would only be good enough for ten years. That sent a very big signal to me that said: well in that case, this is a ridiculous project, because presumably in ten years' time you'll be saying to my successor: 'Please can we have another three lanes each way?' I couldn't accept that.

In April 1995 Mawhinney announced the abandonment of the plans. Some sections of the motorway would still be widened to 10 lanes (12 for a short stretch), while Norris would lead a review of possible rail improvements between Heathrow and Gatwick airports, which generated much of the traffic along those sections.

Mawhinney used a conference on air quality in December 1994 to call for a 'ceasefire' between environmentalists and road lobbyists, appealing to both to join a national transport debate, which he launched with a series of speeches over the following months. To the consternation of business lobbyists, he made it clear that all aspects of transport policy, including the road-building programme, were now under review. Once all contributions to the debate had been considered, he promised a consultation paper on new government policies before the end of the year. In the event, Mawhinney was promoted out of the DTp in July 1995, immediately after his approval of the Newbury Bypass.

His autobiography describes the dilemma this issue posed to him as a Christian committed to 'caring for God's creation': 'I still remember that beautiful countryside around Newbury which is no more and how much I enjoyed walking through it as a preliminary to making my decision – even as I know that tens of thousands of people live better lives as a result of that decision.'[6]

Norris disagreed with that decision, which he describes as an 'aberration' to their emerging consensus to consider other alternatives before environmentally damaging road schemes. What was behind Mawhinney's decision? 'He knew the people of Newbury were dead keen on the bypass, even though Swampy might not have wanted it, so the shrewd thing to do was give the consent and have the chance of winning the seat back [from a Liberal Democrat, who also supported it].'

Charles Secrett recalls both civil servants and a senior minister telling him afterwards:

> The government was on the verge of conceding defeat … We were told in no uncertain terms that if other things had happened between [the rally FoE organised in] March and the decision, to keep the pressure up, to hold the government's feet to the fire, that the decision would probably have gone our way.

The Bicycling Baronet and the Parsimonious Treasury

The new Transport Secretary, Sir George Young, was known as 'the bicycling baronet', as he would often arrive at the Houses of Parliament by bike. He came from the left of the party and was a member of FoE. A right-wing columnist once wrote of him in the *Mail on Sunday*: 'What is a man who rides bicycles, drinks beer and sends his children to comprehensive schools doing in the Conservative Party?' He was less of a showman, and more consensual in his style of management, than Mawhinney. In briefing him on his appointment, John Major's main concern was to force through the privatisation of the rail industry. This would take up much of Young's attention over the following two years; road-building was slipping down the political agenda.

Like Norris, he had no opposition to new roads in principle – and he had no intention to reverse any earlier decisions – but he was concerned at the mismatch between the size of the programme and the available funds. The large number of approved schemes was generating a larger number of compulsory purchase orders, swelling the DTp's portfolio of blighted properties. As many of these schemes could not be funded in the foreseeable future, he wanted to stop what he came to regard as a waste of limited resources. With budgets shrinking he also wanted to protect the funds available for rail and a couple of tram projects in Manchester and Croydon, and to start taking cycling more seriously. All of this pushed him to accelerate the contraction of the road-building programme.

The public finances were still suffering from the aftermath of 'Black Wednesday' when Britain crashed out of the European Exchange Rate Mechanism in 1992. A civil servant recalls how that event 'traumatised the Treasury', which started to feel that 'public spending was out of control.' In that context they were relieved to find an area of spending which a minister was willing to cut back. As Norris explains:

> There was a very long tradition ... that infrastructure was basically just money. Rather than it being viewed as an investment improving our social and economic efficiency it was seen as a big lump of money that either had to be borrowed or taxed, neither of which was particularly attractive.

A civil servant within the Treasury said: 'The whole atmosphere was one of "we must save money" ... It was indifferent to whether this was operating spending or capital spending. It's easier to cut a road scheme than to cut [staffing] ...' In the budget of 1995 the road-building programme was cut back again. Seventy seven schemes were cancelled; only nine schemes plus 11 design, build, finance and operate schemes were now scheduled to start before the Spring of 1997, which was the latest date for a general election.

The Treasury's lack of interest in the economic impacts of capital spending left Young more latitude than some later transport ministers would have, to rewrite national transport policy as he saw fit – as long as he made no spending commitments. Young had inherited the unfinished business of Mawhinney's Great Transport Debate, to which he responded in April 1996 with a Green Paper (a consultative report), 'Transport the Way Forward'. In summing up the contributions to the debate it reported a 'strong preference for improved public transport over expanded road capacity' adding that 'The Government believes there needs to be a shift in priorities to reflect this.'

A whole chapter was devoted to public opinion, drawing on several long-running national surveys and some commissioned for the DTp. All of these told a similar story, that public opinion was turning against road-building, towards more investment in public transport and greater acceptance that some forms of restraint on motor traffic were necessary. Of particular interest with hindsight is the British Social Attitudes Survey, which continues to this day. It asked people to express their agreement or disagreement with a range of statements, one of which was 'the government should build more motorways to reduce traffic congestion'. In 1993 slightly more people agreed than disagreed with that statement. By 1996, during the Newbury Bypass evictions, only a quarter agreed; half the sample disagreed – the largest majority ever recorded against motorway building.[7]

Although the Green Paper's analysis and sentiments were strikingly different from earlier government policy statements, it did not make many new commitments. Its most specific measures had already been announced, such as the fuel duty escalator, below-inflation increases in rail fares and a technology trial for cashless motorway tolling. The challenge of restraining traffic in urban areas was placed on local authorities, who were promised unspecified new powers, to be developed through further discussion.

Shortly before publication an anonymous source described the government's intention to produce 'a sensible, but unheroic' document.[8] With an election approaching, radical solutions were to be avoided. One journalist interviewed environmentalists and road lobbyists about the Green Paper, commenting that they both viewed it as a 'damp squib';[9] another newspaper wrote of a continuing 'policy vacuum.'

The Road Traffic Reduction Bill

One attempt to fill that vacuum came through an unusual route – a private member's bill promoted by FoE. Private members' bills are presented by backbench MPs. Governments rarely allocate enough parliamentary time to enable them to become law. The first attempts to introduce a Road Traffic Reduction Bill were made by Plaid Cymru MP Cynog Dafis in 1994, 1995 and again in early 1996. The bill would have set national targets for reducing traffic volumes and placed a duty on national governments to work towards them. In the Green Paper, the government accepted 'the need for measures which influence traffic and reduce traffic growth' but rejected national targets. Without government support, the bill went no further.

Each autumn, on the day after the state opening of parliament, backbench MPs seeking to promote private members' bills enter a ballot. A few successful ones are allocated some debating time; these 'ballot bills' have a greater chance of success, although they still depend on government support. In October 1996 Liberal Democrat MP Don Foster was drawn seventh in the ballot. He took the opportunity to introduce another Road Traffic Reduction Bill. *The Guardian* noted that the government was offering no support and 'with the general election so close the bill had no hope'.[10] This assessment overlooked a change in ministerial attitudes and what Foster described as 'a model operation of how to get a private member's bill through'. He explains:

> I had already learned the art of writing amendments to legislation and I did a lot of work on the bill, but the real heavy lifting was done by FoE and [their parliamentary officer] Ron Bailey. They arranged all the public meetings, the material that was sent to each MP … We organised mass rallies; we gathered a cross-party coalition of MPs … I was the figurehead; they would say: 'we've arranged for a thousand people to be in Methodist Central Hall; you are speaking to them along with four other people; you will wind up. Here's a draft of what you might want to say', and so on.
>
> Members of the public [would] go into meetings with constituency MPs to persuade them to back the bill, to promise to write to the minister. Ministers then received lots of their own [Conservative] backbench MPs lobbying them, saying: support this.

Meanwhile, FoE branches and some local Lib Dem parties collected signatures on a petition supporting the Bill. I was the Lib Dem parliamentary candidate for Plymouth Sutton at the time. Over three or four days I cycled from Plymouth to London to present a sheaf of petition forms to Foster outside the Houses of Parliament.

Civil servants at the DTp were initially resistant, particularly to the idea of national targets, which they might become responsible for achieving, or failing to achieve. As the pressure from backbench MPs grew, John Watts, the junior minister with responsibility for roads, began talking to Foster about a compromise, which the government could support. The revised bill was, in Foster's words 'considerably watered down'. The national targets were replaced by a duty on local authorities to review the traffic situation in their areas and produce a report, explaining how they intended to reduce traffic or at least to restrain its growth. The bill gave no new powers to help local authorities do this. Examples of specific measures, such as pedestrianisation and traffic calming, were removed from the draft bill, to be addressed by government guidance at a later date.

Several of the bill's supporters accused Foster of 'selling out' but he and FoE took a tactical decision that a watered-down bill with government support was better than a stronger bill with no chance of becoming law: 'I wanted to find a way of changing the way the government provided funds to local government ... I wanted my local authority to have money to support measures that reduced traffic, by funding for local transport initiatives, pedestrianisation, traffic calming, et cetera.'

The Road Traffic Reduction Act received royal assent in March 1997, two weeks before John Major called the general election that swept his government from office. Although it was unlikely to make much difference to national traffic volumes, it did help to lay the foundations for a different approach to local transport planning under a new government.

The roads lobby were sceptical about the bill but were not particularly active in opposing it. One lobbyist, who asked to remain anonymous, recalls a conversation with the late John Watts:

It may have been the day, or the day after, Major called the '97 election, which everyone knew in their heart of hearts the Conservatives didn't stand a hope of winning. They'd just allowed the Road Traffic Reduction Bill to go through parliament and I asked him: 'Why on Earth did it go through?' and he said: 'Not going to be our problem to deal with, is it? The new government's going to have to deal with this bit of legislation and we'd love to see how they're going to cope with it'... I think there was a bit of 'leave them with some problems to pick up'.

The End of 'Roads for Prosperity'

The budget of November 1996 completed the dismantling of 'Roads for Prosperity'. A few days before the budget an internal DTp report was leaked to the media; it showed that with current budgets the road programme would take 30 years to build, and that 'many of the remaining schemes were considered necessary to relieve congestion created by previous road-building.' A Treasury civil servant recalls:

> My day-to-day job was totally about cutting the roads programme and the local transport programme. My predecessor had reduced the 'Roads for Prosperity' programme in half. I effectively reduced it to nothing ... [apart from previous commitments, where contracts had been awarded] I reduced their forward programme to the Spalding bypass and re-signing of the M60 Manchester Ring Road ...
>
> At no point did my seniors in the Treasury object; at no point was there more than the most superficial consideration of the effect on the economy or society ... There is a little bit of me that feels guilty that you participate in something that's not rational, that's not a good outcome ...

By that time, Norris, persecuted by the tabloid media over his private life and suffering from a 'hole in my personal finances'[11] had returned to the back benches. Freed from ministerial constraints he was interviewed by the BBC on the site of the Newbury Bypass, where he said:

> I don't think this route should have been used ... The protestors had a message which was fundamentally the right message, namely, that we could not go on simply pandering infinitely to increased car use and traffic growth, that we had to come to terms with managing

traffic, perhaps even seeing traffic volumes reduced. That was a sea change. They were the first to say it, and they got it right.[12]

Although successive ministers had recognised the shift in public opinion against the road-building programme described above, they did not seek to make political capital from its demise. The leaked report said that, in the past, cuts in the road programme were 'inevitably perceived as "bad news"'. However, in 1995 'we took great pains to issue the results on Budget day, and with considerable success: the department as such was not blamed for the very substantial cut-back. Officials propose that we should deal with this year's announcements in the same way.'

Labour's Shadow Chancellor Gordon Brown accused the government of 'under hand and devious' tactics.[13] The British Road Federation protested that the cuts would 'cost Britain thousands of jobs', but in the final months of a government struggling with many problems, the biggest road programme since the Romans passed quietly into history with little protest or celebration.

5

Integrated Transport,
the New Labour Ideal (1997–2000)

New Labour, New Conflicts

Transport rarely features prominently in general election campaigns. The Labour manifesto of 1997 devoted fewer than 300 words of generalities to it, carefully avoiding any suggestion of radical change. A poll conducted a few weeks before the campaign found that Swampy, identified by 6 per cent of the public, was twice as well-known as Sir George Young. None of the 1,000 people interviewed could name Labour's Shadow Transport Secretary Andrew Smith.

The only Labour politician who had raised the profile of transport was John Prescott who had held the post from 1988 until 1993. An adviser recalls:

> Integrated transport was the mantra of the Labour Party and had been during the previous Labour Government. No one knew what it meant in practice … Prescott's starting point was that he wanted integration. He was pro-rail. You could say that he was an early environmentalist, before it became fashionable, but he also drove a Jag, so he was quite committed to decent roads and was pragmatic about the importance of the motorist.

Prescott was the son of a railwayman, had worked as merchant seaman and became a shop steward for the National Union of Seamen. As a mature student he struggled to gain a third-class degree while taking time out to stand for parliament. His autobiography conveys a recurring 'sense of inferiority' born of his working-class roots. It also affirms his 'Old Labour' identity at a time when the 'beautiful people', the 'college boys' around Tony Blair and Gordon Brown were determined to marginalise him.[1]

Ironically, one of their attempts to exclude Prescott led to his eleva-
tion. In 1994 Prescott was elected Deputy Leader of the Labour Party,
a position which should have secured him a place at any discussions
about election strategy. Late in 1995 he discovered that Blair, Brown,
Peter Mandelson MP and several others had organised 'a secret
meeting at a country house on the south coast'. When he confronted
Tony Blair about this, Blair admitted that Brown and Mandelson had
asked him not to invite Prescott to the strategy meeting. To placate
Prescott, Blair promised to make him Deputy Prime Minister if
Labour won the election.[2]

When Labour won with a large majority, Prescott expected to play
a leading role in the new government. His preference was to become
a 'Cabinet enforcer', operating across all ministries but an adviser
says he told Prescott: 'in government you need troops – you need a
department.' Several options were discussed and it was only on the
morning of Prescott's meeting with Blair that he learned of a plan
for a new 'super ministry' combining the environment, transport and
local government. The idea was not new; it had existed under Labour
governments in the 1970s; it was resurrected with a new emphasis on
regional devolution as the Department of the Environment Transport
and the Regions (DETR) with Prescott, as Deputy Prime Minister,
at its head.

At the same time Gordon Brown was made Chancellor of the
Exchequer, the *de facto* number two of the government, despite Prescott's title. An adviser recalls that Brown was 'resistant to Prescott
becoming Deputy Prime Minister', although he was unable to prevent
it. A Treasury civil servant recalls:

> Gordon was head and shoulders above the others [in the cabinet,
> apart from Blair] in terms of aggression and punching power. John
> Prescott wasn't a more sophisticated thinker than, say, George
> Young but he had a degree of clout and chutzpah, a sense of purpose
> … Gordon Brown had no time for John Prescott. He had no under-
> standing of the things John was passionate about.

The scene was set for a conflict with lasting consequences, although
in its first round Prescott and Brown would find themselves on the
same side.

The Politics of Roads Claims Another Victim

In allocating cabinet places Blair struggled with two instincts: to create a 'New Labour' government in his own image or open a 'big tent' to keep potential opponents on his side. He had already decided to exclude two members of his shadow cabinet. Another member, Gavin Strang, posed a problem. Strang was a left-leaning MP of 27 years' standing who had been a junior minister in the 1970s. Blair did not want him in the cabinet,[3] but Strang was popular among Labour MPs; he had topped the ballot for places in the shadow cabinet. The creation of the DETR offered a potential solution to this dilemma. The Treasury had two places in the cabinet, for the Chancellor and his deputy; the same principle could be applied to the new super ministry. Strang, who expected to become Minister for Agriculture, was 'gobsmacked' by his appointment as deputy to Prescott, in charge of transport with a place in the cabinet.[4] Prescott reluctantly accepted the arrangement. An adviser explains: 'Prescott needed his status recognised ... He would have seen Gavin as a threat ... Poor old Gavin sat on his own in [DTp Headquarters] Great Minster House, completely frozen out by Prescott.'

The first and biggest issue of conflict between them concerned the road-building programme. To reassure wavering voters Labour's manifesto had committed to keep public spending within the limits set by the Conservatives for the first two years. Despite the cutbacks made by Mawhinney and Young, the list of approved road schemes still exceeded the available budget, while civil servants continued to work up new schemes. An adviser recalls:

> The general impression was that the previous government had put a block on [the road-building schemes] for financial reasons rather than a change of heart ... we had moved the priority from road-building to public transport so one of the first measures was to put a moratorium on new projects while they were all reassessed.

Another adviser says this move was:

> viewed as a problem by the DTp, who had a very big roads lobby at that point, who were very frustrated. There were a lot of people

who had built their careers on being involved in roads. [The anti-roads] protests came as an added bonus [for the moratorium and review] but there were still people protesting that their bypass was *not* being built ... Tony Blair wasn't that interested; it wasn't a high political salience issue, but he accepted that we didn't have money to build roads.

Twelve of the road schemes were subject to an accelerated review. Although the DETR was now one department, its constituent parts continued to work independently in separate locations. Their cultures and priorities were very different. The principles of sustainable development, which had gained ground within the former DoE, had not yet made much impact on the former DTp. The civil servants who conducted the roads review included people who had worked to implement 'Roads for Prosperity'. Not surprisingly, their report to Strang recommended that 11 of the 12 schemes should be retained. Strang agreed with them; as he told the *Scotsman* many years later:

I supported cutting [the roads programme]. However, the difference was I still take the view that for many communities and small towns a bypass was an excellent thing – and in opposition I had spent a lot of time campaigning for the Musselburgh bypass – so the idea that building a bypass was an environmental negative I thought was wrong.

This justification was slightly misleading. Some of the schemes were traditional bypasses; others, such as the Hastings Bypass only made sense as sections of new long-distance routes, while plans to widen the A40 into London were remnants of the 1970s approach to urban transport planning.

Prescott disagreed with these recommendations, but could not prevent Strang from making them directly to the cabinet. Prescott felt personally bypassed but, on this occasion, he had the support of Gordon Brown whose first objective was to control public spending. In July 1997, at a meeting in the Chancellor's country retreat, the cabinet backed Prescott. Five of the schemes were approved, including what became the M6 Toll motorway around Birmingham; two were scrapped and the remainder were deferred to a wider review leading towards a White Paper on integrated transport.

Strang would later play down reports of his fallout with Prescott but this incident probably sealed his political fate. In a pattern that will recur later in this story, anonymous sources close to Prescott began briefing against Strang to the media. One source told the Independent that Strang 'had 'not got a grip' or 'attended to the detail'. By October 1997, just five months into his post, Strang was angrily rebutting a 'whispering campaign' that said he 'wanted to leave the cabinet because he had a kidney disorder.' In May 1998 the *The Times* cited allies of Blair's confidante Peter Mandelson, saying of Strang and another minister: 'there is no longer any profit in keeping obvious duffers in place'. Two months later he was sacked, returning to the backbenches until he left parliament in 2010. Strang told the *Scotsman*: 'Part of the difficulty was John Prescott was more interested in transport than anything else in the department … It's a mistake to have transport in with another area because it's such a major part of the economy it should be a separate department.' Prescott wrote of Strang: 'The DTp tried to use him to undermine me in order to secure control of the department themselves. So in the end he didn't last long.'[5]

A New Strategy to Reduce Traffic

By 1997 Prescott's slogan that 'we cannot build our way out of congestion' had become a consensus, accepted by the government, the opposition parties and much of the media. Public opinion had become more critical of road-building and more favourable towards other alternatives. Even the British Roads Federation was willing to acquiesce, for the time being. Richard Diment describes their attitude:

There had been one of those once-in-a-generation political revolutions in the country. The New Labour government could virtually do what it wanted. There was a view that, if it's convinced it can create this revolution in transport – it can reduce the demand for transport, it can persuade people and industry to shift off the roads and reduce other modes – let's see what it can do.

A month after the election Prescott announced the government's intention to consult on a new transport White Paper, adding: 'I will have failed in this if in five years there are not many more people using public transport and far fewer journeys by car. It is a tall order but I want you to hold me to it.'

In August 1997 Prescott launched a consultation document, saying 'We want to take a wider, more strategic view of transport policy.' He also announced that a 'group of experts' led by Professor Phil Goodwin, the author of 'Transport: The New Realism', would advise his department when writing the White Paper. A political adviser recalls: 'They were a very influential group ... They were proposed largely by the civil service but we didn't want people who were predisposed to large-scale road-building. We wanted people who would challenge [past practice].'

Goodwin had given some advice to Prescott when he was deputy shadow transport minister in 1980. He was also approached before the 1997 election by some other Labour MPs, including Jack Straw, who thought that they might be made Transport Secretary, but he was surprised to receive a call from Prescott shortly after the election:

He said 'Can you come down for a chat?' I said 'When?', getting my diary out. 'Well, now.' I thought: 'He is the Deputy Prime Minister', so I jumped on a train. He showed me the list of names that had been assembled by the civil servants. He said: 'Yours is the only name I recognise; tell me what you know about them.' I went through the list; it was sensible enough but there were some obvious missing people and there were some that I thought: do you really want advice from them? Then I said, if you are going to set up a committee you are going to need a Chairman; I could do that if you want. I don't know if that was [already] the intended outcome.

The final list included eight others: academics, representatives of industry and the transport trade unions, Stephen Joseph of Transport 2000 and transport leaders from Edinburgh and Manchester, two cities that were making big efforts to shift travellers onto public transport. Prescott attended a couple of the meetings from start to finish, and one interviewee recalls Gavin Strang: 'like a fish out of water ... a quiet man, totally overwhelmed by Prescott'.

The main challenge faced by the group and the government in trying to reduce pressure for road-building was how to manage demand for limited road space. Traffic growth had slowed since the early 1990s, but the trends and the forecasts were still upwards. If a new policy was to endure, then ways would have to be found to constrain that growth, particularly at peak times. Popular positive measures, such as improvements to public transport, would not be enough on their own.

In its first budget the new government announced that the fuel duty escalator would increase to inflation plus 6 per cent each year. That would dampen overall demand, but it was indiscriminate; it would fall equally on cars queuing in urban rush hours and on uncongested rural roads. To reduce congestion, the most effective measure, as recommended in 'Transport: The New Realism', was road pricing, nationally or within cities, where it became known as 'congestion charging'. This was also one of the most controversial measures.

To persuade the leaders of cities – and urban voters – to accept congestion charging, the advisory group believed that cities must be allowed to retain the revenue ring-fenced for spending on transport. This proposal, and some others, such as taxes on out-of-town retail parking, faced opposition from two sources. Goodwin recalls the opposition of the Treasury to ring-fencing, and a more fundamental objection to the principle of road pricing from Tony Blair and his advisers: 'There was a Downing Street minder, who came to the meetings and said very little – he mostly sat there glowering – but you definitely got the feeling that his brief was: "We don't want a fight with the motorist."' An adviser close to Blair corroborates this: 'He didn't see any part of his political project as wanting to place excessive restrictions on people's use of their car and he would not want to be characterised as anti-mobility. He did say that to John Prescott, but possibly without great emphasis.'

A civil servant recalls how the proposals for the White Paper were received by the Treasury:

For a moment, there was a conversation about whether Treasury should block it, and just stop him from writing it … There was no political desire to be nice to John Prescott, so he was running a real risk of producing a White Paper that changed the grammar but was otherwise identical to George Young's. He only had two or three policy friends: Alistair Darling was one, Ed Balls was another. But the Treasury under Gordon Brown was like Henry VIII's court. Everyone had to mind their Ps and Qs, otherwise your head was chopped off. That put Alistair in a difficult place.

Uniquely among the Treasury officials I could see the transformational potential of road pricing in our major cities. I went out on a bit of a limb, but that only went so far; at least when other officials tried to dismiss it. It was only Alistair's sympathetic hearing that gave me enough space ...

At a certain point, John's proposals for the White Paper were going to a cabinet sub-committee chaired by Gordon Brown ... We were called up to see Gordon. The Cabinet Secretariat person came along. Gordon opened by saying: 'thanks for the advice, so I think it's all agreed, we block this.' I was quite junior and Gordon is a frightening person to deal with, so I just sat there and looked at him. It was quite clear that he hadn't read the advice and had no interest in reading it. So the Cabinet Secretariat person said: 'Well no, that's not the advice, Chancellor.'

Apparently, it was an absolute car crash of a cabinet sub-committee. John Prescott was kicked around the table, humiliated and told to go away. I wasn't there but I got phone calls afterward from DETR people who said: what do we do? I can't quite remember the sequence of events but through what I did, with Alistair Darling and Ed Balls we got to the point where the Treasury acquiesced. In the end, it was only Alistair Darling and Ed Balls's sympathy for the policy that nudged the Treasury towards acquiescence, without Gordon ever really endorsing the measure as such.

Road pricing was one of several demand management measures that worried Blair, Brown and their advisers. The early drafts of the White Paper also included proposals to tax parking at workplaces and out-of-town retail parks. Everyone agreed that transport and land-use planning should be better 'integrated', but there was less agreement on how this might be done. The early drafts suggested stronger planning guidance, directing new development towards urban areas with better public transport, to reduce the need to travel. Gordon Brown and the Treasury did not support more directive planning; an adviser says:

'Brown saw the planning system as an impediment to productivity growth.'

An adviser close to Blair raised some more fundamental objections:

Some of the arguments we had were about the desirability of mobility *per se* – not the mode of mobility. There was a strand of the thinking that said: we need to have a less mobile society, which I think is an extraordinarily reactionary position. The [advocates of demand management] were a very long distance from your average transport user, rightly or wrongly. If we went out and talked to a shopper, a mum picking up their children from school, a dad making their way to work, transport and mobility could be very important to them. Prescott had a tin ear to that.

Between formal cabinet meetings Blair and Brown left the negotiations to their advisers, who would 'drill down to the lieutenants in the civil service', often annoying Prescott. An adviser recalls:

If he heard something like this he would get straight onto Tony Blair, which very few cabinet ministers would have done, and say: 'so I hear you've got these concerns. Do you have these concerns?' To which Tony Blair would often say: 'No, of course not; I don't know anything about it.' Which may have been true or may not have been true.

In May 1998 one of Blair's advisers wrote to a DETR official expressing concern that a draft of the White Paper might be perceived as 'anti-car'. The memo was leaked to the press. Prescott hit back in a television interview, accusing 'teeny boppers' in Blair's Policy Unit of 'undermining' ministers. One of Prescott's own advisers said to him: 'You do realise that this man is about 40 years old?'

On that occasion Blair told his advisers to 'back off', but on many issues, in the White Paper and more widely, Prescott was forced to compromise. Another adviser remembers how the proposals to tax out-of-town retail parking were frustrated, after Tesco lobbied Tony Blair:

I remember a meeting at Prescott's residence attended by [DETR ministers, trade union leaders and advisers]. Stupidly, I said: 'Look, there's no point in talking about this car parking tax ... In the end Blair's going to veto it.' Prescott went up the wall, saying: 'Blair's fucking not going to veto it!' [Laughs] He did – entirely predictably.

The White Paper published in July 1998 reflected both the original principles and several compromises. It confirmed that building new roads was no longer a priority for the government. It talked about improving public transport and aimed to reduce traffic *growth* and urban congestion but not to reduce traffic *volumes*. New legislation would enable road pricing, starting with 'pilot schemes' on motorways or trunk roads. Decisions on whether to introduce urban congestion charging or workplace parking levies would be left to local authorities. If they chose to do so, these measures would 'provide those authorities with significant new sources of revenue for funding improvements, for example in public transport, walking and cycling'. This implied that Prescott had won the battle on ring-fencing (as Goodwin believed) although the wording was rather vague, leaving the detail to later leg- islation. A similar commitment was made to review national planning guidance, aiming to reduce the 'dispersal of development so reducing the need to travel', but the details would follow later.

Local authorities would be required to produce Local Transport Plans, which would promote integrated transport in their areas, and follow the requirements of the Road Traffic Reduction Act. They would 'promote green transport plans for journeys to work, school and other places' but there was no suggestion of a 'war on the school run' as the *Daily Mirror* had speculated.

The White Paper was broadly welcomed by campaign groups, business organisations and even the motoring organisations, although the Automobile Association added that 'the case for more charges on the average motorist is thin'. The Conservatives' Shadow Trans- port Secretary, Gillian Sheppard also attacked the proposals for more charges but not the main aims of the White Paper. For the Liberal Democrats, Matthew Taylor described it as: 'long on words and short on action', which was true; it was a strategic report, with the actions and the details to follow.

Today, the adviser who was close to Blair describes the White Paper as 'not as consequential as the energy spent on it'. A civil servant adds:

The 1998 White Paper was the culmination of thinking [on more sustainable transport] but who was buying into it? John Prescott, bought into it ... but in the arts of government John Prescott was not a first-ranker. Phil Goodwin, Stephen Joseph and the others bought into it, but the chattering classes weren't buying into it, the senior politicians who mattered weren't buying into it. The CBI wasn't bought into it, so it was insecure.

The Retreat Begins

A few days after the publication of the White Paper, the DETR published its review of the remaining road-building programme. From 150 schemes inherited from the previous government, 37 were scheduled to start over the following seven years. Among them were a widening scheme in Prescott's Hull constituency, as Conservative MPs pointed out, and plans to widen a section of the M25 to 12 lanes, which angered Friends of the Earth. For the longer term, the report announced the creation of 'multi-modal studies' in each of England's seven regions (in Scotland and Wales transport would be devolved to newly elected executives). Their aim was to study problems which would have led to road-building in the past, and look for broader solutions, involving different modes. As with the White Paper, the people around Blair and Brown were not convinced. One adviser recalls 'a Prescottian wheeze: "We're not delaying, we're having a multi-modal study." I could see the attractions of trying to think holistically but it was also an excuse for inaction.'

As the new government began to put its commitments into law, some of the fudges in the White Paper flared into new conflicts. A manifesto commitment to a directly elected mayor for London posed new problems for Blair, as support grew for Ken Livingstone, the left-wing former leader of the Greater London Council, to stand as the Labour candidate. The draft law for the new Greater London Assembly (GLA) appeared to renege on the White Paper's ring-fencing commitments. The new mayor could introduce congestion charging but the Secretary of State – Prescott – would decide where the revenue went. But, when Prescott presented the Bill in Parliament, he made a surprising commitment to pass 100 per cent of the revenue to the Mayor and 'review the situation after ten years'. An adviser recalls what happened behind the scenes:

> Gordon would avoid having an argument with John. He would get his officials to basically say: 'you can't do that.' So Prescott said: I'm not talking to his official. If Gordon wants to stop it he can tell me himself, but of course Gordon wouldn't come to the phone. So Prescott went ahead and made the announcement and then got bollocked afterwards by Blair and the Permanent Secretary to the Cabinet.

Notwithstanding that incident, in grappling with the problems of government, relations began to improve between Prescott and Brown, as another adviser explains:

> Gordon realised that this was the second biggest capital spending department in the government now, so he started to pay a lot of attention to it and work constructively with it. We never had the sort of concerns we heard from Downing Street with the Chancellor's people. On the big picture they were on board, for relieving congestion by investing more in public transport.

At the same time, Blair was becoming more concerned about a lack of visible progress across all departments. He and his advisers became more focussed on accelerating 'delivery.' By mid-1999 unnamed 'Blairites' were 'gunning for a clique of Prescott supporters' at the 'leftist' DETR; some were calling for transport to be separated from the rest of the department. Prescott was aware of these machinations and fought to resist them, but a cabinet reshuffle removed some of his allies and installed Lord Macdonald, a Blairite television magnate, as Minister of State for Transport, still within the DETR.

While working towards a new transport strategy, Prescott had also been grappling with inherited problems on the railways. The fragmented structure of the newly privatised railways created misunderstandings and conflicts of interest, which had already contributed to one fatal crash at Southall in 1997.[6] Then in October 1999 two trains collided at Ladbroke Grove in west London, killing 31 people and injuring 425. Prescott went to visit the site of the disaster, where he made another rash promise: that money would be 'no object' in making the railways safer. Inevitably Prescott became a target for grieving relatives. These events further weakened Prescott's position in the government. In December 1999 Prescott's own comments to the *Sunday Telegraph* seemed to imply that he was passing more control over transport to Macdonald. Although he later claimed that nothing had changed, advisers confirm that Macdonald was the driving force behind 'Transport Ten Year Plan 2000', published in July 2000.

Compared to the White Paper, the Ten Year Plan marked a further retreat from the principles of the 'new realism' (Goodwin was not invited to advise this time). There would be more road-building, including 100 new bypasses and 80 other trunk road schemes. It set some highly optimistic targets for reducing congestion but mentioned no plans to restrain growth in national traffic volumes. It assumed that eight local authorities would implement urban congestion charging and 12 would go for workplace parking levies, but it did not explain how national government might help that process. On fuel duty and road pricing on trunk roads it said: 'such choices do not have to be made now'.

One choice had already been made: to scrap the fuel duty escalator. After six years of increases faster than inflation, petrol and diesel were more highly taxed and more expensive in Britain than in any other European country. A coalition of motoring, retail and road haulage organisations met Gordon Brown, arguing that they were suffering from unfair competition; their call to scrap the escalator was supported by several Labour MPs. In the budget of 2000, Brown announced that fuel duty would rise in line with inflation this time, and the policy of automatic increases would be scrapped. Would that be enough to satisfy the government's critics? No one I interviewed anticipated what was about to happen next.

6

The Fuel Protests and
their Aftermath

Over eight days in September 2000 a few loosely organised groups of farmers and hauliers blockaded oil refineries and fuel depots around the country, stopping the flow of fuel to petrol stations, causing panic buying and shortages in shops. These events provoked a political crisis with lasting consequences for national transport policy. They took the government, and most other commentators, by surprise although with hindsight the warning signs seem clear enough.

The Origins of a Revolt – and a False Start

During 1998 the price of crude oil fell to its lowest level since the 1970s. Although the oil companies did not pass all the savings on to the consumer, prices at the pump fell in the early months of 1999. In March of 1999, OPEC, the cartel of oil producing countries, agreed to cut their production to increase prices. Between November 1998 and mid-2000, the price of crude oil nearly trebled. Prices at the pump, which were more influenced by taxation, rose by around a third.

Ironically, the people hit hardest by these increases were users of 'red diesel', which is untaxed, so much cheaper but more sensitive to international market prices. Tractors and other agricultural vehicles use red diesel, although deliveries to and from farms, as well as farmers' personal vehicles, use normal taxed fuel.

In the early years of the Labour government livestock and dairy farming were in crisis. Exports of most British beef remained banned four years after the outbreak of BSE ('mad cow disease'). The price of milk fell below the cost of production in 2000, due to a strong pound and the deregulation of milk marketing, which pitched individual farmers against the buying power of supermarket chains. In late 1999 a group of livestock and dairy farmers, led by a Welsh farmer Richard

Handley, formed Farmers for Action, to highlight their plight through direct action. South Devon farmer Richard Haddock recalls:

> Because we had all worked together during the BSE crisis and linked up, we had learned one thing: new technology. And the new technology back then was a brick, called a mobile phone. And we used to talk to each other. We would bump into each other in the market, we'd have meetings around the country ... A lot of farmers work by day on the farm and by night will drive lorries, to keep their business going ...

Rising fuel costs were squeezing farmers and hauliers and anger was rising among both. In March 1999 a group of hauliers borrowed the French tactic of an *opération escargot*, a slow-moving convoy of around 500 lorries, which blocked some motorways and Park Lane in West London for several hours.

In June 2000 an IT consultant, Gary Russell, hit on a new idea for organising protests. By 2000 about a quarter of UK households were connected to the Internet, making it a viable channel for mass communication for the first time. His campaign 'Dump the Pump' called on motorists to boycott petrol stations for one day on 1 August. A 'Hauliers and Farmers Alliance' planned a 'French style blockade' of the port of Dover on the same day. Neither of these actions made much impact, despite enthusiastic support from the tabloid media. The leader of the failed Dover protest said of the poor turnout: 'It sends out all the wrong signals to the Government and makes them think hauliers don't mind paying the high taxes on fuel.'

The Protest Begins in France

Direct action, often blocking roads, ports or the distribution of goods, is a recurring feature of French politics and industrial relations. In 1996 and 1997 striking lorry drivers blocked fuel depots, causing petrol stations across parts of the country to run dry. Their actions won significant concessions from employers and the government on pay and earlier retirement.

In August 2000 fishermen in the Mediterranean and the English Channel began blockading ports, calling on the government to compensate them for their rising (untaxed) fuel costs. As queues grew on both sides of the Channel, Kent police closed a section of the M20, to create a temporary lorry park. The fishermen's leader, nicknamed 'Monsieur Misery' by the *Daily Mail*, told their reporter: 'The English people are always so selfish. They don't understand teamwork and the need to fight together for what you believe in.'

As the French government had little influence on the price of untaxed fuel, they offered to cut harbour fees and social security contributions, reaching an agreement to lift the blockade on 31 August. The British media reacted with a mixture of contempt and *schadenfreude*. Mary Ann Sieghart wrote in *The Times*:

> I asked a member of the Government yesterday what it would have done had British ports been barricaded by protesting British fishermen. 'We would have let them demonstrate for a bit, then we would have sent in the police', was the reply. No question of giving in, as the French did yesterday.'[1]

Organisations representing French hauliers were already in fraught negotiations with the government over a law which would limit their working hours, when rising fuel prices began to squeeze their operating margins.[2] Encouraged by the success of the fishermen they agreed to organise a blockade of oil refineries and petrol depots starting on 4 September. The largest organisation expected 4,000 lorries to join its protest; in the event only about 1,500 turned out, but this was enough to block most of the flow. By the end of the day petrol stations across the country were running out of fuel.

Protest Crosses the Channel

As these events unfolded in France, on 4 September a farmers' leader in North Wales, Brynle Williams, called a meeting to discuss direct action. The meeting was 'chaotic' but a 'small huddle' after the main meeting agreed the outline of a plan to blockade fuel depots. Richard Haddock recalls:

> We never did anything in writing, for obvious reasons, but we verbally agreed that Brynle Williams and his colleagues would shut

the first fuel depot on the Monday night [11 September]. My Welsh colleagues always get a bit excited and they went on the Thursday night [7 September], and caught us all out.

Why did this happen? On 5 September, as the new French blockade hit the headlines in the UK, BP and Texaco announced that the price of fuel would be rising yet again. A friend told Williams of mounting anger among the hauliers and persuaded him to call another meeting.[3] About 200 farmers and hauliers turned up at St Asaph livestock market at 6 p.m. on Thursday 7 September – day 1 of the protests. They debated different options, then someone suggested a blockade of Stanlow oil refinery near Ellesmere Port. One of the farmers said they should go straight away 'when we are motivated'. Williams put the suggestion to a vote. When it was carried he said to the meeting: 'If you're not with us then leave now. No one will think the worse of you.' No one moved. The mood of the meeting changed as they talked about potential risks; it was agreed to allow deliveries of fuel for the emergency services and to keep the action non-violent. Then nearly all of those present got into their tractors lorries or cars and drove the 30 miles to Stanlow, where they blocked the entrances for six hours.

The refinery management called on the local Labour MP to ask the protestors to move; they refused until the police arrived and told them they were committing an offence by blocking the highway. At 4.30 a.m. the blockade was removed and most of the protestors went home, believing their point had been made, but although the road was now clear, the tanker drivers refused to leave the refinery. A spokesman for Shell, the owners of Stanlow, said that it was 'too dangerous' for them to cross the picket line, which had dwindled to just 40 people by the following morning. Over the next week there were many claims of intimidation and there was some minor damage to lorries but little evidence of actual violence and only two arrests, prompting accusations that the oil companies were tacitly supporting the blockades, to put pressure on the government to cut fuel duty. However, at most of the sites, including Stanlow, the drivers were no longer employed by the oil companies. Haddock explains: 'We knew the tanker drivers were very disgruntled because most of the fuel companies were handing over their transport to P & O, and P & O at the time were trying to change drivers' safety and policy rules. They wanted to cut the prices and bring cowboys in to drive tankers.'

A government adviser went with a minister shortly afterwards to meet the drivers and hear their grievances; he says: 'a more alienated group of people it was hard to imagine'. At Stanlow, one of the farmers told the *Daily Mirror* that 'we have the full support of the tanker drivers and are confident they will not leave even if the authorities break the protest'.

Over the next few days, the 'jungle telegraph' sprang into action; reinforcements from Northwest England began arriving at Stanlow and the action spread to other refineries and fuel depots across the country. Only around 2,500 people were involved, but as in France, their actions were enough to disrupt the flow of fuel to petrol stations. Haddock explains:

> We looked at a map. I said: 'Stand the map on end; look at the UK as a funnel. We've got to shut the fuel depots one by one and work our way down the country, 'cause the fuel tankers will run to the next one down to load.' So we set a trap, never thinking they'd walk into it, 'cause we're just country bumpkins. We couldn't believe that it was working.

On day 3 Milford Haven refinery in Wales and depots at Pembroke and Avonmouth near Bristol were blockaded in a similar way; others in Manchester, Hampshire and Lincolnshire followed on day 4. Later that day Haddock told the media in Devon that they planned to blockade the Cattedown fuel depot in Plymouth at 6 p.m. on day 5. The statement provoked panic buying across Southwest England, where petrol stations ran dry before the blockade had even begun.

The attitudes and actions of the police were a critical element in the events that followed. Relations between the police and the fuel protestors were much more cordial than during the anti-roads protests a few years earlier.[4] Haddock recalls:

> The police had a lot of sympathy [for the protest] because they were taking police cars off the road, because they couldn't afford the fuel to keep them on the road. We were being told off the record, overtime was being cut; they were pissed off... The police liked us

because we kept our own people under control; if someone got upset they knew that we wouldn't thump a copper on the nose. We would sort our own problems out and they just monitored us. I phoned up to say: we are going to shut the fuel depots from 6 o'clock tonight. I got a call at quarter past four from some farmers and hauliers who'd got there early. They said: 'The police have closed it all off; there's bollards everywhere.'

So we all turned up. I was asked to see the inspector. What did we plan to do? I said: 'We're here for 48 hours, round the clock.'

He said: 'We haven't got much money, in the police. Can you step down the numbers after ten o'clock?'

'Of course we will. We don't want to cause any problems, as long as you don't try to get any lorries in or out.'

'No, no, nobody's going to go in or out'.

So we came to a fair compromise with the local police. We agreed that there would be garages designated for the fire, police and ambulances. We were then asked to go in and meet the fuel companies, and we made an agreement with them that they wouldn't try to run the blockades. 'We're only here for 48 hours and then we're bogging off.'

By six o'clock a crowd had assembled outside the gates, not just the original farmers and hauliers but members of the public who had heard through the media or word of mouth. People began bringing food and other supplies, while fishermen blocked access to the depot on the seaward side. As at Stanlow, when the original protestors left to take some rest, the numbers dwindled but the only tankers leaving the depot were those supplying the emergency services. On day 6, Haddock went home to get some sleep, leaving a low-key protest to run for one more day, or so he thought.

The Government Reacts

On day 1 of the protests Tony Blair was at the UN General Assembly in New York, where President Chirac reassured him that his government would not make further concessions to the farmers and hauliers blocking petrol stations across France. They had already offered a backdated cut of around 14 per cent in the fuel tax levied on hauliers and a 30 per cent cut for farmers. This placated some, but not all, of the protesting groups. Two weeks later his government made further concessions, creating a new mechanism, which would cut the tax on all fuels if prices rose by more than 10 per cent. On 9 September (day 3 in Britain) the protests spread across the border to Belgium, followed by several other European countries over the next few days.

In Britain, the speed and impact of the protests took the government entirely by surprise. Looking back today one adviser says: 'what happened was slightly inexplicable.' To begin with, they tried to play down the impacts. On day 4 the Scottish Secretary, John Reid, told GMTV that cutting fuel tax made no sense, adding that people in Britain 'do not react to the French way of doing things, which cause massive disruptions and inconvenience to fellow citizens'.[5] But behind the scenes ministers, civil servants and advisers were struggling to manage the situation. The adviser recalls: 'Getting a good flow of information in real-time [on the blockades and their impacts] proved incredibly difficult … the major source of information was Sky television news.'

Over the weekend (days 3 and 4) Blair was in Chequers, dealing with the liberation of hostages in Sierra Leone. On the morning of day 5, after reading a report on the crisis from civil servants, he called the Home Secretary Jack Straw to invoke the government's crisis procedure, seeking emergency powers from the Queen and convening a meeting of COBRA, the cabinet's emergency sub-committee. At the same time, Blair wanted to maintain a public impression of business as usual, so he decided to go ahead with a speaking tour of the Midlands and Yorkshire. On the evening of day 5, he was due to speak at a function in Hull City Hall, celebrating John Prescott's 30 years as the local MP. An adviser recalls that Prescott was aware of the deteriorating situation when Blair arrived to find Hull City Hall surrounded by 200 protestors. The function went ahead, with Blair heaping praise on Prescott, acknowledging their political differences but adding: 'We are closer together than ever.'

When it was over, Blair was escorted to a side door by police who advised him that trucks, lorries and taxis were blocking the roads to the restaurant where the celebrations were planned to continue. He decided to go straight to Sheffield, his next destination. That night, he received a report prepared for COBRA. It described a situation 'near breaking point' with tanker drivers refusing to leave the depots. Despite the protestors' attempts to maintain emergency supplies, hospitals were running short of vaccines and blood. During the 1980s supply chains began to shift to the 'just in time' principle, aiming to keep stocks of parts and raw materials to a minimum. This had made the whole economy much easier to disrupt. As panic buying spread to food supplies some supermarkets began rationing certain products;[6] if the blockades continued food would begin to run out in a few days. On the morning of day 6 Blair cancelled his tour and returned to London.

Ministers and officials were trying to work out what was happening, secure emergency supplies and put pressure on the oil companies, police, and tanker drivers to re-start deliveries. An adviser recalls:

> The police were clearly saying they couldn't stop people protesting, and because there were protestors the tanker drivers said they wouldn't drive. We don't live in a police state and we didn't want to repeat the actions of the miners' strike [under Margaret Thatcher] … There were issues about trying to get soldiers to drive tankers. The army didn't have very many people who could do this, and they needed to be trained. The Ministry of Defence supposedly had a pipeline network that could move oil around, and then we discovered that it was unusable.

During day 6 Blair called the chief executives of five major oil companies, asking them why their tankers were not moving. His autobiography, which says very little about transport, devotes six pages to his version of the fuel tax protests, where he stars as the tough leader, threatening the oil companies and unleashing the police and the army to 'stop the protests'.[7] In reality, the government's advisers knew the oil companies had little power over the drivers, who would probably defy them anyway, but greedy oil companies made a better media target than disgruntled tanker drivers. John Prescott told the press: 'we are quite convinced that the oil companies can face up to their responsibilities to see that oil is distributed properly' while unattributed government sources accused them of colluding with the protestors.[8]

Blair also called Bill Morris, the General Secretary of the Transport and General Workers Union, to urge their tanker driver members to restart deliveries. Reassured by Morris's promise, Blair made a stronger statement to the media, reiterating that the government would not back down, and adding 'we hope in the next 24 hours to have the situation on the way back to normal'.

That evening the first few tankers began to leave Stanlow and three other sites with police escorts and officers riding in some of the cabs, but as day 7 dawned it became clear that this would not be enough. Although the government could ensure emergency deliveries, it could not satisfy demand across the country. The adviser recalls: 'We were desperately hoping that a shift of these drivers would turn up and then drive.'

As the press and the opposition taunted Blair for his unfulfilled '24 hours' promise, the government and its supporters began to harden their rhetoric, and to put more pressure on the police to break the blockades. The General Secretary of the Trades Union Congress condemned 'this bosses' blockade', which was 'holding the country to ransom', adding: 'It's not good enough to let supplies through to ambulances, if doctors, nurses and hospital staff can't get to work.' That evening, Blair made his strongest statement so far, saying: 'There is a real danger now for the NHS and other essential services. Lives are at risk.' The Ministry of Defence put the armed forces on standby and said that emergency powers could be used to commandeer privately owned tankers.

Public Threats and Private Promises

Back on the picket lines, some of the protestors took Blair's declaration as a challenge. Richard Haddock recalls:

> I'd gone home because I was knackered to get a couple of hours' kip. After Blair's statement, a senior police officer phoned me saying things were going to happen; they needed me back down there to make sure people didn't kick off, and I said: 'I've got a bit of a problem.'
>
> 'What's your problem, Mr Haddock?'
>
> Because the fuel protests had happened faster than we expected – because the boys in the north had gone two days early – 'my car's empty of fuel!'

An hour later a police car arrived at Haddock's farm to take him back to Cattedown: 'They took me right to the front of the demonstration and dropped me off, and everyone was clapping and cheering – couldn't stop laughing.' Later that day, several hundred riot police, flown in from London following Blair's orders, arrived at Cattedown. Their attempt to break the blockade hardened the protestors' attitudes; they decided to prolong their blockade until 8.30 a.m. on day 8 to 'stick two fingers' to Tony Blair.

Meanwhile, the messages in the media about the impacts on the NHS were beginning to worry protestors elsewhere in the country. In the early hours of day 8 the protestors at Stanlow voted to 'stand down while we still have the moral high ground' as Brynle Williams put it. At around the same time, the trade unions, helped by the Chancellor Gordon Brown, persuaded the protestors to leave Grangemouth refinery in Scotland. In mid-November Brown would make his pre-budget statement; hints of concessions were privately made and publicly denied,[9] offering a face-saving formula. Across the country, with some arguments and reluctance, the protests came to an end with a promise to re-start them in 60 days' time if the government did not cut fuel tax.

Surveillance and Concessions

On 20 September, as supply chains across Britain returned to normal, a group of the original protestors and some new ones met in a hotel near Manchester to form a new organisation, the People's Fuel Lobby (PPL) 'to maintain pressure on ministers'. David Handley was elected as its leader. Neither Brynle Williams nor Richard Haddock were at the meeting, though Handley said he hoped to persuade Williams to join. The group's key demand was a cut of 26 pence per litre in fuel duty, just over half of the duty rate at that time, and clearly much larger than any concession the government might be contemplating.

The 60-day pause offered a challenge and an opportunity to the government to prepare for new protests. While officials worked with oil companies and the army to ensure continuity of supplies, thousands of people in the intelligence services, Special Branch, the trade unions and the media were deployed to infiltrate, divide and discredit the protest movement.[10] Several of its leaders were openly placed under surveillance. Haddock remembers hearing clicks on his telephone line and joking with the Special Branch officers who followed him for several months after the first protests.

The intelligence reports mentioned divisions between Handley and some of the other leaders, particularly Williams and Haddock, both members of the Conservative Party, whose instincts were more cautious. Haddock says: 'I didn't want to bring the government down. Some did, I didn't … We were not politicians; we were not anarchists as some people tried to portrays us … We frightened ourselves, to be truthful. We didn't realise how vulnerable this country was.'

As the PFL debated options for more and bigger disruption, the government began a divide and rule strategy. Blair invited Williams to meet him in Downing Street and ministers talked constructively to Haddock, while the government's media machine set out to discredit Handley and the PFL. The *People* revealed that he owed £44,000, mainly to agricultural suppliers, and had 37 County Court judgements against him.[11] They interviewed his wife, who said 'I can't even remember how much we owe, it's in that pile of paperwork somewhere', and his ex-wife, who said 'I wasn't sorry to see the back of him.'

In late October the PFL announced that it would organise a 'people's convoy' of vehicles, starting in the northeast on 10 November and finishing at Hyde Park in London on 14 November, the day after the 60-day deadline. Williams attacked their plans to start before the deadline and Haddock said none of his supporters would take part.

As the PFL planned their next action the government began a media offensive with one key statement each day and a concerted attack on Handley and the PFL. Jack Straw talked up the government's plans to deploy the military and threatened to revoke the licences of hauliers who broke the law. The *Daily Mirror* ran a picture of Handley on its front cover with the headline: 'Stop This Silly Fuel'.

During the first wave of protests, opinion polls conducted by ICM showed strong public support for the protestors. Eighty-nine per cent said they wanted a cut in fuel tax; most wanted this immediately but 38 per cent said they were willing to wait until the next budget. By November that support was slipping but 55 per cent still said they supported further blockades in support of lower fuel taxes.

On 8 November Gordon Brown made his pre-budget statement including a cut of 3p per litre (around 6%) in the duty on most fuels.

The road tax for lorries was also cut by up to £2,000 a year. This came nowhere near the demands of the protestors, but Brown believed that it would be enough to placate public opinion without appearing to capitulate.

A heavy police presence awaited the drivers who joined the people's convoy. Each driver was given a letter listing 12 offences which would lead to arrest; hauliers were told of the threat to their licences if they failed to follow police instructions. Police with video cameras filmed the convoy, while a helicopter accompanied them on their route south. Around 70 vehicles made it as far as Newcastle, accompanied by counter-protestors from Greenpeace and Friends of the Earth.

Throughout these events the environmental movement, and the environmental arguments for higher fuel taxes, hardly featured in any reporting; an opinion piece by Charles Secrett in the *Daily Mirror* was a rare exception. He now regrets their low profile:

> We had a discussion at FoE about what we should do about it and the key question was: do we confront the picket lines? We decided that we wouldn't because of the danger of it flaring up … It would be the picture, not the reasoned interview that would make the story … A month later, I thought: we made a wrong call.'

By the time the convoy arrived in North London it had grown to around 100 vehicles, with about 300 other people making their own way to Hyde Park. The disruption it caused was minimal. Handley made an impassioned speech, saying 'we'll be back in the New Year' but then resigned saying 'I've got a business to run and we're all tired.' Although fuel tax remained one of several grievances for local protests, the national movement was effectively over. The government's strategy seemed to have worked, but the political consequences of the protests were only beginning.

The Political Consequences of the Protests

The blockades and threats to restart them compelled the competing factions in the government to work together, for a while. One adviser recalls:

Tony Blair and Gordon Brown, in particular, became very wary of continuing fuel duty escalators. John wasn't against putting a pause on that. He said: the thing that will determine whether people are driving is the price of fuel, not the tax on it, and the price was going up faster than people had expected when the escalator started.

But as normality returned, the crisis reinforced the shifts of power and policy, which had already begun with the reshuffle and the Ten Year Plan. The same adviser says: 'there was definitely more wariness about being anti-motorist'.

Another adviser, closer to Prescott's critics, says:

The fuel tax protests weren't an anti-Prescott integrated transport protest... but for a strategy that was losing momentum anyway, it gave added reasons for the politicians to think, 'Well, I'm going to focus my attention on other things.' Prescott was generating a Catherine wheel of ideas ... everything was being thrown up into the air. Some of it was perceived as half-baked by colleagues in government and parliament. He wasn't getting a great press for his transport strategy ... He wasn't a good person manager and wasn't a very good Deputy [Prime Minister].

In October 2000, during the pause in the fuel protests, a third major rail crash killed four people and injured over 70 at Hatfield in Hertfordshire. The cause was traced to a broken rail and incompetent maintenance by Railtrack, the private company which now owned the track. Under pressure from Prescott and the media they imposed speed restrictions across the network and began an emergency programme of rail inspection and renewal. The ensuing disruption lasted for several months, adding to the political pressure on Prescott and the DETR. People in government and the media began to question the effectiveness of the 'superministry'. The same adviser says:

It was an incoherent department. You had Prescott and his gang in Eland House and [the transport ministers] in Great Minster House. Prescott had set lots of hares running and was struggling to deliver. It was a department that had lots of breadth but wasn't very coherent ... It was an underperforming department.

Others who were more sympathetic to the integrated strategy make some similar observations: 'The transport people didn't like being there. They wanted their own department. They wanted to talk about trains and roads and they weren't really interested in integrating with anything else.'

In November 2000, the *Independent* called for the 'monolithic' DETR to be broken up, and the *Daily Express* reported Peter Mandelson's desire to become Minister of a newly separated Department of Transport. Ironically, around this time Prescott and the DETR instigated the most enduring legacy of Britain's brief experiment with integrated transport and planning. Two planning guidance documents with the snappy titles of PPG3 and PPG13 kickstarted the regeneration of Britain's inner cities, by constraining greenfield sprawl, reducing land allocated to parking and forcing developers to build upwards on brownfield sites. Over the following decade they would help to halt the inexorable growth of traffic and support a new generation of young adults who would move to the inner cities with fewer cars and drive less than their predecessors.[12]

None of that was apparent to the public or rival politicians at the time (and few people have made those connections with hindsight). Prescott fought a rear-guard battle to prevent the break-up of the department he had created, although he knew he was likely to leave it after the next election. For a short period during and after the fuel protests the Conservatives, who kept a low profile during those events, moved ahead of Labour in the opinion polls, but by May 2001, when Blair called the election, Labour had recovered its lead. Their manifesto promised to reform the railways, build 25 new tram systems and a lot more roads, offering 'real hope to motorists and passengers alike'.

Labour was returned to power and Prescott was given the job he had originally sought, as a 'Cabinet enforcer'. The DETR became the DTLR – Department of Transport, Local Government and the Regions – minus the environmental part. Stephen Byers was appointed DTLR Minister, with resolving the chaos on the railways as his overriding priority.

The wariness of politicians over taxing fuel would outlast Blair, Brown and the protests. As fuel duty is set in pence per litre, its value falls each year unless the Chancellor uprates it in line with inflation, which few chancellors have done since 2000. What is usually called a 'freeze' is really a cut. By 2019 the duty on petrol had fallen by 30 per cent; over the same period rail fares increased by 22 per cent more than inflation.

In 2001 no one knew how long future chancellors would continue that policy, but one of the most powerful demand management tools seemed to have been laid aside. This left road pricing as the most direct alternative. A few days after the protestors made their way home from Hyde Park the Transport Act 2000 passed into law, enabling transport ministers to charge for driving on trunk roads and local authorities to levy congestion charges. This is where the supporters of demand management, including local politicians, academics and much of the transport planning profession, increasingly turned their attention.

7

How Road Pricing Came to London – and Nowhere Else

The idea that road use should be priced to raise revenue and make more efficient use of limited space originated among right-wing ('neo-classical') economists. Milton Friedman, who advised Margaret Thatcher, was an early advocate. Several Conservative transport ministers investigated the idea, starting with Ernest Marples in the early 1960s. John MacGregor, the arch-enemy of the anti-roads protestors, coined the term 'congestion charging' to describe urban road pricing, when he published a study confirming its feasibility in 1993. A congestion charge had operated in Singapore since 1975 and in Oslo since 1988 but in Britain the idea did not progress until the early 2000s, when it became more associated with the left following an extraordinary story of political double-dealing.

How Congestion Charging Nearly Didn't Come to London

During the 1980s, Ken Livingstone, the left-wing leader of the Greater London Council (GLC), was frequently in conflict with Margaret Thatcher's government. One issue of conflict was the GLC's 'Fares Fair' policy, which subsidised public transport fares until the Law Lords ruled it unlawful. In 1986, the government abolished the GLC, replacing it with several London-wide bodies for different purposes. By the mid-1990s these fragmented arrangements were frustrating London's business community, which made common cause with the Labour Party in calling for a directly elected mayor.[1] Some of their frustrations related to transport and congestion, leading some business groups to propose a congestion charge.[2] For Livingstone, this situation offered an opportunity. A lifelong Londoner who had never learned to drive, he held, and still holds, strong views on urban transport. He says: 'In great world cities like London or New York with 8 million people,

people have to use public transport, unless you're going to treble their size and build vast numbers of new motorways.'

As the mayoral legislation was under discussion, Livingstone set out a manifesto with transport improvements at its core. He would not seek to repeat Fares Fair because, he explained, unlike the 1980s there was no longer spare capacity on the Underground. Instead, he planned to use the new congestion charging powers to pay for public transport improvements and reduce traffic passing through central London. However, he had drawn one important lesson from Fares Fair, as he wrote in the *Independent* in July 1999:

A few days before we cut the fares by increasing the rates, Thames Television commissioned an opinion poll that showed that 64 per cent of Londoners were opposed to our policy, and only 24 per cent supported us. The Labour group realised that opinion polls cannot make policy and we went ahead with the fares cut. Within a few weeks the polls had turned round, and two-thirds of Londoners supported us. The real lesson for Mr Blair and the Government is that we have to lead. We cannot expect the public to support in advance. They will have to judge us by results.

That was a lesson which some other cities would learn the hard way.

For Labour's leaders, particularly Gordon Brown, and some of their advisers Livingstone represented a throw-back to the hard-left politics, which had kept the party out of power during the 1980s. When internal polling suggested that Livingstone would comfortably win a ballot of party members, the New Labour majority on the Party's National Executive voted to set up an electoral college, giving a third of the votes to MPs and GLA candidates. An anonymous party source told the *Independent*: 'We want to see Ken's blood on the carpet. This is the way to do it.'[3] The same article reported that Blair's favoured candidate Frank Dobson was 'likely to back official government line' in favour of congestion charging.

As expected, Dobson won the electoral college vote, by just 3 per cent, in a contest marred by allegations of vote-rigging. Steven Norris, the Conservative candidate, called it 'an electoral system that would not be out of place in North Korea'.[4]

Encouraged by supporters and some newspapers, Livingstone decided to run as an independent. In a desperate attempt to claw back support two months before the election, Dobson, supported by the Labour leadership, decided to oppose congestion charging – the policy they had voted into law. Labour's manifesto for the London Assembly took the same stance. The tactic failed; Livingstone was elected with a large majority and Labour won just nine out of the 25 seats on the Assembly, the same as the Conservatives.

Dave Wetzel, the Vice-Chair of TfL, remembers that 'with one or two notable exceptions the Assembly Labour Group were generally hostile to Ken and his policies' during his first term, but they had no power to stop a specific measure, such as congestion charging. That did not mean that implementation would be easy. Some of the challenges were political, others were more practical. Wetzel recalls: 'Ken had four years and he wanted the scheme up and running in two years so he had two years to tweak it, if necessary, before he stood for re-election.'

But timing was not the only concern. Livingstone says: 'Seldom, if ever, had any politician in Britain brought in an IT scheme that wasn't a disaster.' To avoid a disaster, the team developing the scheme chose tried and tested technology: number plate recognition cameras, already in use for security purposes. Then in 2001 TfL appointed a new Commissioner, Bob Kiley, the former head of transport in New York. Wetzel recalls: 'Kiley was sceptical of this [old technology] so he delayed the scheme while he ran a review with his American team, but having reviewed it he was sure that we were on the right track ... [Some of us were] tearing our hair out because we could see the clock was ticking.'

In June 2001 John Spellar was appointed transport minister, reporting to Stephen Byers at the DTLR. An adviser remembers: 'John was an old infrastructure union man. He was not a great lover of Ken and the left. He used to joke with me that I was a sandal-wearer because I was a bit too interested in the environment and [the] effects [of transport]. John was more: "Let's build stuff."'

David Begg, a member of TfL's Board, remembers Spellar being hostile to congestion charging and 'dragging his feet'. In December 2001 Spellar publicly reminded Livingstone that he had the power to obstruct the scheme (by redirecting its revenues to the Treasury), which he would do if he was not satisfied that London's public transport system could cope with additional passengers. He added that Livingstone's 'performance in office has not encouraged confidence in his ability to run the scheme successfully'.

Behind the public war of words, people on both sides remember the government taking a hands-off approach. The government adviser recalls:

> We really didn't know how people would react. Would people disobey? None of us knew whether the technology would work, really. I remember some discussions about: if the day it comes in it all goes wrong, do we say: 'You idiot, Mayor', or do we try and help? John [Spellar] wouldn't have wanted to get too close to Ken if the whole thing failed. It wasn't: 'Let's deliberately try and make it go wrong', it was: 'If it goes wrong it was on his watch' and I think that was sensible politics, in a way.

The Mayor's proposals, published for consultation in July 2000, aimed to charge vehicles entering eight square miles of central London between 7 a.m. to 6 p.m., Monday to Friday. Following the consultation and lobbying by affected groups, concessions and exemptions were agreed – too many, according to Wetzel:

> Originally we were talking about a £7 charge; we reduced it to £5 [per day]. We changed the exempt areas, where residents only pay 10 per cent of the charge [wider than the charging zone itself]. It was too generous: 10 per cent, ridiculously generous. That was one mistake. Another was that we didn't include motorcycles.

Taxis, private hire vehicles, minibuses and disabled drivers were also exempt and concessions were made to Conservative-controlled Inner London Boroughs, including Westminster City Council, who launched an unsuccessful legal challenge to the scheme. Peter Hendy, then Manager of Surface Transport, recalls:

> There was a congestion charging complementary measures fund, and it didn't half fund a lot of stuff in Westminster and Kensington & Chelsea. In a sense, that's the politics of local government,

they're bound to extract things on behalf of their residents. Actually, everybody knew, if you lived within the [charging] zone you did rather well.

These concessions did little to placate the scheme's critics. As the work progressed, media reporting turned increasingly hostile. Retailers, teachers, West End actresses, restaurant chefs, animal welfare inspectors and a rabbi all attacked the plans, claiming that it would threaten their services. Workers at Smithfield meat market, dubbed 'the Smithfield Martyrs' by the *Evening Standard*, threatened not to pay the charge and were 'prepared to go to jail in defence of their cause.' Although initial opinion polls had showed a clear majority of Londoners in favour, Livingstone says: 'as we got closer the undecideds got bigger and bigger.' Wetzel recalls: 'There was a real wobble late in 2002. [Livingstone's political advisers] thought: 'how's he going to win an election with all these people against him?' ... Those who had faith that it would work knew that they wouldn't be against it once it was in and settled down.'

At a private meeting, his advisers urged him to delay the scheme until after the next mayoral election; he heard them out, then said he 'wasn't persuaded'.[5] The implementation date was set for Monday 17 February 2003 – a school holiday, when traffic volumes would be lower.

Although opposition to the charge was widespread it was fragmented, and protest actions were small in scale. On the morning of implementation Steven Norris and Conservative Leader Iain Duncan Smith addressed a rally of around 200 workers at Smithfield Market, while Conservatives, and a few Labour members led by a London MP, demonstrated at different points around the Congestion Charging Zone. By 6 a.m. journalists were gathering outside Livingstone's house. He recalls: 'I walked out to the start of it; there was a huge mob of journalists and it dawned on me they were expecting by the end of the day I would have to announce my resignation, as London collapsed into chaos. They all believed this crap.'

A protestor followed Livingstone dressed as a snail, but slow traffic was nowhere to be seen. In TfL's new traffic control centre Livingstone watched images of deserted streets and 'feared I had overdone it'.[6] Spellar phoned to congratulate him, adding 'the Devil looks after his own' and media critics grudgingly conceded that the introduction had gone well. Livingstone says: 'Within two weeks of it coming in my poll ratings had gone up ten per cent. The 2004 election was a foregone conclusion. Even the *Standard*, which hoped to get rid of me at that election, had to wait until the one after.'

The congestion charge achieved many of its objectives but also caused some unintended consequences. It reduced traffic volumes and improved air quality. It helped to fund more buses, used by more people. It enabled the city's transport planners to close some through roads, pedestrianise others, improve pedestrian crossings and allocate more space to cyclists. Those measures reduced road capacity, while the exemptions attracted more motorcycles, taxis and private hire cars. As a result, congestion, which fell in the early years, returned to its original level by 2008.[7]

London's experience attracted interest from across the world; Stockholm and Milan introduced congestion charges shortly afterwards. Several British cities were also considering the possibility, led by Edinburgh, where plans were already well advanced.

Edinburgh Puts Congestion Charging to the People

The option of a congestion charge for Edinburgh was first raised in a study in 1992, then written into the Regional Transport plan in 1994, although the legal powers to levy a charge did not yet exist.[8] David Begg was the Regional Transport Convenor at that time:

> I was very influenced by what I witnessed in some of the enlight-ened European cities [with excellent public transport, but rising congestion]. I realised early on that just supporting better public transport wasn't going to address the issues. My instincts were not to go for a city centre charge. I would have put it around the perim-eter of the city. I would have started by charging people to come into Edinburgh, on the basis that you're not going to affect people who are voting in the Edinburgh election. I'd have started there and tried to win support for the concept.

In 2001, the newly formed Scottish Executive passed a law enabling local authorities to implement congestion charges. Compared to the situation in London, this gave the Scottish Executive more power to influence and ultimately approve or dismiss proposals from a local authority for a congestion charge. Their influence, though lightly applied, would prove critical to the events that followed.

As the legislation passed through the Scottish parliament, the ruling Labour group on Edinburgh City Council announced their intentions. Motorists would pay £2 a day for entering the city, with the proceeds used to improve public transport including a new tram line. The Conservative opposition vowed to lead an 'anti-toll tax campaign' if the powers were ever used.

In August 2001, the Scottish Executive published guidance on congestion charging, which called for 'fair treatment of those who pay the charge and those who benefit from the scheme.' This effectively ruled out Begg's idea to exempt Edinburgh voters from a city-wide charge. It also required an authority submitting a plan to provide 'evidence of consultation *and support* from business, the community and other affected stakeholders' (emphasis added).

The City's plans, published for consultation the following year, were based on a flat-rate daily charge of £2. This would be triggered when drivers crossed *either* an outer cordon encompassing most of the city *or* an inner cordon around the city centre, heading inwards (only). No one would be charged twice. Research conducted afterwards showed that element was not well understood; many drivers believed they could be charged more than once in the same day.[9] Begg says: 'The officers are less interested in the politics, they are interested in evidence. The evidence would say that the main congestion was in the city centre so that's where you should charge, but it's not something that I would have [gone for].'

In October 2002 the Conservatives won a council by-election by campaigning against the charge. The Liberal Democrats, who came a close second, also opposed the charge, despite their party's support for the principle of congestion charging. The Labour vote collapsed. With full council elections due in May 2003, the Labour leadership decided that the plans would be put to a referendum, after the election. As a tactic to deflect opposition, it worked; Labour was returned to power with a comfortable majority. But there was another reason behind this decision; among the people who responded to the consultation 51 per cent of Edinburgh residents expressed support but more people from the surrounding areas opposed it. The councils and some MSPs representing those areas were vociferously opposed. As in London national politicians (including the Scottish Executive) distanced themselves from a controversial policy which they had initiated; a councillor complained that it was 'impossible to find a national Labour politician to speak in favour of the scheme'.[10] The council would have to convince a potentially sceptical Scottish Executive that there was 'support' for the scheme. By late 2002 it seemed the only sure way to do that would be through a referendum.[11] Some supporters of the congestion charging were sceptical of the council's chances of winning; Begg suggested that Edinburgh would be better to follow the example of Stockholm, which was planning to introduce a charge on a trial basis, then hold a referendum a year later.

The referendum date was set for February 2005. As in London, media coverage turned more hostile as the date approached but unlike London there were no major stunts or demonstrations. A 'yes' and a 'no' campaign fought it out in the media, each accusing the other of misinformation. The council was caught in the middle, unable to wholeheartedly promote the scheme, for fear of legal action. In the event, three surrounding councils launched a legal challenge in January 2005; the Court of Sessions adjourned the case until after the vote.

The referendum result was decisive: three-to-one against on a turnout of nearly two-thirds, which was much higher than most local elections. A study commissioned by the Scottish Executive concluded: 'Residents had made up their minds quite soon after they heard about the scheme ... this was not based on a detailed understanding of the proposal, but on a reaction to the idea of paying to use Edinburgh roads.'[12] The message was clear; no scheme changes, no clever communication would have changed the result (although Stockholm's approach of trialling a scheme before a referendum, did eventually produce a yes vote).

The referendum result provoked much criticism of the council, and calls for its leaders to resign, which they ignored. Many commentators wondered whether the result would kill off interest from other cities. Others argued that London had shown the right way to do it. John Curtice of Strathclyde University told the *Glasgow Herald*: 'You start with the possible rather than the ideal. Secondly, you do it and you take the rap and you are willing to take the risk of losing an election.

Probably you don't hold a referendum and do things gradually and get it right first time.'[13]

Would any other British cities, or the national government, follow this advice?

An e-Petition Halts Plans for National Road Pricing

In 1999 David Begg left Edinburgh to head the Commission for Integrated Transport (CfIT), a body set up by John Prescott to advise him on transport policy, 'because he never quite trusted the transport department' [within DETR] according to an adviser. Over the next 11 years CfIT would support, provoke and sometimes embarrass governments with its critical reports. In 2001 CfIT published a report which estimated that a national road pricing scheme could reduce congestion by 44 per cent while costing motorists no more than they paid already. Big cuts in road tax and small cuts in fuel duty would make the scheme 'revenue-neutral'. Traffic volumes would fall by 5 per cent but most of the benefit would come from drivers changing their times of travel.

A wide coalition (including the CBI and the Freight Transport Association) backed the report, but it made little impact on the government until Alistair Darling became Secretary of State for a newly independent Department for Transport (DfT) in 2002. Begg recalls:

> At first Alistair was really hostile to CfIT. He wanted to abolish it; he thought I was giving him too much criticism because I kept on banging the drum for road pricing and saying we were never going to tackle to congestion without it. But [DfT civil servant] Robert Devereux was really persuasive and Alistair became the biggest convert to road pricing.

In July 2003, Darling announced a new programme of motorway widening, not as big as 'Roads for Prosperity' but enough to anger his environmental critics. Partly to assuage those critics, he announced a new study into road pricing, to 'lock in' the benefits, so the newly widened roads would remain uncongested. Devereux headed a study steering group including business leaders, campaigners and civil servants from the Treasury as well as the DfT. Treasury interest in road pricing was growing as revenue from fuel taxes was declining, after the fuel tax protests.

The report, published in 2004, called on the government to lead a national debate and build 'a consensus' on road pricing. Darling endorsed the findings and announced that a 'pilot scheme in a major conurbation' would begin with five years. The opposition parties seemed supportive, prompting the *Daily Telegraph* to conclude that 'few seriously doubt that road pricing will be introduced. The question is no longer if, but when and how.' Shortly after Labour's victory in the 2005 election Darling launched the 'national debate' on road pricing, leaving all options open. A political adviser says with hindsight:

> The fundamental mistake he made was to create a vacuum into which other people started saying what road pricing meant. It became a totemic issue that had other issues hung off it. You had 'big brother spy-in-the-sky' concerns, as well as 'it's my right to drive where I want to and when I want to' ... The national scheme was going to be many many years down the line. The local ones were going to be more likely to happen sooner, but all of these issues were put out there, and that meant it became defined by its opponents.

In November 2006 the government created a new method for opponents to mobilise: online petitions addressed directly to the Prime Minister. By 2006 just over half of UK households had Internet access, but the potential for this new channel was untested.

A few days later, Peter Roberts, an account manager from Telford who drove a lot for his work, remembers reading about the road pricing proposals on the hearing and thinking:

> I really don't fancy the idea of anyone sticking a GPS system in my car, tracking where I go and what I do and then charging me for the privilege. I had a look at the Downing Street petition site and thought: that looks like a place where I can try and make a differ-ence with the government. So I did a bit of research on how to word petitions and sat there and wrote this petition [which read 'We the undersigned petition the Prime Minister to scrap the planned vehicle tracking and road pricing policy', plus explanatory notes].

As I was about to press the 'go' button I sat there and I thought: 'Do I really want to do this? Because this is going to change my life.' Anyway, I pressed send and I sent it out to 20 friends with a link saying: 'Please will you sign this and send it to everyone you know?' A week later it had got something like 35,000 signatures.

I also sent a press release out to all of the national papers and the following week David Millward from the *Daily Telegraph* called me and said: 'I see your petition's doing well. It's number one on the Downing Street website. I want to do a story about it, and the *Telegraph* will support you.' They came and spent the day with us, did some video work and it was on the front page of the *Telegraph*.

Roberts had no experience of campaigning or dealing with the media. He had recently joined the Association of British Drivers (ABD), the hard-line anti-environmental motorists' organisation, although they did not get involved until 'they saw it had legs, then they put it on their website.' (He later broke with the ABD, particularly over their attitude to air pollution and electric cars – he now drives one.)

By early January 2007 the petition had attracted 200,000 signatures, causing the website to crash, and Roberts was in demand. 'I accepted every media interview', he says. He stressed three key arguments against road pricing: it was unfair, particularly for poorer drivers; it would be expensive to administer, and the GPS tracking would be an invasion of privacy. The right ways to tackle congestion, he argued, were road-building or widening and removing traffic lights. These arguments found a receptive public, and wrong-footed leading politicians: 'I emailed [Conservative opposition leader] David Cameron a few times. He wrote something like "we would be supportive of road pricing", then after the campaign had got halfway through, they inserted a "not" in front of "be supportive"!'

The government decided not to respond to the petition until it was closed, creating the appearance of a policy vacuum once again. In July 2006 Blair had appointed Douglas Alexander as Transport Secretary with a strong brief to 'advance the debate' on road pricing. The adviser who favoured starting with local congestion charging schemes says: 'It was petitioning against a misrepresentation of our policy. My advice to Douglas was: "You should sign the petition, Douglas, and say: 'If this is what I was proposing, I'd be against it as well.'" It didn't matter. We'd lost the political argument by that stage.'

Alexander did not follow that advice. Instead, the DfT said: 'no decision has been taken on whether to implement a national road pricing scheme'. Blair's spokesman acknowledged the strength of public feeling but added: 'doing nothing is not an option'.[14] The preparatory work and planned trials would continue. A colleague of mine, Professor Glenn Lyons, was leading a research project for the DfT into the public acceptability of road pricing at the time:

> I remember being in a lift in the DfT around then. One of the civil servants said: 'We're going to go for it.' That was probably before the petition … This was a big piece of social research for the DfT, highly sensitive, as you can imagine. We were conducting workshops with [members of the general public], building up their understanding and assessing their reactions … Some of the public reaction was: 'Clearly the government wouldn't be talking about this in the media unless it really was going to happen. They know how provocative it is, so clearly they're going to do it.'

The petition began to circulate around work places, prompting some employers to reprimand their staff. An academic at our university sent an email to all staff urging them to sign it, which prompted Lyons to send a terse reply: 'I remember being appalled that an academic colleague was saying "do this" instead of "this is a topic which needs [research and debate]". You wouldn't circulate a petition [to all staff] for or against Brexit, for example.' By the time the petition closed on 20 February 2007 it had collected 1.8 million signatures, believed to be a UK record at the time, although a civil servant says 'the powers that be hadn't twigged how easy it was to open multiple e-mail accounts and sign several times from different e-addresses'.

In his reply to the petitioners, Tony Blair wrote: 'we have not made any decision about national road pricing… we need to explore the contribution road pricing can make to tackling congestion … Before we take any decisions there would be further consultations.'[15] A few days later he changed his tone. In an interview on *Top Gear*, the BBC's motoring programme, he compared road pricing to the poll tax, which had brought down Margaret Thatcher: 'In the end it didn't matter whether it was the right policy or the wrong policy, the public would not buy it. I wouldn't personally as a politician engage in that type of kamikaze politics.'

There was no formal abandonment of national road pricing. The research projects were completed and published, while the government became increasingly distracted by a growing financial crisis from September 2007 onwards. An adviser says: 'In the abstract, [national road pricing] looks the perfect demand management tool and so we can all agree in the seminar room on the desirability of this, and it chugs along and then when it emerges into the light of real politics it gets shot down.'

Manchester – the Last Attempt at Urban Congestion Charging

The prospect of a national road pricing scheme faded after the petition and the Edinburgh referendum halted any prospect of urban congestion charging in Scotland. However, a few English cities remained attracted to the idea. In 2004 Alistair Darling had published a Transport White Paper with a new Transport Innovation Fund (TIF), offering £2 billion a year to local authorities willing to combine 'radically enhanced' public transport with 'plans to tackle congestion, through measures such as congestion charging'. Thirty-three authorities applied for 'pump priming' funds, including Greater Manchester.

Among the fragmented arrangements governing England's larger provincial cities, Manchester was an exception. The Association of Greater Manchester Authorities (AGMA) had few formal powers or resources but it had proved surprisingly effective in persuading its ten member authorities to work together. In 1992 Manchester became the first British city to build a new tram network, Metrolink, which the AGMA was keen to extend.

A senior council officer involved in these plans explains the background:

> We had been successful up to that point, largely through Metrolink and a renaissance in rail, to support the growth in commuting to the city centre through modes other than the car, but as we looked forward we could see capacity constraints on the system, so a step-change would be needed …

As other cities hesitated, Manchester used its position as a pioneer to press for concessions. Eventually the government agreed that grants to pay for public transport improvements would be paid several years before the congestion charge began (in 2013). The AGMA would retain the revenue and be able to borrow against it. In total, around £3 billion would be spent on: new Metrolink lines, an expanded bus network, more frequent and longer trains on the local lines into Manchester, improvements to 40 stations, expansion of park and ride and 120 miles of new or improved cycle routes. It was a more impressive and more specific package than the one offered to Edinburgh.

The AGMA commissioned consultants to examine the feasibility of a congestion charge, and public attitudes towards it. Their plan, published in May 2007, would involve two cordons, as in Edinburgh, but with a twist, which made it even more complicated. Drivers would only be charged if they crossed a cordon during peak hours travelling with the peak flow i.e. inwards in the morning or outwards in the evening. The charges would be £2 for crossing the outer cordon and £1 for crossing the inner cordon, with a maximum payment of £5 per day.

The announcement prompted some members of the Association of British Drivers to set up a local campaign group, Manchester Against Road Tolls (MART). They set up a website, began attracting people to their meetings and the attention of the media. Once the principle was established, they argued, the charges would rise and spread. Their spokesman told the *Daily Mirror*: 'what we are getting is "road pricing lite". This is the version they hope will get them through consultation.'

At that stage, AGMA intended to consult, but not to hold a referendum. The precedent set in Edinburgh offered MART a potential line of attack. One of the first people MART contacted for help was Peter Roberts, who went to meet Peel Holdings, the owners of the Trafford shopping Centre:

> The Trafford Centre was in the congestion charging zone, which meant that people coming off the motorway would have to pay the charge ... They put money into the campaign against it and also employed a PR team to work against it, which gave us some useful videos and bought some advertising space. There was also a political side where we worked, surprisingly, with a Lib Dem guy.

An opinion poll conducted by MART showed that nearly 80 per cent of the public opposed the congestion charge. A survey commissioned by Peel Holdings revealed a similar result among businesses. Armed with these findings MART began lobbying councillors across the ten authorities to support a referendum. In council elections held in May 2008 they targeted the seat of Roger Jones, the Labour Chairman of the Transport Authority and a leading supporter of the plan. He was beaten into third place by a member of the local Community Action Party, who campaigned against the charge.

Although the elections made little difference to the political balance on AGMA, the officer says Jones's defeat 'was definitely a factor which unnerved a lot of politicians.' A second consultation, on the detailed scheme, was due to begin. With more councillors now opposed to the charge, the AGMA board agreed to proceed subject to a referendum. The consultation and the referendum campaigns would run in parallel, putting the council officers in a difficult position. The officer recalls:

> It made for a confused period … I remember going to a series of events where I would stand up and give the objective 'here is a policy that we are consulting on', then sit down and the 'yes' camp and the 'no' camp would then do their bit, and I would just sit there, not contributing one way or the other.

The 'no' campaign was unconvinced by this supposedly neutral stance. A month before the poll AGMA ran a television advert explaining the consequences of a 'yes' or a 'no' vote. Following several complaints, the regulator Ofcom ruled that it was biased towards the 'yes' arguments and ordered ITV to stop screening it. From that point on, the officer recalls, they took 'a very conservative approach to informing around the consultation'.

While MART concentrated on the local media, Roberts recalls, 'I kept in contact with the national media more than the local media. They weren't interested to start off with; they saw it as a local issue … until a week before, then all of a sudden it was big news.' The media and the government had noticed a groundswell of public opposition; a government adviser recalls: 'people knew it was dead before the referendum.' By the time the votes were counted in December 2008, the no camp knew they had won, but the size of the margin was a surprise: 79 per cent no, 21 per cent yes.

The officer says in retrospect:

> I went away to find out more about referenda generally ... I think there was a naïve assumption in some quarters that those people who didn't have access to a car would take the view that the improved public transport offer was a good thing and would come out and vote yes in large numbers ... the evidence suggests that people project themselves forward into a position where they might have a car and look at the proposal that way.

Roberts went on to fight congestion charging proposals in the dwindling number of other places still interested in the idea. As the TIF funds remained unspent governments found other ways to fund local transport projects. Through those and other means the Manchester authorities eventually made most of the public transport improvements they had planned. Over a decade later, London remained the only British city with a congestion charge.

The End of Demand Management?

In 1991, the authors of 'Transport: The New Realism' identified two options for managing demand for road space. Their preferred option involved road pricing although some of the benefits could still be obtained through other means. 'A New Deal for Transport' in 1998 identified rising fuel duty as a key element of demand management, with or without road pricing. By 2009 neither of those policies seemed politically feasible. Local transport authorities seeking to manage traffic in towns and cities could still fall back on parking controls or road capacity constraints (through pedestrianisation or bus lanes, for example[16]) but no comparable measures would prevent traffic from rising on inter-urban roads. In time, this would create pressure for a return to large-scale road-building. In the short term, the global recession and some more fundamental changes to British society dampened traffic growth and delayed that pressure for a few years. Declining car use among urbanising populations and particularly young adults confounded official forecasts of rising traffic from the late 1990s onwards,[17] but that respite would not last indefinitely, as Chapter 12 will explain.

The story so far has focussed on road transport, but the same tensions also apply to other modes of transport: tensions between growing demand and environmental concerns with public opposition to expansion and also to constraint. The next four chapters will look at two other issues that spawned protest movements in the mid- and late 2000s: airport expansion and high-speed rail.

8

Airport Expansion
and Climate Change

UK Airport Policy: A History of Expansion and Broken Promises

The history of airports in the UK is one of expansion driven by consumer demand, local opposition and broken promises, particularly in southeast England, where over half of UK flights are concentrated. During the public inquiry into plans to build a fifth terminal at Heathrow in 1999 BAA's Chief Executive wrote to residents around the airport saying: 'We do not want, nor shall we seek, an additional runway. I can now report that we went even further at the Inquiry and called on the Inspector to recommend that, subject to permission being given for Terminal 5, an additional Heathrow runway should be ruled out forever.'

The inspector ruled in favour of Terminal 5, subject to a new ceiling of 480,000 flights per year. A third runway, he wrote, 'would have such severe and widespread impacts on the environment as to be totally unacceptable'. He welcomed the government's intention to review aviation policy and called on that review to rule out any further expansion of Heathrow. Among the reasons he cited for his recommendations climate change was absent; ten years after Margaret Thatcher's speech to the UN, it was yet to feature as a major issue for aviation policy.

Stephen Byers picked up the inspector's report when he became DTLR minister in May 2001. An adviser recalls:

We were ready to make the decision and then it turned out we couldn't because somebody hadn't taken account of a stream going through the site. [Byers] just wanted to get on with this. We'd had endless reviews, but you have to be very careful; you have Greenpeace and everybody else challenging every decision you make, so you've got to watch your words ...

Meanwhile Blair and Brown were deeply frustrated with how long the planning system took for major infrastructure projects ... How did you get private capital into infrastructure (which you needed a lot of)? They would say: 'The uncertainty's too much ...' The trouble is, the private sector thinks: 'Can't you take these decisions out of political hands?' And the answer is: 'No, you can't, but you can at least create some kind of consensus on infrastructure.'

In the late 1990s John Stewart, the founder of ALARM UK, switched from campaigning on roads to campaigning on airports and aircraft noise. His new organisation, ClearSkies, began in South London where the expansion of Heathrow was increasing noise pollution. In 2000 ClearSkies merged with a longer-standing group HACAN; Stewart became its Chair and paid employee. His experience of working inside and outside official mechanisms would transform airport campaigning over the following years.

Shortly after the 2001 election, private lobbying for a third runway at Heathrow began in an unusual way. An adviser recalls:

British Airways were the first people who began to work on the notion of a third runway. I remember them floating it with Number 10, who were quite sympathetic, and with [new Transport Secretary] Alistair Darling ... The officials were asked by ministers to assess the proposal and consult with BAA [Heathrow's owners]. Interestingly, BAA were initially opposed to it. They didn't see that it was necessary, because in the end, they would have to fund it.

Their opposition did not last long. In May 2003, under pressure from MPs who blamed them for congestion at London's airports, BAA ditched their commitment to residents and backed a third runway.

A Generation-Spanning White Paper – at the End of an Era

Later in 2003 Darling published the White Paper on aviation. His foreword talked of a 'measured and balanced approach' with a brief mention of climate change (to be addressed through international negotiations and 'voluntary action' by the industry) but its main concern was airport expansion. The first priority would be a second runway at Stansted, followed by a third runway at Heathrow. There would also be new runways at Birmingham and Edinburgh, while most other regional airports would expand in some way. It did contain one important caveat, however. Airports would only be allowed to expand if they complied with European air quality legislation, which would become more stringent from 2005 onwards. This could present a problem for Heathrow. An adviser comments:

> Those of us who think a productive economy is important can see a strong case for it ... Unless things change and adapt they can die ... The Treasury were very keen; their [estimates] show a third runway at Heathrow [produces a] fabulous [economic return]. There was some disagreement but the British Labour Party has never had a big green anti-growth faction – [Climate Change and Energy Secretary] Ed Miliband began to voice a bit of it. The political logic for us was: Scotland, Merseyside, Greater Manchester, they all want to be connected to London and beyond. Heathrow generates 50,000 jobs. If you are a manual worker in West London Heathrow is extraordinarily important ... I think those were the views of most Labour MPs and ministers.

There were some critics within the party and government. Chris Mullin MP, who had ministerial responsibility for aviation under John Prescott, wrote in the *Evening Standard* of a 'fundamental contradiction between the demands of the aviation industry and the government's goal of sustainable development'. Another adviser, who became involved after the 2005 election, says: 'The air transport White Paper was a generation-spanning document written at the end of an era. It didn't fully account for the climate change challenge.'

In the years that followed, the aviation White Paper would foster growing conflict between government objectives on aviation and on climate change.

The Big Ask – for a Climate Change Law

By the mid-2000s concern about climate change was rising. In August 2003 a heatwave hit Europe, provoking 20,000 premature deaths and breaking the all-time temperature record in Britain. Even the *Daily Mail* cited expert opinion that this was 'further evidence of climate change'.[1] In January 2004 Sir David King, the government's Chief Scientific Adviser, courted controversy by writing that climate change was a greater threat than terrorism.[2]

Labour's 1997 manifesto promised a 20 per cent cut in CO_2 emissions by 2010. During their second term in office it became clear that this target would be missed. Ministers began to emphasise a longer-term target, for a 60 per cent cut by 2050. In March 2005 Friends of the Earth responded to a government policy review criticising this failure, particularly in surface transport and aviation where emissions were rising.[3] They argued that a new 'top down approach' was needed to hold ministers to account and prevent them from deferring difficult decisions. Their solution involved five-year 'carbon budgets'; in each five-year period slower progress in the early years would require deeper cuts later.

The idea for a law mandating timely cuts in carbon emissions emerged 'in an ad-hoc conversation in late 2004 in a stairwell in the FoE offices' between two of FoE's national campaigners.[4] A small team formed to develop the idea. Mike Childs, who was FoE's Campaigns Director, says:

> We were used to running campaigns about getting new laws through parliament. It wasn't an uphill struggle [internally]. The government were way off track. If they're not even delivering what's in their manifesto you've got a very good argument to say: we need to up this to a different level.

In February 2005 FoE met other Environmental NGOs to seek support. Childs recalls:

> It was all very pleasant and positive and it was kind of 'you go with it and we'll see how it goes, and we might jump on board'. Generally NGOs work well together but there's a competitiveness as well, so people don't automatically latch on to other people's ideas. There's a greater rivalry between FoE and Greenpeace ... Out of all NGOs they were less likely to jump on a FoE idea than anyone else's.

So to begin with, FoE decided to act alone, with some free assistance from an advertising agency, who suggested the campaign title: 'The Big Ask'.

In April 2005 a draft bill was presented to parliament by three backbench MPs with a record of supporting environmental initiatives: Michael Meacher (Labour), John Gummer (Conservative) and Norman Baker (Liberal Democrat). The bill set a target to reduce CO_2 emissions by 3 per cent a year and placed the responsibility on the Prime Minister to ensure that these annual targets were met. With no government support, the bill was not debated and parliament was dissolved shortly afterwards for a general election.

On 24 May, a few days after Labour was returned to power, six MPs, including the original three, put down an Early Day Motion (EDM) calling for a climate change bill. The purpose of an EDM is to show strength of feeling among MPs to put pressure on the government. As with the Road Traffic Reduction Bill eight years earlier, any new bill would require government support, which was not forthcoming. Opinion within government was divided. The Department for Environment, Food and Rural Affairs (DEFRA) was broadly sympathetic, particularly after the appointment of David Miliband as DEFRA minister in May 2006. However, the Department for Trade and Industry (DTI) feared additional burdens on businesses and the DfT feared constraints or taxes on the aviation industry.

Persuading the government to support legislation was the first aim of the Big Ask. The campaign was launched on 25 May, fronted by Radiohead lead singer Thom Yorke. Alongside gigs and celebrity endorsements, FoE groups around the country (including the local group I had helped to set up) distributed postcards with a space for the name of a local MP, urging each one to support the EDM. They organised over 50 public meetings in different parts of the country, targeting the constituencies of wavering MPs. By November 2006 130,000 people had sent a postcard or written to their MP; two-thirds of MPs had signed the EDM, one of the highest proportions ever.

Later in 2005, FoE brought together 15 charities and campaigning organisations, including WWF, Oxfam, Christian Aid, the Women's Institute and Greenpeace, to form Stop Climate Chaos, a coalition which would eventually encompass over 130 organisations (called The Climate Coalition today). This enabled Greenpeace to join the campaign. In November 2006 20,000 of us marched through London, calling for stronger action on climate change from the UK government and internationally.

The campaign encountered surprisingly little opposition. There were occasional articles in newspapers questioning the science of climate change or the cost of trying to avert it. A few MPs, mainly Conservatives, shared those views; Childs recalls that they 'weren't particularly vocal'. Some Labour MPs and ministers disliked environmental groups, including FoE, for different reasons. Gordon Brown and John Prescott felt let down by their low profile during the fuel tax crisis, but they refrained from public criticism. Throughout 2005 and most of 2006 the government maintained that climate legislation was unnecessary; government targets would suffice.

Two factors helped to change that stance. The first was a review commissioned by the Treasury into the economic impacts of climate change, led by economist Lord Nicholas Stern. The Stern report, published in October 2006, concluded that the costs imposed by climate change would be far greater than the costs of acting to avert it. A civil servant at the DfT remembers that period as one 'with Stern staring everyone in the face'.

A second factor was the election of David Cameron as Conservative leader in December 2005. After two election defeats for the Conservatives, Cameron saw environmental issues as one way to re-brand them as a more progressive, less 'nasty' party. Responding to criticisms that he was 'policy light' he supported the principles of The Big Ask and proposed an additional element, an independent 'carbon audit office' to model and forecast the UK's performance against legally binding carbon targets. Theresa Villiers who became Shadow Transport Secretary says:

> We genuinely felt that climate change was an issue that had to be tackled. As a party we had always had 'conserve' in our name and had always been concerned about conserving the natural environment but perhaps we hadn't been explicit enough about that. I suppose the traditional view of Conservatives protecting the countryside needed to be adapted to modern environmental threats – and it was very much the mood of the time.

They remembered the conflicts over road-building in the 1990s, but by that point the party had 'moved on', she adds.

In May 2006 Cameron attended a gig with Thom Yorke in support of the Big Ask and in September he appeared on a platform with FoE director Tony Juniper to call on the government to table a climate change bill in the next parliamentary session. On the same day, the Liberal Democrats gave their support. Ed Miliband decided that Labour must not remain the only major party opposing climate legislation.[5] Pressed by his Conservative shadow in parliament in October he said the government was 'looking carefully at the idea of legislation'.

Over the following months Miliband worked to build a consensus among ministers, including Brown and Darling, who had moved to the DTI. Some people in the Treasury and Blair's Policy Unit wanted to make the new law conditional on action by other countries. Miliband convinced the cabinet that the UK should lead by example. In March 2007 he presented a draft bill to parliament. It included the existing target to cut CO_2 emissions by 60 per cent by 2050, five-year carbon budgets and an independent climate change committee to advise the government on the difficult decisions that all of this would require.

Nicholas Davies, an FoE campaigner who went on to work in parliament, wrote: 'I remember us watching it like sad political anoraks on a big screen in the William Pub nearby. We cheered when the BBC's political correspondent Nick Robinson bigged up the Big Ask on live TV.'[6]

The Campaign to Include International Aviation and Shipping

Despite these celebrations, FoE remained concerned about some aspects of the draft bill; the latest science was suggesting a need for deeper cuts, of 80 per cent by 2050. Although the five-year budgets were originally FoE's idea, they also wanted a target to cut emissions by 3 per cent each year. And critically for this story, international aviation and shipping were excluded from the draft bill, prompting FoE's Executive Director to comment: 'Introducing a climate change law which doesn't cover emissions from planes and ships is like introducing a drink driving law that doesn't count whisky.'

Why were those two sectors excluded? Passenger movements through UK airports had more than doubled since the launch of low-cost airlines in the early 1990s. The 2003 aviation White Paper supported further expansion of flights and airports. The government argued in parliament that constraining aviation emissions would require international agreement. They hoped this would begin within the EU and in the meantime 'we would not want to cut across our parallel efforts to reach wider international agreement'.

Childs was sceptical of this reasoning; the DfT, he observes 'has always acted as a lobby for the aviation industry'.[7] In 2009 documents leaked to *The Guardian* confirmed his suspicions. Flying Matters was (until 2011) a lobby group funded by airlines and airport owners which aimed to counter the influence of the environmental movement on government and public opinion around aviation. The leaked documents revealed that the DfT had approached Flying Matters 'for support on key issues' including the Climate Change Bill. As with road-building in 1989 (see page 4) it seems the DfT was once again lobbying the lobbyists. Flying Matters approached the All-Party Parliamentary Aviation Group, with an offer to provide various services (the details were disputed). The Group rejected the offer because the MPs felt that Flying Matters were 'pressurising' them.

In July 2007 FoE launched a new phase of their campaign to strengthen the bill, to include international aviation and shipping, annual targets and an ultimate 80 per cent cut. The Big Ask Online March used another recent technological advance, enabling supporters to send personal video messages to their MPs, who were becoming increasingly receptive. Two parliamentary environmental committees called for the bill to be strengthened. In January 2008 six Labour MPs tabled a new EDM supporting two of FoE's demands: the 80 per cent target and the inclusion of aviation and shipping. Two hundred and sixty MPs eventually signed it.

While the bill was making its way through parliament, the government decided to set up the Climate Change Committee to begin its advisory work. In October 2008 it recommended that the 60 per cent target should be increased to 80 per cent and applied to all greenhouse gases (not just CO_2) and all sectors, including international aviation and shipping. The government accepted the first two recommendations, but not the third one.

Shortly before the bill came back to the House of Commons for its third reading a Labour MP proposed an amendment to include international aviation and shipping, saying: 'Politicians from all parties have been inundated with letters and emails from constituents who want a strong climate change law that covers all the UK's emissions.'

Fifty four Labour MPs signed the amendment – more than the Labour majority in parliament. Facing the prospect of defeat on the issue, the government opted for compromise. They introduced an amendment of their own, requiring the Climate Change Committee to advise the minister on aviation and shipping emissions. The minister would then make a statement to parliament explaining how those emissions would be treated in each five-year carbon budget. With that amendment, the bill finally passed into law in November 2008.

The Climate Change Act was a major achievement for FoE and the wider coalition. Unlike most of the other campaigns described in this book The Big Ask achieved nearly all its goals through entirely legal means. After the Act became law, the UK Foreign Office worked with FoE to promote similar legislation elsewhere. Six other European countries eventually passed climate legislation[8] and the Act is often cited as a model for countries considering a similar step.

Although the Act was described as 'historic' and 'revolutionary',[9] doubts remained around its enforceability. The legal duty to enforce it fell on the environment minister (in departments whose names and functions have changed over time), who might need to persuade cabinet colleagues with different agendas. The environment minister must report to parliament each year on progress and plans to comply with the Act, but the consequences for governments which failed to comply were, and are, unclear. An environmental organisation might apply for a judicial review, but the courts have limited powers to compel ministers to respect their judgements. As a FoE campaigner told me at the time: 'there is no global policeman, so we've tried to maximise the political embarrassment if they don't comply'.

The ambiguous treatment of aviation and shipping increased these uncertainties. Aviation emissions (much larger than shipping) rose sharply in the early 2000s. They peaked in 2005 at somewhere between 6 per cent of UK carbon emissions, according to the official statistics, 17 per cent according to some other estimates (depending on the method of measurement).[10] They began falling before the global recession, but the long-term forecasts remained strongly upwards. For road transport, the Climate Change Committee recommended fuel efficiency in the short term and electrification in the longer term as nuclear, wind and solar power replaced coal and oil. But aeroplanes, which were already highly efficient, would continue to burn fossil fuels for the foreseeable future. If aviation continued to grow unconstrained, they estimated that it would take up around two-thirds of all UK carbon emissions by 2050. Some airport expansion might be possible, but unconstrained growth would not.

In the years since 2008, the work of the Climate Change Committee has commanded growing respect. Governments of different political persuasions have nearly always accepted the Committee's recommendations but have failed to act on many of them. Despite the Labour government's backing for the new law, the DfT and the Treasury continued to support airport expansion and oppose constraint. Meanwhile, growing concern about climate change had re-invigorated the long-running, and long-failing, campaigns against airport expansion.

A New Campaign Begins

John Stewart remembers the early 2000s as 'difficult years' for the airport campaigners, some of whom gave up and moved away.[11] Reflecting on the history of past defeats he drew several conclusions. The previous campaigns had been too narrow; they needed to build a broader coalition, inside and outside the establishment. Previous campaigns had focussed almost exclusively on environmental impacts; they also needed to challenge the economic arguments for airport expansion. NIMBYism played into the hands of the authorities; campaigns against *all* airport expansion would be stronger than competing campaigns undermining each other. Too much effort had been wasted on futile consultations and public inquiries. From now on, they needed to 'set the agenda', using direct action, breaking the law if necessary. On that point, Stewart was in a minority within HACAN. If his plan was to work, he would need to find others willing to go further.

As the DfT and BAA worked on their plans to expand Heathrow, Stewart worked to build a coalition against them, including a cross-party group of MPs. John McDonnell, MP for Hayes and Harlington, which encompassed the airport, became its chair. McDonnell was a left-wing Labour MP, who often rebelled against the government, but he chaired the group 'in an inclusive manner', according to Stewart. Justine Greening, Conservative MP for Putney and a future Transport Secretary, was another active member of the group.

Local authorities surrounding the airport had opposed the previous expansion plans through public inquiries and legal action. As the campaign began to gain momentum they were joined by others. The 2M group, representing 2 million people living underneath the flight paths, grew to include 26 authorities. The Mayor of London, Ken Livingstone, and his challenger, Boris Johnson, also pledged their support.

BAA's draft masterplan, published for consultation in 2005, showed the new runway obliterating a village, Sipson, and threatening several others. A local action group, NoTRAG, was formed in 2002, led by Geraldine Nicholson, whose home lay 100 metres from the planned runway. Publication of the masterplan re-energised NoTRAG; some residents told journalists they were now ready to take direct action, but they would need help from outside.

9
The Campaign Against a Heathrow Third Runway

Plane Stupid: Direct Action against Airport Expansion

In his search for activists to strengthen the campaign against Heath-row's third runway, John Stewart turned to his old friends from the anti-roads movement, including Jason Torrance, who was now working for Greenpeace. Torrance introduced him to Joss Garman and Richard George, two younger activists concerned about climate change and keen to take direct action against airport expansion. A few weeks later they formed Plane Stupid.

During 2006 some veterans of the anti-roads protests proposed the first national climate camp, which met near Drax power station in August. Stewart and Garman offered to run a workshop. Stewart remembers the tension, sitting in an empty tent, hoping more people would turn up. One of the first people to arrive was Leo Murray, who recalls:

> I had been very inspired by the anti-roads protests as a teenager. I went on some of the Reclaim the Streets events. By 2005 things were starting to coalesce around climate change. The values were shared; the ways of organising had evolved and become more sophisticated but built on the general principles [of the anti-roads protests] like consensus decision-making ...
>
> I had met Joss briefly a few months before, so I dragged my mates along to this workshop. We had a galvanising conversation. John and Joss set out the context – the 2003 Air Transport White Paper, which set out plans to expand every airport in the country with no notion of limits to growth and no regard to environmental impacts ...
>
> Civil disobedience is very well suited to stopping infrastruc-ture projects ... and you could see how this could play out with

Heathrow ... It was already unpopular and it was just not consistent with emerging policy around climate change ... So we left that meeting going: 'Yeah! Come on, let's do something about this!'

Two of Plane Stupid's first actions were a 'sermon on the runway' of East Midlands Airport from a Methodist minister and a blockade of EasyJet's London headquarters. They were helped by Greenpeace, who brought their expertise, resources and a more professional approach to action planning and media handling. Whereas the anti-roads protestors had eschewed the conventional media, Plane Stupid aimed to use it to their advantage. Murray became their principal spokesperson:

We very quickly established ourselves as the go-to people for comment on anything to do with aviation and environment. We established good relations with professional people at NGOs, so I would get a call from a newspaper saying: what's your position on... [for example] Prince Harry's flying 30 km in a Chinook helicopter? And then I would call up some people in NGOs and say: what's the per kilometre emissions of a Chinook helicopter? So we were funnelling a lot of expertise from professional campaigners.

Why did the journalists not call the NGOs directly? 'Because we were spiky and interesting. The media love conflict. A lot of what Plane Stupid did was leveraging spectacle and the media's appetite for that to put a radical message on climate and aviation into the [wider public] discourse.'

Meanwhile Stewart found himself in a similar role to the one he had played in the 1990s, as a link between the radical and respectable wings of a protest movement:

The relationship was secret. I went to nearly all Plane Stupid's meetings. Direct actions [were discussed] on a 'need to know' basis ... I wouldn't be involved in the detailed planning of actions but I would be involved in the broader strategy, particularly to link to the wider campaign, so Plane Stupid's activities fitted in with the time scale of the wider campaign, and latterly to use my links with local residents to encourage them to take direct action with Plane Stupid.

While Plane Stupid captured the headlines, HACAN continued its more prosaic work, lobbying MPs and commissioning research. While they sought funding for an economic study, late in 2006 they published a short report on 'Short-Haul Flights: Clogging up Heathrow's Runways'. This revealed that many of Heathrow's most frequent destinations were well-served by direct rail links to London; Heathrow's top destination was Paris. Instead of expanding Heathrow, the government should tax short-haul flights, reduce the landing slots allocated to them and improve the rail alternatives. These arguments made little impact at the time, but they found a few receptive readers within the Conservative opposition, which was rethinking its environmental and transport policies.

In March 2007 Plane Stupid gatecrashed an aviation conference where Transport Secretary Douglas Alexander was due to speak. Among the protestors were several residents they had trained, including a woman in her seventies walking with crutches, who told journalists what it was like growing up near Heathrow before the airport expanded. She never got to confront Alexander; he was ushered out of hall by a side exit and driven away.

In the summer of 2007, as the Climate Change Bill was passing through parliament, BAA were alarmed to hear that a second climate camp was planned on land they hoped to use for their third runway. Their response gave the protestors an unexpected boost. BAA applied to the High Court for an injunction against: Murray, Stewart, Garman, Nicholson, Plane Stupid and Airport Watch, an umbrella organisation encompassing the National Trust, the Campaign to Protect Rural England and eight others. In total, the injunction would have banned five million people from travelling on sections of the M4, the M25 and the London Underground indefinitely. Police could arrest any of these people found in possession of a spade, a whistle, a balloon or a kite. During the hearing the judge revealed that she was a member of some of these organisations, so she could have been setting herself up for arrest!

The hearing brought opprobrium and ridicule for BAA and useful publicity for the climate camp. The judge granted a limited injunction preventing Murray, Stewart, Garman and Plane Stupid from 'disrupting the airport' within its perimeter. All of them were free to attend the climate camp. Stewart said: 'BAA's legal adviser claimed he was a legal rottweiler – today he looks like Scooby-Doo.'

The climate camp attracted around 1500 people, including several MPs, and the interest of the world's media, but as Murray recalls: 'There were some tensions between Plane Stupid and the "proper anarchists" … Fundamentally climate camp was an anti-capitalist project. Plane Stupid wasn't. It was much more instrumentalist.'

George Monbiot, writing in *The Guardian*, regretted that some sympathetic journalists were turned away. He also noted how the protest movement was becoming better organised and more democratic, with small 'affinity groups feeding decisions upwards to general meetings'.[1] These were important pointers to the future of protest movements, as we shall see in Chapter 13.

A Dodgy Consultation, a Parliamentary Mole and a Plane Stupid Spy

In the summer of 2007 the officials working on the plans for Heathrow encountered a problem. The 2003 White Paper had set conditions on noise, pollution and road traffic. Their initial analysis showed that a third runway would breach those conditions. Then Greenpeace obtained documents through the Freedom of Information Act, revealing how DfT officials worked with BAA to change the assumptions behind the analysis. An unnamed official working on the report told *The Times*: 'It's a classic case of reverse engineering. They knew exactly what results they wanted and fixed the inputs to get there. It's appalling'.[2]

In November 2007 Transport Secretary Ruth Kelly launched the consultation. This was not just about the details; it asked whether a third runway should be built, whether aircraft movements should increase and whether more night flying should be permitted. However, Kelly's public statements cast doubt on this apparent openness. Speaking at a London business meeting she said a third runway was 'essential to Britain's economic competitiveness'; any limit on airport expansion would drive business overseas, leaving the UK 'feeling purer but poorer'.[3] Her comments were reinforced a few days later by the new Prime Minister Gordon Brown.

The opponents of expansion sensed an opportunity. Here was a government conducting a consultation on questions it had already decided. The leader of Richmond Council, a member of the 2M group of authorities, said it would take legal advice on grounds for a judicial review. Judicial reviews are expensive and rarely succeed, so this was not a decision to be taken lightly; the threat of legal action was repeated several times while the broader coalition worked on plans to pay for it.

Learning from past experience, HACAN spent little time on the formal consultation, treating it as an opportunity for publicity. Shortly before the consultation closed in February 2008, they published the report they had commissioned on the economic impact of a third runway. In a room at the London Stock Exchange former transport minister Steven Norris presented the report to an audience of business people and financial journalists. It concluded that the government and BAA were exaggerating the economic advantages of expanding Heathrow; constraining its expansion would not damage the competitiveness of London, as they had claimed.[4]

Meanwhile, Plane Stupid were planning an action to discredit the consultation and also grappling with an internal threat. As Murray explains:

> We had very strict security protocols. We would never have our phones in meetings. Every time we met we would put the phones in a fridge or microwave, batteries out. We had a strict 'need to know' [policy]. I never discussed any of this with my partner, and I think everyone else was pretty strict as well …
>
> At the height of our stuff we had such a high profile that there were a lot of activists who wanted to be involved in some way. You have a tension between maintaining security and being open to new people coming in …
>
> We decided to set up a Plane Stupid London, which would be more open, but with the awareness that some of those people who were strangers to us might not be trustworthy. So we tested it. A fake action was proposed at one of those meetings, and we waited to see. It appeared in the *Evening Standard* a couple of days later. There weren't many people at that meeting so it had to be one of them.

Their suspicions fell on a young newcomer, who called himself Ken Tobias. 'He was always on time for meetings, which is very unusual in the world of activists, and he would arrive wearing things like a Ben Sherman shirt and a kaffia. You could smell a rat.' Another activist remembered his keen interest in hardcore action, in which he never took part himself. The core of the group continued to plan their actions without him, while feeding him an occasional red herring.

A few days before the end of the consultation, HACAN organised a rally attended by nearly 3,000 people at Central Hall in Westminster. One of the speakers, alongside experts and politicians, was Leo Murray. Stewart describes this as a deliberate tactic 'to confuse the powers that be' about the relationship between the local protestors and Plane Stupid, who were planning their most audacious action yet.

An opportunity to take their protest to the centre of power emerged through a chance conversation. A member of Plane Stupid had a friend, Laura (not her real name) who had recently left a job at the Houses of Parliament but had not yet handed back her parliamentary pass. Murray recalls that Richard George worked for an NGO and used to attend occasional meetings in the committee rooms:

> Every time he visited, he would have a little nose around to see if there was a way onto the roof, and he discovered that the alarm had been disabled on a door at the top of a stairwell ... MPs were able to smoke on the members' terrace, but not the staff, so there was this place to have a cheeky cigarette on the roof. There was no camera on it. We spent some time poring over Google Earth to plot our way onto the roof.

John Stewart says:

> They felt there should be a small number of people, a mixture of men and women ... The head of their media team said: 'You mustn't look scruffy. You must look like the sons and daughters of *Daily Mail* readers.' One of the girls [Olivia Chessell] borrowed her mother's pearls. This was very different from the direct-action protests of the 1990s where there was a lot of antagonism towards the media. Plane Stupid were cynical about the media but they used it to their advantage.

The aim of the action was to highlight the rigged consultation. Five activists, including Murray, George and Chessell, would climb onto the roof, handcuff themselves, unfurl a banner reading 'BAA HQ' and launch paper planes made from government documents. The next steps were planned like a spy movie:

> Laura took a cycle pannier in with our banner and handcuffs, which we obviously couldn't have got through security. We then entered through the public entrance with an identical cycle pannier. We all went and had a cup of tea in the Commons cafe. Laura was on the next table from us. When we got up we did the secret agent bag swap; we left with her pannier and she left with ours. We then went up onto the roof … We had someone down in Parliament Square who we notified as soon as we got up there. He went over to Security and said: 'excuse me, there are some peaceful protestors on the roof. Don't shoot them, will you?' The officer looked round and the guy was gone.

Chessell wore a camera around her neck, which beamed images down to someone with a camcorder in the Square, who took the footage to the television stations based in nearby Millbank. The media strategy was a great success. Several television channels aired the protestors' own footage. Most national newspapers quoted their key messages about the consultation and climate change. The *Daily Mail* ran the type of story Greenpeace had hoped for, impressing their readers with the 'oh-so smart backgrounds' of the five. They interviewed the protestors' parents, who were kept 'in the dark' along with everyone else. Stewart asked Chessell what her mother made of the protest: 'She thought the action was great but said "don't you ever wear my pearls again!".'

Another person kept in the dark was the hapless spy Ken Tobias, whose real name, they had discovered, was Toby Kendall. When trying to impress women (failing to notice that some of them were gay) he had been boasting of his 'hush-hush' work 'infiltrating an extremist group'. Tamsin Omond, one of the five on the roof protest, volunteered to confront him in a cafe, while some of the men waited nearby in case of trouble. After fifty minutes of evasion and denials, Kendall disappeared. 'Fortunately for us', Omond wrote in the *Mail on Sunday*, 'he was more Johnny English than James Bond.'

Who had employed him? BAA denied all knowledge, and Murray believes them. Suspicion fell on British Airways, who had been forced to apologise and pay damages to Virgin Atlantic after a campaign of 'dirty tricks' (for example, poaching customers through phone calls pretending to come from Virgin) in the 1990s.[5] This time they refused to comment.

Heathrow Expansion Becomes a Party-Political Issue

Although the government appeared to be standing firm on Heathrow, opinions were shifting within the Conservative opposition. In 2007 an internal commission chaired by John Gummer, published 'Blueprint for a Green Economy', which cited evidence from HACAN and recommended 'scaling back airport expansion plans'. It recommended a new high-speed rail network to replace many domestic flights but made no specific mention of a third runway at Heathrow.

Theresa Villiers, who became Shadow Transport Secretary in July 2007, remembers that aviation was a contentious issue among her colleagues:

> I researched [the issue of Heathrow expansion] with my team and I spoke to David Cameron and his team about it ... My recommendation to him was that we should oppose it because I thought the economic benefits were overstated and the environmental impacts would be very strong, but for the moment we decided we'd listen to the debate; we set a series of tests for deciding what our position would be in the future.

In June 2008 Cameron made a speech attacking the government for using the issue of Heathrow 'as a fetish' and ignoring the serious environmental concerns.[6] He stopped short of opposing a third runway, but some newspapers interpreted his speech as a move in that direction. Villiers continues:

> That was followed by some intensive work by members of my team and the Conservative Research Department on high speed rail and

the possibility of air-to-rail switch ... ultimately the conclusion was to commit to a new high speed rail line, to link it as effectively as possible to Heathrow ... to provide an alternative to many of the short haul flights and free up space at Heathrow, particularly if it was linked in to HS1 [through the Channel Tunnel] as well, so it would provide an alternative to flights to Paris, Brussels and other [European] locations as well [as domestic flights].

At a meeting before the Conservative Party conference in 2008, despite anxiety about the banking crisis, Cameron approved what Villiers was planning to say, committing the party to opposing a third runway and building a high-speed rail link to Heathrow instead.

The Liberal Democrats had a long-standing commitment to oppose the expansion of airports and aviation. In 1996 I was selected as their parliamentary candidate for Plymouth Sutton. In the run-up to that election, commercial interests began to pay more attention to the UK's third party. The Independent commented on the 'cornucopia of free food and drink' around their 1996 party conference.[7] A smart young woman employed by British Airways cornered me at one of those events to tell me why I must support Heathrow Terminal 5; if it didn't go ahead flights from regional airports would be cut back, and that could threaten the future of Plymouth Airport. I smiled and said nothing. Terminal 5 was approved, then a few years later Plymouth Airport closed down anyway.

At the party conference a year later, I proposed an amendment stating that 'indefinite expansion in aviation is incompatible with sustainable development' and calling for 'medium term targets for air traffic reduction'. I was strongly opposed by supporters of the aviation industry. One of them, I discovered later, worked for British Airways and was linked by the *Independent* to their 'dirty tricks' campaign against Virgin Atlantic. The vote was close, but the amendment was carried.

I withdrew from party politics a few years later and forgot about that debate until the life-changing events described in Chapter 13, so I cannot not claim much credit (or blame), but the Lib Dems remained committed to constraining aviation. Their stance would prove critical to national airport policy between 2010 and 2015.

The Conservatives' change of policy left Labour as the only major party supporting a third runway at Heathrow. Many Labour MPs, including some inside the cabinet, were uncomfortable with this. The issue came to a head at two cabinet meetings in January 2009. The new Transport Secretary Geoff Hoon put the economic case for a third runway, supported by Prime Minister Brown. Climate Secretary Ed Miliband and Environment Secretary Hilary Benn opposed them. Miliband argued that expanding Heathrow was incompatible with the targets in the new Climate Change Act. Several other ministers supported him. With no agreement by late evening, Brown ordered the different ministers to agree a solution, and bring it back to the cabinet the following day.

Hoon and Miliband spent most of the day negotiating a deal, which Hoon announced in parliament the day after. The third runway would go ahead, subject to a cap on the additional flights. This would mean that only half the capacity of the new runway would be usable when it opened. Any increases in the longer term would depend on the UK's performance against its legal carbon budgets. For the aviation sector the government was setting a new target, to keep its carbon emissions by 2050 below the level in 2005. The target was a political compromise, unrelated to any expert advice, but it would remain national policy over ten years and three changes of government.

Responding on behalf of the opposition, Villiers was scathing: 'Frankly, if this is the result of the great row in the Cabinet, his colleagues did not get a very good deal out of it. Let us be in no doubt: this is a bleak day for our environment and for all of us who care about safeguarding it.' Norman Baker, for the Lib Dems, asked if parliament would be allowed to vote on the decision. When Hoon refused, John McDonnell condemned this 'betrayal', then grabbed the ceremonial mace prompting the speaker to expel him from the chamber.

Although none of his colleagues stood up to support him on that occasion, several of them declared their unhappiness over Hoon's decision. Seeing a split in the Labour ranks, the Conservatives decided to allocate some of their parliamentary time to an Early Day Motion urging the government to 'rethink its plans for a third runway'. The debate was scheduled for 28 January 2009. Coincidentally, on that day I was in a meeting in Portcullis House, the MPs' office building opposite parliament. What happened next provides a curious footnote to the story of Plane Stupid.

I had arranged the meeting between the Shadow Housing Minister and representatives of several transport and environmental organisations. As I went through the airport-style security I saw on a screen that MPs were debating Heathrow across the road and decided to go there when the meeting was over. A few minutes into the meeting a large man in a sharp suit with an intercom put his hand on the shoulder of the small woman next to me and said 'come with me'. When she questioned why, the man barked: 'now!' Then we all watched in astonishment as a senior representative of a respected national organisation was frogmarched off the premises. That was the last time I ever saw Laura.

Afterwards, I walked through the private tunnel under the road to the Houses of Parliament and entered the public gallery as the Scottish Labour MP Tom Harris was saying:

> There is astonishment among grass-roots Conservatives, and especially in this country's traditionally Conservative-supporting business community, that the shadow Secretary of State for Transport [Villiers] is beginning to sound more like a Green party spokesman – or, heaven help us, a Liberal Democrat.

Twenty-eight Labour MPs defied the party whip, but it was not enough; the motion was defeated by 19 votes. If Labour remained in power then a third runway at Heathrow now seemed inevitable. But in early 2009 the Labour government, grappling with a deepening recession, fell behind the Conservatives in the opinion polls. The latest date for the next election was May 2010.

Victory – for the Time Being

In April 2009 the opponents launched their legal challenge; whatever the outcome, delay could work in their favour. By this point Stewart believed the Conservatives would win the election, but all the opponents agreed that they needed to prepare for an unexpected Labour win. While the local authorities prepared for a public inquiry, activists from Plane Stupid moved into houses in the threatened villages and began training people for direct action. Some of them gate-crashed events with companies supporting the runway or hoping to win contracts for it. Their message was simple: if you get involved, you will be targeted.

During 2009 the aviation industry began to take the prospect of a Conservative government cancelling the third runway more seriously. The British Chamber of Commerce published a report claiming the runway would bring far greater economic benefits than even the DfT was forecasting. Meanwhile industry lobbyists worked on the Conservatives' leaders behind the scenes. One of my interviewees described the mixture of frustration and contempt they felt for Villiers, who just wasn't getting their message. One of their arguments concerned the rail alternative. On its own, a high-speed link would not replace enough flights to satisfy demand with only two runways. The elephant in the room was the same beast Goodwin and the New Realists had grappled with over road-building; if you don't want to keep expanding supply, how do you constrain demand? 'Blueprint for a Green Economy' provided one answer: constrain capacity and let the market prioritise higher-paying business flights (most beneficial to the economy) over low-cost leisure flights. That was clear and logical but not likely to win many votes.

In March 2010 a High Court judge gave the opponents an unexpected boost. The judgement stopped short of halting the expansion but criticised several aspects of the government's case, particularly the inconsistency between its aviation policy and its obligations under the Climate Change Act. The National Policy Statement on Airports, due in 2011 would have to reconcile the two. The new Transport Secretary, Lord Adonis, claimed they were going to do that anyway, but the conflict between aviation and climate policy would remain unresolved for over a decade. The judgement allowed both sides to claim victory, but the most important comment came from David Cameron, who had faced some criticism within his own party: 'I have made it very clear time and again that under a Conservative government the third runway is not going ahead: no ifs, no buts.'

A few days later Prime Minister Brown called the general election. Labour's manifesto committed to build an additional runway at Heathrow, but nowhere else. The Conservatives and Liberal Democrats both said they would build no new runways at any of the main airports in the Southeast. The decision now rested with the voters.

The outcome was a hung parliament; the Conservatives were the largest party and the Liberal Democrats held the balance of power. As the parties negotiated and the country waited for news a group from my university visited the protestors' unofficial headquarters in a pub near Heathrow, where I heard John Stewart speak for the first time. While some of my colleagues were hoping the smaller parties might support a minority Labour government, Stewart seemed to speak with inside knowledge when he talked of a coalition, which would scrap the plans for a third runway. He talked of the lessons he had learned about successful campaigning: avoid NIMBYism, tackle the economic arguments and don't waste your energy on official consultations or inquiries. I can't remember what he said about Plane Stupid, but he would later write:

> [Direct action is] illegal and that worries people. It's eye-catching – and that can lead to the perception that direct action is all a campaign is about. It wasn't direct action alone that won this campaign … [but] I'm not at all certain we would have been drinking champagne if the direct-action activists had been missing from the campaign.[8]

A few days later, his confidence was vindicated when the Conservatives and Lib Dems published an agreement outlining their policies for a coalition government. These included a commitment to cancel the third runway at Heathrow and refuse permission for additional runways at Gatwick and Stansted. It was a historic victory for the campaigners, but it came with a time limit. The commitment would apply for the duration of the next parliament, which would last for five years. Meanwhile, the plans for high-speed rail, which were also affirmed in the Coalition Agreement, were stimulating a new protest movement.

10
High-Speed Rail
False Starts and Big Decisions

The history of high-speed rail in Britain, stretches back to the 1960s, including several false starts and the national humiliation of British Rail's experimental tilting trains in the 1980s, which frequently broke down, made passengers feel sick and were soon withdrawn from service.

By 1994, when the Channel Tunnel opened, high-speed rail was well-established across Europe, but was new to Britain. The first Eurostar trains ran on a high-speed line from Paris to the tunnel but were forced to follow conventional tracks on the British side. This prompted French President Mitterrand to warn passengers:

> They will race at great pace across the plains of northern France, race through the tunnel on a fast track, and then be able to daydream at very low speed, admiring the landscape … until the day when someone over there in London decides to harmonise the way of doing things between the continent and the island.

Mitterrand's mockery raised a sensitive point, often raised in future debates around high-speed rail: if the French (and Spanish and Japanese) can do it, why can't we?

A spokesperson for the DTp replied that a new line was not needed yet; but there was another reason for the delay. BR's original plans for a direct high-speed line had provoked mass protests in Kent and south London. In 1989 6,000 people marched through Maidstone, led by Conservative MPs who put considerable pressure on the government to reconsider. In 1996 John Major's government approved a longer route through East London and Essex to the Channel Tunnel. The private sector was supposed to finance and build the line but the project ran into difficulties obliging the government to intervene.

When the new line finally opened four years late the construction cost had more than doubled to £6.8 billion. It was named 'HS1' anticipating more high-speed lines in future. A civil servant responsible for high-speed rail reflects: 'I feel about HS1 a bit like the Scots feel about the Scottish Parliament. Did it cost more than you thought it was going to? Well I'm afraid it did. Did all the development you thought it was going to unlock happen? Not yet. Do you wish you'd never done it? Not really.'

Studies and Lobbying Under Labour Governments

In 2001 the Strategic Rail Authority (SRA), a body created by John Prescott to oversee the rail network, commissioned consultants Atkins to write a report on the potential for high speed rail. It concluded that 'there is a business case' for a North-South high-speed line, which would serve most of Britain's main cities. The main justifications, it noted, were 'meeting future transport needs and delivering value for money.' Their preferred option would cost £32 billion. On that basis, they estimated that each pound spent on the project would create £1.40 of benefits across the UK. This was a modest ratio compared to most schemes funded by the Treasury, although the authors suggested that it could be improved by making some related changes to the rest of the rail network.

The technique which produces those estimates, known as cost–benefit analysis, is familiar to everyone who works on transport projects in the UK. The biggest element of the benefits comes from time savings to rail passengers or car drivers, which are greater on faster journeys. The benefits are sometimes called 'economic benefits', which is misleading; some of the time saved may be used productively but most travel is for leisure purposes; the impact of shorter journeys on the economy is difficult to assess. The usefulness of cost–benefit analysis was, and still is, controversial. Whether transport projects make any difference to national economic performance has never been proven,[1] but many people working in transport and in government believe that they do and believe that cost–benefit analysis can help to show this. As one civil servant puts it:

DfT was far better at appraisal than any other department. Long-standing, very capable, very sophisticated on appraisal ... We had numbers which would suggest that building roads was a good thing ... These numbers were a big part of DfT's dealing with Treasury ... The more interesting thing is why does rail still get so much capital spending, when their numbers – both the cost–benefit and the number of trips – are mediocre compared to roads?

That argument would recur in different ways over years of controversy surrounding HS2.

When the final report was sent to the DfT in 2002 Alistair Darling had become Transport Secretary. As one adviser describes his appointment: 'Alistair was there to avoid trouble.' This made him sceptical of the arguments for large risky infrastructure projects. In the financial circumstances of 2002, a price tag of £32 billion was enough to shelve the idea but by the mid-2000s the economy was improving and calls for a high-speed network began to resurface inside and outside government. In 2006, Jim Steer, a transport consultant who had worked at the SRA, set up a not-for-profit company, Greengauge 21, to research and lobby for high speed rail in the UK. Their manifesto attracted little media attention at the time, but their work behind the scenes with MPs and local authorities helped to keep the issue on the government's agenda.

Although Darling remained unconvinced, he allowed a working group to study the issue. That work was ongoing when Douglas Alexander replaced him in May 2006. An adviser recalls: 'The Treasury were always deeply suspicious [of high-speed rail]. Other people weren't massively against it, in that period. It was like being against something that would never happen.' In March 2008 the Rail Minister Tom Harris set out the government's view in parliament: 'a lot of the debate on high speed lines is basically saying, "Well, here's a solution. Now let's look for a problem to answer."'

Lord Adonis Commits Labour to HS2

Those attitudes changed quite rapidly after the appointment of Lord Andrew Adonis as rail minister in October 2008. A few days into the job, he told *The Times* why he supported high-speed rail: 'our projections show we will be at saturation point on some lines in 15 to 20 years'. Interestingly, he singled out Waterloo station, which was indeed suffering from overcrowding – on the opposite side of London from the proposed high-speed line. Some of the lines north of London were also nearing capacity but there was no clear pattern suggesting a new line to Birmingham as the top priority. If there was a case to be made it would depend on future growth.

The project would take 20 years to realise, Adonis said, so it would need cross-party agreement. The Conservatives had already proposed high-speed rail as an alternative to expanding Heathrow, but Adonis was sceptical of that argument. The country needed both, he believed.

In January 2009 Geoff Hoon, Adonis's boss, announced the government's support for a third runway at Heathrow with 'better surface access'. At the same time the DfT published a plan for a publicly owned company, HS2 Ltd, initially 'to help consider the case for new high-speed services from London to Scotland'. As the project progressed, the role of HS2 Ltd would extend to managing the project itself. It would also become increasingly embroiled in the politics of high-speed rail, but its first step was straightforward enough: to advise on a new line between London and Birmingham with a connection to Heathrow.

The study was expected to take at least a year; if Hoon was content to wait and see what it recommended, Adonis was not. An adviser recalls:

> Geoff Hoon was pretty ineffectual; he was not proactive. You had a very active individual in Andrew as the number 2 in the department, who was a transport enthusiast and was very knowledgeable, and politically understood that he needed to find a 'stand out' issue he could campaign on, that defined what he was trying to achieve. Academies were his example in Education; HS2 was his example in Transport ...
>
> The Tories had stolen a bit of a march and people were asking whether we'd left a gap; did we have to make a similar move? But nobody was really pushing for it, and then Andrew came in and began lobbying for it big-time ... He would talk to Gordon, to people in the Number 10 Policy Unit ...

While the study was under way two issues were changing British politics. The biggest one was the global financial crisis and the second was a scandal, which touched a raw national nerve, about the lavish expenses claimed by MPs. One beneficiary was Hoon, who was claiming expenses for a second home while living in a 'grace and favour' apartment. In June 2009 he resigned and was replaced by Adonis. The adviser continues: '[Prime Minister] Gordon [Brown] was changing his view of investment after the financial crisis. We started to see lots more stimulus measures and Gordon became more comfortable with advocating significant public infrastructure investment into the future.'

With an election due the following year, a commitment to a big rail project seemed to make political sense, but what type of project? In future years, many people and organisations would argue that there were better alternatives to HS2. How thoroughly were those alternatives considered before the decision was made? The adviser's comments are revealing:

> Work was certainly done. Upgrading the West Coast Main Line and the Chilterns Line was considered as well. The [cost–benefit analyses] were not as good. Andrew did challenge the analysis. It wasn't purely done by the economists in the department. He would challenge their numbers if some of the alternatives were getting closer to HS2 than might be comfortable... You are making a polit- ical judgement; it's not just about numbers on a spreadsheet. He had made his judgement that it was the right thing to do. I think it is fair to say that the analysis that was then done on the alternatives, by and large, was to use arguments as to why they were not as good.

Could the new line have taken a slightly slower route, following motorways or disused railway lines (as some critics have suggested) to minimise the environmental damage?

> That's a fair challenge. There were some historic bits of old line [the Great Central Line] and they were considered but I think the truth is that Andrew did become very, very focussed on speed [which] means that you needed a line as straight as possible to reduce journey times. His defence would be that ... that this was transforming the

economic geography of the country. You were bringing together the main population centres of the country.

In March 2010 the DfT published the government's response to the study by HS2 Ltd. They recommended a Y-shaped route, starting at London's Euston station with a spur to Birmingham and the main route dividing to serve Manchester in the northwest and Leeds in the northeast. The estimated construction cost was 'in the region of £30 billion'. The report deferred the question of a direct link to the Channel Tunnel and preferred an interchange at Old Oak Common in West London over a detour via Heathrow. With an election looming Adonis was concerned that ruling out a direct link to Heathrow might offer an election issue to the Conservative Party, so he appointed former Conservative Transport Secretary Lord Brian Mawhinney to review the issue, and report on it after the election.

Most controversially, the new line would cut through the Chilterns AONB (Area of Outstanding Natural Beauty), with some tunnelling but mostly overground. The report included a map with a blue line showing a 'preferred route' from Lichfield to London with a spur into Birmingham. The line alerted communities along it to the potential threat.

The Campaign Begins – and Splits in Two

One of the places close to that blue line was Quainton, a picturesque village in Buckinghamshire. Penny Gaines, a mother at home who had previously worked in IT, remembers finding the report online and seeing how the line would pass within a mile of Quainton. She phoned the Chairman of the parish council, who knew nothing about it. Shortly afterwards she learned that the Chairman of the local Conservative Association was organising a meeting at the Parish Hall where the local MP, John Bercow, would speak. Reassured by this, she helped put up some posters and took one small initiative of her own:

I had been online for a long time. I knew that if you want a website, the longer it's been in existence, that matters. So I set up a website called HS2 Action with the thought that when the real campaigners came along I could say: 'Here, have a website; it's got three months' history.' And it turned out, well, the real campaigners – that was me!

The meeting was arranged for a Saturday evening, nine days after the announcement. The weather was bad, but the parish hall was packed, with the public, journalists and television cameras.

The announcement had created a problem for Bercow. As Speaker of the House of Commons he would have to chair debates about HS2 where he would not be allowed to express any opinion. How could he represent the views of his Buckingham constituents? Two of his comments are interesting with hindsight: 'I hope you will not accuse me of an excessive cynicism if I say in respect of all governments that that the estimated cost with which you start, is invariably very much on the low side …' And: 'It is true that I can't speak in debates, but … I get quicker replies from ministers then I ever did before … If anybody refers to impartiality, I say it's nonsense on stilts … I can speak on anything that affects our interests.'[2]

Accusations of partiality (particularly on Brexit) would eventually damage his relations with his own party, but for the time being he could expect a sympathetic hearing, though no change in policy, from Theresa Villers, the Shadow Transport Secretary. A few days later the election campaign began. All three of the main parties included a commitment to high-speed rail. The Conservatives repeated their commitment to a line 'connecting London and Heathrow with Birmingham, Manchester and Leeds.'

Meanwhile over 40 separate local protest groups were forming along the route. Gaines became the secretary for the Quainton Action Group. A few weeks later they were invited to a meeting to discuss the formation of a national campaign. Apart from the people from Quainton, she knew none of the others, who seemed more experienced, so she assumed that her role would be a minor one.

South of Quainton, in the Chilterns AONB, the preferred route would pass within a few hundred metres of a mansion owned by management and transport consultants Bruce Weston and Hilary Wharf. Wharf and Weston circulated a proposal in advance of the meeting. They wanted to challenge the business case for HS2 and propose alternatives but did not want to run a 'stop HS2' campaign. They presented their proposal to the meeting and explained that they had set up a not-for-profit company for the purpose. Gaines continues: 'A lot of the people at the meeting weren't terribly happy about this, but the chair of the meeting said, "Well, this is the only proposal on the table.' Then the meeting voted, that if anyone else wanted to come up with an alternative "stop HS2" proposal they could go ahead with that.'

The outcome was two separate campaigns. Stop HS2 was formed with Lizzy Williams as Chair, Joe Rukin as Campaign Director and Gaines as Social Media Director. Wharf and Weston set up the HS2 Action Alliance and published an alternative to HS2, making better use of the West Coast Mainline. For a while both organisations claimed to be the umbrella group representing many others. Gaines says: 'A lot of people assumed that HS2 Action Alliance would be the lead and that we would be a minor [campaign].'

The picture was further complicated when some of the local protest groups decided to create a third umbrella organisation, AGHAST (Action Groups Against HS2). Over the following years, the different groups would generally cooperate, sometimes conflict and sometimes focus on different issues, but Stop HS2 would endure the longest and become the best-known voice of opposition to the scheme.

The 'Preferred Route' is Confirmed

In September 2010 Lizzy Williams, who was off work recovering from a car crash, set out on a walk along the preferred route from Lichfield to London's Euston station. She wanted to alert people living along the route, publicise the campaign and encourage people to get involved. She was surprised to find people living right next to the route who were unaware of the plans, particularly in London. She arrived in Euston 23 days later, then took a train to walk the Birmingham spur to the International Convention Centre, where she joined a small group of protestors outside the Conservative Party Conference.

Inside the Centre, the new Transport Secretary Philip Hammond announced a consultation on HS2 in the New Year. Ironically, in a speech mainly attacking the Labour Party, he announced the government's preferred route, which sounded rather like the one published by Adonis.

In September and October of 2010 Hammond arranged a series of meetings with MPs and campaigners along the route. At the first of these meetings in Brackley, Northamptonshire, 200 people turned up to protest. Gaines remembers:

> I'd never been to a protest of any sort before. Philip Hammond came outside and there was this moment of silence, and suddenly someone started hissing and booing, so everybody else started hissing and booing ... At later meetings we would have a chant: 'HS2 – no thank you', but at that first one a lot of people there, myself included, didn't really know what they were doing.

In December 2010 Hammond announced that he had reviewed the proposal he inherited from Adonis and decided that it was the best option, with a few minor adjustments.[3] There would be an extra 150m of tunnelling in the Chilterns. The line would be moved further away from Lichfield and from Hartwell House to placate the National Trust. A short tunnel north of Euston would link HS2 to HS1 and the Channel Tunnel. Following Lord Mawhinney's recommendations there would be no direct link to Heathrow in the first phase, but they would study the potential to build a spur to Heathrow as part of the second phase.

Hammond's announcement dismayed local authorities along the route, particularly in Buckinghamshire, where the line would pass through the Chilterns. Buckinghamshire County Council announced a fighting fund to oppose HS2 and invited other councils along the route to join them. Martin Tett was their Cabinet Member for Planning and the Environment at the time:

> I remember when HS2 was first mooted, there was a view that we should be opposing it but not very actively. Then in 2011 I decided to stand as Leader of the County Council and part of my platform was a more vigorous opposition to HS2 and that was one of the reasons I got elected as Leader... We quickly identified there were a number of councils along the route, all of whom were pretty hostile to HS2. It needed someone to step forward and take some leadership on this, so I agreed to chair a meeting pulling all of those councils together, and that evolved into what became 51M. We called it 51M because we worked out that at that time, the budgeted

cost divided across the country would have meant £51 million for each constituency.

The 13 councils who formed 51M were joined over the following year by another six. They ranged from 'red Camden' to 'true blue Stratford-on-Avon' and Tett recalls 'everybody worked really well together'. They worked alongside other groups, particularly the HS2 Action Alliance, who brought useful technical expertise; Tett describes Hilary Weston as 'a star'. They noticed some of the friction between the various groups, however, and had mixed feelings about some of their tactics. In the summer of 2011 Stop HS2 acquired what became its public mascot – a ten-feet-high inflatable white elephant, which appeared at many of their demonstrations. Tett explains: 'We had cordial relations [with the protest groups] but it wasn't close. We were local councils spending public money ... We had a mandate [from our voters] but we felt had to so on a reputable basis, so inflatable elephants and stuff was not really what we wanted as an image.'

Although Stop HS2 and its member groups organised many noisy and provocative actions, they remained within the law, for the time being. Gaines explains: 'We always felt when the bulldozers came, people would be willing to lie in front of them but [as yet] there were no bulldozers.'

During 2011, 51M had several meetings with Philip Hammond who, like several transport ministers, 'really didn't like the scrutiny' according to Tett. Their questions focussed on the economic case and affordability of HS2. As with many big transport projects, the positive cost–benefit analysis was mainly due to projected time savings, particularly for business travellers, but:

At that point, it rested heavily on the issue of no one working on trains, therefore arriving 15 minutes earlier in Birmingham was worth billions to the economy. It was clearly nonsense and it was really easy to articulate. Whenever I went on radio or television in those days I would say: 'here's a mobile phone. These don't exist in the world of the DfT because no one works on trains.' You could feel the way the DfT were wriggling on this and really trying to gerrymander the business case to get around this 'no one works on a train' argument.

In the summer of 2011 campaigners gained a powerful ally in London's Mayor Boris Johnson. Johnson objected to the impact of the line on parts of West London and overcrowding on the Underground serving Euston station. As the government was making no commitment to expand the Underground connections 'I cannot support the current proposal' he said. One of the West London suburbs most affected was Ruislip, where 500 people marched in the rain behind the inflatable elephant to a Stop HS2 rally at the local rugby field. They were joined by John Randall, the MP for Ruislip South and the government's Deputy Chief Whip. The MP for the neighbouring constituency, Nick Hurd, was also a government minister. Meanwhile, Cheryl Gillan, the Welsh Secretary, who represented a Chilterns constituency, was telling the media that she would resign if prevented from campaigning against HS2. The campaigners were gaining powerful supporters, but would they be able to sway enough MPs and the government?

The Conflict Moves into Parliament

In February 2011 Philip Hammond launched a public consultation into the government's plans for HS2, which would run until the end of July. In June 2011 the Transport Select Committee of the House of Commons launched its own inquiry to run in parallel. As supporters and opponents gave evidence, both sides ratcheted up their war of words in the media. A business lobby group, Yes to High Speed Rail, paid for posters showing an arrogant-looking man in a bowler hat with the caption 'Their lawns or our jobs?' David Begg, their Director, who gave evidence to the inquiry, talked of opponents 'in a very, very privileged position economically, while a number of people who would benefit from high-speed rail are not in the same position'. Joe Rukin, Stop HS2's Campaign Director, replied through the press: 'As a single father hardly surviving on income support I find the idea that I am "economically privileged" from a man who charges thousands of pounds just for speaking utterly disgusting.'

The Committee's final witness in September 2011 was Hammond. Stop HS2 supporters paraded outside parliament with their inflatable elephant as he gave evidence. A Labour MP asked him for reassurance that HS2 would not become 'a rich person's toy'. His answer would be quoted against him on many occasions:

The railway is already relatively a rich man's toy – the whole railway. People who use the railway, on average, have significantly higher incomes than the population as a whole ... If you are working in a factory in Manchester you might never get on HS2, but you will certainly be benefiting from it if the salesman and sales director of your company is routinely hopping on it to go and meet customers.

In October 2011, Stop HS2 handed an old-fashioned pen-and-paper petition signed by 108,000 people to Downing Street. It called for a parliamentary debate, which took place a few days later. There was no vote, but most MPs outside of the affected areas appeared to support the project.

The Transport Committee published its report in November 2011. It declared its support for HS2 in principle but found much of the government's case unconvincing. It said that more work was needed on: the policy context, the assessment of alternatives, the economic case, environmental impacts, connections to Heathrow and the justification for the proposed route. Supporters were relieved that HS2 had cleared another hurdle, while Stop HS2 described the report as a 'scathing' call for the government 'to go back and do it again properly'.[4]

A few weeks later, Justine Greening replaced Hammond as Transport Secretary. In January 2012 she gave the government's response to the public consultation and Committee report. Over 54,000 people and organisations had responded to the consultation, mostly opposing HS2, but the government remained convinced of the case. HS2 was approved with a few more concessions to the objectors. A new tunnel, nearly three miles long, would reduce the impacts on Ruislip and three other tunnels would be extended to reduce impacts on the Chilterns. Compensation terms would also be improved. Despite these changes, the estimated cost of the project remained around £32 billion. The line from London to Birmingham would open in 2026 and the second phase to Manchester, Leeds and Heathrow by 2033.

How realistic were those estimates? That question was in the minds of most participants at another inquiry, by the Parliamentary Accounts Committee into the finances of HS1, in April 2012. HS1 had run over time and over budget; why would HS2 be any different? Under its Chair, Margaret Hodge, this committee had a fearsome reputation and on this issue some of its members scented blood. One civil servant says (with a little irony): 'I always enjoyed my afternoons at the Public Accounts Committee – did it not show?' Another says:

> Ostensibly the Public Accounts Committee was asking questions about HS1 but it was pretty clear to us all that the real object of their interest was HS2 and what the comparison between the original business case forecasts and actual patronage on HS1 might imply for the forecasts underpinning HS2.

Within the Cabinet Office a Major Projects Authority rates the government's biggest projects on a traffic-light scale. Hodge asked one witness how they had rated HS2. His answer was 'amber-red' (the second highest risk level), to which Hodge replied: 'Amber-red isn't good enough.' The civil servant says:

> I was thinking: I bet the risk register for D-Day was amber-red. Some things you do will always be amber-red … If we had brought you a risk register that was amber-green you would have accused us of delusion … What does HS1 tell you about HS2? Well, we've got a bit better at forecasting, a bit better at analysis. We've got a bit wiser about projecting things in ranges but fundamentally, what we've learned is: building big railway lines is a risky business.

In presenting the Committee's report in July 2012, Hodge was damning about HS1 and the government's failure to learn from it:

> HS1 was supposed to pay for itself but instead the taxpayer has had to pay out £4.8 billion so far to cover the debt on the project. The root of the problem is the inaccurate and wildly optimistic forecasts for passenger numbers … The Department must revisit its assumptions on HS2 and develop a full understanding of the benefits and costs of high-speed travel compared to the alternatives.

Her comments conflated cost–benefit analyses, which are purely theoretical exercises, with budget overruns, which cost real pounds to governments and taxpayers; but on both measures, the message was clear: the DfT's numbers were suspect.

11

HS2

'On Time and On Budget'

In April 2012, the local authorities and campaign groups separately made the first of several legal challenges to the HS2 project. The High Court rejected the authorities' claim but upheld one of the grounds advanced by the campaign groups; the consultation on compensation to property owners was 'so unfair as to be unlawful'.[1] The government decided to re-run the consultation instead of appealing.

In the cabinet reshuffle of September 2012 Cameron appointed Patrick McLoughlin as Transport Secretary and sacked Cheryl Gillan, who used her new freedom to launch a fierce attack on HS2. A civil servant describes McLoughlin as a 'consummate parliamentarian', sensitive to the opposition inside and outside parliament. Before incurring any larger costs, he wanted to secure cross-party support. Although there was no requirement for parliamentary approval at that stage, he decided to present a paving bill to parliament.

A paving bill confers powers on a public body, including the power to spend money. How much money was not defined in the bill, allowing Stop HS2 to call it 'the Blank Cheque Bill'. When McLoughlin rose to present it to parliament, he made the first of several admissions over the years, that HS2 was going to cost more than expected. The new budget would be £42.6 billion. Some of the extra £10 billion was due to the design changes but he also stressed the 'prudent' contingency of £12.7 billion to allow for unexpected increases in future.

Why did the costs of HS2 keep increasing? The civil servant says:

There are any number of reasons why things cost more than you think they are going to. Until you start digging into the ground you never know what you are going to hit. Railways are particularly trying because the global rail supply industry isn't that big. In an average year, not many people go down to the shops to buy a railway signalling system, so the suppliers are supplying a one-off bespoke system every time ... every commission is a voyage of discovery for them ... We did our best to come up with a range of costs that had sufficient optimism bias in them. We weren't trying to massage the costs.

In later years whistle-blowers would allege that HS2 Ltd was indeed trying to massage the costs,[2] but in 2013 no such evidence was available.

Although the costs had risen, the cost–benefit analysis was now showing £2.50 of benefits for every £1 of costs. These ratios would be recalculated several times over the years. Each time, the costs would rise and so would the projected benefits. Were those figures being 'massaged'?

You're conscious that the Secretary of State wants to make the most positive statement. He's arrived with a manifesto commitment to do something and it's going to take something pretty earth-shattering for him to have to go back and say: 'You know we committed to do this, but actually I'm not so sure' ... At the same time, we civil servants are obliged to tell the truth... I think it's fair to say that the DfT economists approach these issues dispassionately. Their job is to do the sums as well as they can, and we will deal with the consequences ... I hope – I believe – that none of us were unduly swayed.

In December 2013 the paving bill was passed by 348 votes to 32. It was the first of several acts of parliament authorising different stages of HS2; all passed with strong support. However, ministers remained sensitive to criticism of HS2's rising costs. In November 2013, McLoughlin instructed Sir David Higgins, the new Chair of HS2 Ltd, to review the project and advise him on how its costs might be reduced.

Higgins's report was published in March 2014; its tone was highly political. It made three main recommendations: to scrap the link between HS2 and HS1, spend more money on rebuilding Euston station and extend the line to Crewe six years earlier than planned to deliver 'faster services sooner' to northern cities. He appealed to government to bring 'civic and business leaders' from the north 'into the discussion', ostensibly to maximise the economic potential of HS2, but also to build a coalition against the critics. His recommendation to scrap the link to the Channel Tunnel was partly a cost-cutting measure but also aimed to provide more capacity for services to other regions, such as north Wales, which were lobbying for high-speed connections. With this change, and a larger contingency, Higgins was 'confident that the budget can be made to work' and even expressed some hope that phase 1 might be built for less than budgeted.

In fact, the costs continued to rise, and the government continued to look for ways to cut back. During 2014, the Davies Review of Airport Capacity (discussed in the next chapter) examined the case for an HS2 spur to Heathrow. They concluded that it would be expensive, carry relatively few passengers and 'represent an inefficient use of HS2 capacity'. In March 2015, McLoughlin confirmed that the government was scrapping the idea. This decision cut some costs, but others were rising faster; the Chancellor's autumn statement of 2015 revealed that the 'funding envelope' for HS2 had increased again, to £55.7 billion.

In April 2014 a hybrid bill (with public and private elements) passed its second reading in the House of Commons; only 41 MPs voted against it. This bill specified much of the detail for the first phase of HS2. Martin Tett remembers it as a turning point, when the authorities in 51M began to accept that HS2 would eventually happen; instead of fighting against it they, and MPs, began to press for concessions. An adviser recalls:

> The bill committee wanted to make a concession to each MP's constituency. You could almost see the MPs sitting round saying 'hmm, so what do we have to give Cheryl?' The politics was a bit like that. When Cheryl Gillan was removed by David Cameron, she became a lot more active in lobbying and she managed to get some extended tunnelling, so instead of coming out at Amersham it was moved to an area near Great Missenden. David Lidington was lobbying for some tunnelling near Wendover; he got some [extended] 'cut and cover', where they dig down and then rebury it. Along the route every constituency got a bit of something.

By the time the hybrid bill reached the House of Lords in March 2016 nearly 30 miles, over a quarter of the route from London to Birmingham, was in a tunnel of some kind. The length of the tunnels had more than doubled since the start of the project, for engineering reasons as well as local concessions. Although some of these changes were expensive, they only explain a small proportion of the project's rising costs. Several reports have tried to explain why civil engineering projects are more expensive in Britain than elsewhere; land and property costs are part of the reason; higher consultancy costs are another. Other studies have tried to explain why underestimates are more common than overestimates when planning mega-projects in Britain and elsewhere.[3] Technical factors and property costs are always uncertain at the start, but the tendency to underestimate is driven by politics; HS2 was no exception to that rule.

Protestors Return to the Trees

Dorothea Hackman is the Chair of the Camden Civic Society and warden of St Pancras Church opposite Euston Station. She recalls several meetings as the hybrid bill was passing through parliament and Camden Council was simultaneously consulting on its Euston Area Plan. The community's concerns included the loss of over 200 homes and air pollution during the lengthy construction period. She recalls:

> We met with Camden Council and consultative bodies. There was this dire consultation where all the shouty men in the community bellowed their existential anger at High Speed Two representatives, which might make them feel better but as far as I can see achieves no outcome. Nevertheless, I believed in the democratic process at that point, so we all prepared petitions as best we could. I'm a governor of the local primary school. The children were amazing. We took a bunch of them to the public examination of the Euston Area Plan. A nine-year-old girl fixed the inspector with her eyes and said: 'If you let them do this you shorten my life by 18 months!'

The children's interventions made little difference to the outcome, but they did not pass unnoticed. One of the commitments made during the passage of the hybrid bill was to fund an educational programme.

The main aim of this programme was to promote the employment opportunities, which HS2 was expected to create. However, part of the programme was aimed at primary schools. In late 2016 HS2 Ltd sent out packs to schools along the route including an exercise for children to consider four different routes for 'Zoom Rail'. The material for teachers explained:

> One of the four options – Route D – is the preferred route. This is not the only acceptable 'right answer'. However, students who have closely understood the opportunities and constraints faced by Zoom Rail as it tries to strike the best balance are more likely to opt for the preferred route.

As the hybrid bill made its way through parliament Camden Council, like the other members of 51M, gradually changed its focus from opposition to negotiation. According to Hackman:

> Camden rolled over in exchange for a hundred assurances, which they don't police and implement because they don't have the finance and they fear they will lose influence if they [object too strongly] … They dismissed all our petitions on the grounds that Camden had been given the assurances.

The full list of these assurances is still available online.[4] Most of them include subjective phrases such as: 'actively engage', 'use reasonable endeavours' or 'insofar as reasonably practicable', which would make them difficult to enforce in any case.

In November 2016 the DfT issued contracts for enabling works to begin. These would entail the felling of hundreds of trees, removal of a small park near Euston station and exhumation of an ancient burial ground. Hackman recalls: 'Fortunately, we were in contact with what was to become Extinction Rebellion [see Chapter 13]. We were all trained up in non-violent direct action …'

In January 2018 Hackman chained the vicar Anne Stevens and another female protestor to one of the condemned trees, surrounded by hundreds of protestors, old and young, from around the area. Images of the vicar and another campaigner with chains around their waists appeared across the national media that day. It was 'partially successful', Hackman says – 26 of the trees were given a reprieve – until the main works begin. Does she expect any more action? 'Oh yes. If the main works start, I imagine they'll want to cut down every tree known, and I'm expecting my Extinction Rebellion colleagues to go up those trees. I'm way too old for that!'

Meanwhile, in the Colne Valley Regional Park west of Ruislip, protestors were digging in for a longer conflict. If you have ever watched news items about HS2 you have probably seen the Colne Valley as the backdrop to a train speeding over concrete stilts through a beautiful landscape surrounded by water and trees. The train and the line are computer-generated, the landscape is real. In a scene reminiscent of the anti-roads protests, security guards working on the project were filmed there in the autumn of 2017 shoving and abusing two women, including Sarah Green, a Green Party activist who went on to organise a growing protest camp on the site.

In February 2018 Transport Secretary Chris Grayling obtained an injunction against protestors who were camping in ancient woodland along the route. In November 2018 protestors succeeded in halting work on the site and two of them, Green and Laura Hughes, were charged with aggravated trespass. In a moment of farce, reminding many of wider failings by HS2 Ltd, the High Court dismissed the case because the company was unable to prove that they owned the field where the two women were arrested.

On Time and On Budget, or On its Way Out?

Throughout 2016 and 2017 there were recurring media stories about mismanagement, rising costs and attempts to conceal them. The website glassdoor.co.uk reveals some interesting comments from former employees of HS2 Ltd. One anonymous employee wrote: 'Nothing is written down or confirmed and when it goes wrong, guess what, no audit trail … When a deadline is missed the stock answer is "I told xxxxxxxxxx to do it". Was that confirmed on email? No I just told them to do it.'[5]

In March 2016 the National Audit Office (NAO) announced that they were planning to investigate the project, a move which reportedly 'spooked' the executives of HS2 Ltd.[6] When Simon Kirby, the Chief Executive of HS2 Ltd resigned in September 2016 the company was forced to deny rumours that his departure was 'due to problems with the project or tensions within government'.

Kirby and his team had attracted criticism from the media and some MPs over the size of their salaries, which were the highest in the public sector. The NAO's report published the following year accused the company of making inflated redundancy payments, despite a DfT instruction not to do so. They criticised the informality of communication and decision-making between the DfT and HS2 Ltd and called for a 'significant improvement in the general control environment'.

In July 2017 Michael Byng, a quantity surveyor who had advised Network Rail, published an estimate suggesting that HS2's ultimate costs would be nearly double the £56 billion budget. The first phase to Birmingham would use nearly all that budget, he estimated. HS2 Ltd disputed Byng's analysis and said it was 'confident we will deliver the project on time and on budget'. When Grayling repeated that assurance in the House of Commons Stop HS2 published an image of him as Pinocchio with a long nose in the shape of a high-speed train.

In July 2018 the *Sunday Times* published some of the most serious allegations against HS2 Ltd.[7] Doug Thornton, who was sacked as the company's Head of Property in 2016, had passed internal documents to the NAO and Lord Berkeley, a Labour Peer who was becoming one of the project's most strident critics. Thornton alleged that HS2 Ltd put him under 'tremendous pressure to accede to an enormous deceit' around the cost of land and property along the line. The original estimates, he alleged, were 'rudimentary map-based analysis by interns.' Over time, more accurate information had been gathered, suggesting much higher costs, but these were not revealed to the board of HS2 Ltd. He alleged that he was sacked after refusing to present misleadingly low estimates to the board. He claimed that he had shared his concerns with civil servants but these concerns were concealed from MPs as the hybrid bill passed through the House of Commons.

HS2 Ltd denied that Thornton and another employee had been sacked for whistle-blowing. They denied that anyone had misled MPs. Chief Executive Mark Thurston told a BBC *Panorama* documentary in December 2018, 'I'm not worried about overspending. I'm confident we've got a budget we can stand by.'

In retrospect it is difficult to interpret the conflicting statements made in 2018 and 2019 as honest differences of opinion. Were middle managers concealing the truth from senior managers at HS2 Ltd? Were senior managers (with or without the knowledge of ministers) concealing the truth from MPs and the public, or were the critics misinformed or venting a grudge against their former employer? Somebody was clearly lying, but who, and why?

In August 2019 I exchanged messages with a former employee of HS2 Ltd who expressed some interest in the book and a possible interview. Then he stopped replying. A few weeks later the trade magazine *New Civil Engineer* revealed that HS2 Ltd had sent letters threatening legal action against former employees who had copied documents or revealed company information. One former employee told them: 'I may believe I am entirely in the right, and entirely in the public's interest and you are exposing what you believe was a fraud and a crime. But to fight HS2 could ... cost someone their life savings.'[8]

HS2 Ltd cited data protection requirements as the reason for wanting to keep certain documents private, but in a (separate) court case in October 2019 they also stated: 'Detractors of the HS2 programme may use such information to renew their criticism of the HS2 programme, which could result in cancellation of the HS2 programme by the government.'[9]

The company had good reason to be nervous. In July 2019 Boris Johnson, MP for Uxbridge and a long-standing opponent of HS2, became Prime Minister, following the resignation of Theresa May. The following month his new Transport Secretary Grant Shapps announced a review of the project to be chaired by Doug Oakervee, a former Chair of HS2 Ltd, with Lord Berkeley, a leading critic, as his deputy. A few days later Shapps made an announcement to parliament which surprised no one, acknowledging that HS2 could not be built for £56 billion. The new budget would be up to £88 billion, approximately £1,600 for every adult in the UK. After allowing for inflation, the cost of the project had roughly doubled since Justine Greening's announcement in 2012. The forecast time scale had also slipped by around five years. Phase 1 was now expected to be completed by 2031, Phase 2 by 2040.

Shapps and Oakervee sent out some conflicting signals over the following weeks. Was cancellation of the project a serious option, or would it just look for ways to cut costs? Was Johnson following the example of Lord Adonis, by pushing a controversial issue past a forthcoming general election? A few days before the review was announced I asked a former civil servant if a future government might cancel the project. He said:

> In principle any government can do anything. The limitations … would be about the parliamentary politics of it. If you were to cancel it, wind up the company, that would be a big thing. I think it's unlikely in the current climate, unless they find it's going through a solid gold Inca city that we didn't know was buried somewhere under Nottingham … I could easily see the government deciding that it can't go as quickly, or that it could only go to Birmingham or Crewe. You get a lot of the advantages by getting as far as Crewe, and then pausing before committing to phase 2.

In November 2019, shortly before another general election, Lord Berkeley denounced the review as a 'whitewash' and asked for his name to be removed from the report.[10] Instead, he produced a 'dissenting report', criticising Oakervee's overreliance on information supplied by HS2 Ltd. The costs of the project, he argued, could be considerably cut by reducing the speed of the trains and the engineering features needed for high speeds.

The conclusions of the final report were widely trailed in the media before its publication in January 2020.[11] It rejected Berkeley's arguments and called on the government to press ahead with only minor changes. The line to Crewe should be built as part of the first phase, while the legislation for the later phases should be paused pending another study, aiming to cut costs and improve the integration of HS2 with the conventional rail network. The word 'fail' was applied only once to HS2 Ltd; they had 'failed to properly address the concerns of local authorities or local people'. The costs had risen again but no one was blamed for that. The authors guesstimated that the total cost could rise to £106 billion, unless savings were made in the later phases. At that price, the project's costs would barely cover its notional benefits.

Ministers were more critical than Oakervee of HS2 Ltd's past failings, but they accepted the report's main recommendations. *The Guardian* commented that Oakervee had given Johnson 'cover' for a decision that was probably his original intention.[12] As an adviser said to me in a different context: 'you never commission a review unless you know what it's going to recommend.'

According to most economists, 'sunk costs' – money already spent which you cannot recover – are not relevant to financial decisions, but they are relevant to political decisions. As Johnson said to a ten-year-old interviewer on children's television: 'In a hole the size of HS2, the only thing to do is keep digging.'

12

Return to Road-building and Airport Expansion (2010–17)

The Coalition Agreement between the Conservatives and Lib Dems in 2010 had little to say about transport. The few points it did make mainly reflected the green agenda which David Cameron shared with his new coalition partners. They would create a national network for recharging electric vehicles. They would prioritise low-carbon proposals including light rail, cycling and walking. They reaffirmed the commitment of the previous government to high-speed rail 'to fulfil our joint ambitions for a low-carbon economy', but it would be phased due to 'financial constraints'. There was no mention of aviation in that section; the commitments to halt the expansion of major airports appeared under 'Energy and Climate Change'. A few concessions were made to motoring interests but they were small by comparison: the government would tackle 'rogue wheel clampers' and end national funding for speed cameras.

Nowhere in the agreement was road-building mentioned, although the Conservative manifesto had promised to 'upgrade' certain motorways and strategic roads. The most important sentence in the agreement appeared right at the end and seemed to contradict most of what came before. It said: 'The deficit reduction programme takes precedence over any of the other measures in this agreement.' The deficit would mainly be reduced through cutting public spending rather than increasing taxation. Big spending on transport infrastructure was clearly off the agenda.

Three days after the agreement was signed Cameron gave a speech to civil servants at the Department for Energy and Climate Change re-emphasising the Coalition's environmental priorities: 'I want us to be the greenest government ever ... nowhere is that more important than in the area of energy, climate change, and reducing our carbon emissions.' Over the next few years, the expectations created by Cameron and the Coalition Agreement for transport would be radically reversed, in ways which few observers (including transport academics) seemed to appreciate at the time. This chapter explains what happened and why.

Recession, Changing Travel Patterns and Cut-backs

The global financial crisis which began in 2007 caused Britain's deepest recession since the 1930s. National output fell by more than 6 per cent from 2008 to 2009. As usual in recessions, public borrowing increased because tax revenues fell and spending on welfare benefits rose. The Labour government had reacted to the downturn with a range of emergency spending increases, including a subsidy for people scrapping cars to buy new ones; but one option they did not seriously consider was more road-building. An adviser explains: 'Swampy had a lasting impact. To build a road now is a lot of aggro. You are going to have to get Securicor to protect your site. And to go round bragging about the size of your road programme looks a bit non-PC.'

When the Coalition came to power the national debt had doubled since 2007. Sooner or later any government would probably have been forced to reduce its borrowing, but economists disagreed on the timing. Should the new government allow the high borrowing to continue for a while longer, to help the economy out of recession, or should they start cutting straight away? Would that provoke a 'double-dip recession'?

These were the most pressing decisions facing the incoming Chancellor George Osborne, who rapidly established his control over other departments, including transport. Norman Baker, a Lib Dem who became Under-Secretary of State at the DfT, explains: 'Cameron was just a Chairman of the Board. He didn't take much interest in policy … Osborne did the detail and Cameron let him.'

In 2009, at the height of the recession, Osborne had steered the Conservatives towards a policy of austerity; they would start cutting public spending as soon as they gained power and would continue cutting throughout the next parliament. Osborne had no training in economics; he believed that austerity was necessary and could be used to blame Labour for causing the problem in the first place. Most Lib Dems were instinctively less hawkish, but their leaders had come to similar conclusions, so they had no problem signing up to the principle of deficit reduction.[1]

If national politics and the public finances were the biggest influences on transport decision-making in 2010, the changing travel patterns of the British public were another. Although few people noticed at the time, the average distance travelled by each person in Britain reached a peak in 2003 then began to decline. Population was continuing to rise, so road traffic volumes flatlined for several years until they too declined during the recession. The only mode which continued to grow was rail. These changes were most pronounced among young adults, who were migrating towards bigger cities, owning fewer cars, driving less and travelling less overall.[2] All of these trends helped to ease pressures on the road network.

Cameron appointed Philip Hammond as Transport Secretary. Hammond had been Osborne's deputy in the Shadow cabinet and would probably have preferred that job in government. Villiers was made second minister at the DfT. She says:

> I was disappointed not to be in the cabinet, but I accepted that the Coalition meant that some of us had to give way. I had done so much work on transport matters, there was a certain logic in keeping me in that department … Philip's view was, as the most senior minister in the department (after the Secretary of State) and as a Conservative, it was important for me to take the aviation brief because of its sensitivity.

She and Baker both describe good working relationships at the DfT, although Baker said that Hammond could be 'hard work'.[3] Opinions did not split along party lines; Baker and Villiers often found themselves agreeing on issues where others differed. However, the whole department was answerable to Osborne and the Treasury. In June 2010 it was Osborne, not the DfT, who announced the cancellation of the A14 widening, the largest road scheme inherited from the previous government.

Although Osborne was more sympathetic to infrastructure than he was to other spending, reducing the deficit came first. In his first spending review in October 2010, the DfT's capital budget was cut by 11 per cent and its resource budget (for everything except capital projects) by 21 per cent. The modest road-building programme they inherited would gradually decline over the next five years.

A civil servant who remembered the 1990s was relieved at this outcome. 'We were expecting the capital programmes to be slaughtered', he says. Another civil servant says that Osborne and two of the four transport ministers wanted to make a 'very public display of hair shirt' on public spending. He recalls one of them saying 'you the civil servants need to understand that we are not postponing these schemes, we are cancelling them'.

In October 2011 Justine Greening replaced Hammond as Transport Secretary. Baker remembers her as being a 'good supporter of public transport'; she was also a strong opponent of expanding Heathrow. Baker, Greening and Villiers worked well together, within fairly limited budgets, for a while.

The Austerity Chancellor Embraces Road-building

Between 2011 and 2013 the attitude of the government towards capital spending, and road-building in particular, radically changed. Several interviewees identify Osborne as the driving force behind this change. The reasons for his change of heart date to back to economic events during the Coalition's first year in office. In the last quarter of 2010, provisional statistics showed the economy contracting again[4] (they would later be revised upwards). For the government's critics, this was confirmation of the 'double-dip recession' they had predicted. Economic growth remained subdued for the next two years, strengthening calls for the government to change course.

The International Monetary Fund, whose opinions clearly mattered to Osborne, initially supported his strategy; but their view rapidly changed. By 2012 they were calling for more public capital spending in the UK to boost economic growth.[5] Business organisations began to lobby ministers more earnestly, particularly for more spending on roads. A civil servant recalls:

Someone like John Cridland [Chairman of the CBI] was very influential … He was very close to ministers. He didn't always understand the ins and outs of the schemes he was lobbying for, but he was very good at boiling down inchoate thinking about the desirability of the roads programme into punchy, compelling sound bites. He was very good at embarrassing ministers about lack of activity – in public and private.

In March 2012 David Cameron was invited to address the Institute of Civil Engineers. He took the opportunity to call for road-widening to ease congestion. How would this be paid for? He said: 'I've asked the Department for Transport and the Treasury to carry out a feasibility study of new ownership and financing models.' A civil servant says:

> This was the first DfT had heard of it. So that committed us to a review. How to get private finance in? That was part of the brief. You don't get private finance in unless you do shadow tolling [where a private company builds a road and the government pays for its use], which is not new finance, or else you do road pricing. So we were inexorably heading towards road pricing again. In fact, a submission did go up to George Osborne saying: this is what we've been asked to do by you and the Prime Minister and the only answer is: road pricing. That submission was never answered, which is a ministerial way of dealing with unwelcome advice ... David Cameron had made the speech, so something had to happen ... In the strange way these things happen, George Osborne clearly decided that although he wasn't going to charge [motorists], he was going to find the money himself.

While the review was under way, the DfT was also assessing bids for major transport schemes from local authorities. When the Coalition came to power they decided to freeze applications for new transport schemes, to consider the ones already in the pipeline and look at changing the system for the longer term. Norman Baker recalls:

> The first two years of the Coalition were mainly about rail, and there was also quite a bit of money spent by me on cycling and walking. Then Osborne noticed and decided – without any evidence but based on prejudice – to rebalance things as he saw them. In the [2012] autumn spending review he said to the DfT: give me all the road schemes you've got in any way worked up and funded the whole lot ... It was a personal decision ... To be fair to him he

had a good political brain; he could see the political sense of doing these things but it completely threw out of the window all the DfT's careful cost–benefit analysis.

Baker also wrote: 'There was a view in the Tory centre that the department was somewhat off-message, that it had become too Lib Dem and not Tory enough.'[6] An adviser close to the 'Tory centre' says 'there was no major disagreement' over road-building, but adds, 'Norman doesn't really believe in driving cars anywhere, but his constituents all do and that's probably one reason Norman's not the MP for Lewes any more.'

In September 2012 the Coalition leaders agreed on a cabinet reshuffle. Deputy Prime Minister Nick Clegg would choose the Lib Dem ministers, while David Cameron would choose the Conservatives, in theory. In practice, Baker believes the key decisions were made by Osborne, who wanted to strengthen his control over other ministries.

At the DfT all three Conservative ministers were replaced; only Baker remained. Patrick McLoughlin became the third Transport Secretary in just over two years. Baker describes McLoughlin as 'more pro-roads than Justine' but he was relieved to find that the new team continued to work well together. However, the biggest decisions were now being made by the Treasury, who were taking more interest in transport. A civil servant recalls:

> There was a growing swell of opinion – I would point to the business organisations – calling for infrastructure. The heads of organisations such as the CBI would say: 'Yes, government needs to rein back on public spending, as any business would seek to minimise its operating costs. Businesses need to control their costs, but businesses also need to invest. Investment is good. Investment in infrastructure is good because it enables business to operate efficiently; and infrastructure is roads and bridges, railways and tunnels.' George Osborne had business voices on all sides saying this, and he listened.

Another factor, mentioned by several interviewees, was Osborne's apparent hostility to environmental constraints. In November 2013 the media reported that Cameron, who had driven the Conservatives' green conversion, had said in a private meeting: 'get rid of all that green crap'.[7] A spokesman for the Prime Minister's office responded that 'we do not recognise that phrase', an ambiguous response, which led reporters and even some academics to conclude that the story must be true.[8] According to Baker there was another reason for the official reticence: the phrase was used in a meeting, not by Cameron, but by Osborne.

Meanwhile, some of the motoring organisations had rebuilt their relationships with ministers at the DfT, which had weakened during the 1990s. David Quarmby was Chairman of the RAC Foundation, originally funded by the Royal Automobile Club but now an independent research organisation. They had some strong views about the Highways Agency, the body charged with managing the nation's motorways and 'strategic' national roads:

I had experience of the railway planning regime, the five-year planning cycles which went into the 2004 Railways Act [with five-year budgets agreed by government] ... As long as the Highways Agency was an agency of the DfT, roads would be at the whim of ministers. We strongly argued to the Department that they should adopt the same planning regime for the Highways Agency, which should be reformed and made into an arms-length agency like Network Rail ... The then Chairman of the Highways Agency was [also] coming to the same views ... During 2011 and 2012 we submitted various papers to the senior civil servants and we had several meetings with Justine Greening when she was Transport Secretary. She was the one who really 'got it'.

These two pressures – for more spending and longer planning cycles for road-building – culminated in 'Investing in Britain's Future', published by the Treasury in July 2013. This report committed the next government to trebling spending on national road-building between 2015 and 2020. The Highways Agency would become a 'publicly owned corporation with long-term funding certainty and flexibility' – now known as Highways England.

The report also made commitments on energy, housing and digital networks, but most of the money would be for transport – high speed rail and road maintenance as well as road-building. It implicitly repudiated the conclusions reached by ministers in the late 1990s, that 'we cannot build our way out of congestion'. Maps of the motorway network showed how congestion was forecast to worsen. The report said the government would '[tackle] the most congested parts of the network' but did not explain what difference the road-building would make to congestion.

Why were those conclusions from the 1990s no longer accepted? Baker explains it as follows:

> Going back to 1994, SACTRA demonstrated that building more roads would generate more traffic... After the Newbury Bypass the lessons had been learnt and it was very difficult for anyone who wanted more roads to get them through ... The road-builders never went away, they just thought they had lost the argument and kept quiet, but as soon as they got the green light from people like Osborne, off they went again.

No research in the intervening years had seriously challenged SACTRA's conclusions (see page 63); several international studies had reinforced them.[9] Research evidence might have little influence on politicians, but what about the officials? A civil servant says:

> Civil servants have to develop the knack of knowing which way the wind is blowing. If senior ministers have given a very strong steer that they are enthusiastic about a particular policy option, be that a presumption in favour of or against road-building, then the civil servants will know that turning up with a whole raft of alternatives is unlikely to be welcomed.

Labour's attempts at demand management were widely viewed as failures. The fuel tax protests had killed off tax increases; the national petition had pushed road pricing off the agenda. How else could governments prevent traffic and congestion from rising? Another civil servant recalls a widespread view that 'we might not be able to build our way out of [congestion] entirely but we can do *something* about it – *surely*'.

After adjusting for inflation, the new road-building budget was similar in size to the one set out in 'Trunk Roads England', which had triggered the anti-roads protests of the 1990s.[10] But the new programme provoked no significant backlash, even from the environmental organisations. Why was this? Stephen Joseph says:

> The environmental movement had gone onto other things ... The new road-building programme hasn't got the same visibility and impacts that the 1990s programme did because it's mainly focussed on smart motorways, widening within existing boundaries. You don't even need planning permission for most of this, so the triggers [for protest] aren't there. We took a view when this first came up that it was going to be really difficult to oppose this stuff at a local level.

'Investing in Britain's Future' included an appendix listing the local road schemes recently approved, the national schemes approved and six feasibility studies to inform the next stages. Most of the national schemes were for road widening, but over the following years a growing number of schemes for new roads through countryside or urban areas would join the programme.

Apart from the big budget increase for national roads 'Investing in Britain's Future' also signalled the government's commitment to spending more on local roads. Some of this new funding would be channelled via a new type of body, Local Enterprise Partnerships (LEPs), which covered wider areas with a mixture of local councillors and business representatives on their boards. Baker says of the LEPs:

> They were a mixed bag. Some of them were very good, like the Coast to Capital one in Brighton. A lot of them became full of people who were prepared to ignore the evidence and argue for what they wanted themselves. They didn't have the same rigour or requirements used by the DfT analysis. We had the ridiculous situation where Colonel Blimps in the shires would say: 'I've been campaigning for this road since 1913. Now we can finally have it.' The reason they hadn't had it before was because it never made any sense! Suddenly there was a green light to have their favourite road built.

The road programme administered by the DfT only covered England, as transport was devolved to the governments of Scotland, Wales and Northern Ireland. However, the national budget increase triggered an equivalent increase to the devolved nations. One of the few road schemes to provoke much opposition was in Wales, as described below. Meanwhile, George Osborne had also turned his interest to airport policy.

A U-Turn on Heathrow

Some of the business organisations who were lobbying the Chancellor over roads policy also began to call on the government to change its policy on airports in the southeast. John Stewart says: 'The aviation industry got the shock of their lives when they didn't get a third runway – particularly from a Conservative government. They took at least a year to reassess, regroup and work out a new strategy.'

During 2011 and 2012 the aviation industry and its supporters launched an intensive campaign of lobbying, against taxes on aviation and in favour of airport expansion.[11] In November 2011 John Cridland of the CBI told the *Times*:

> The coalition agreement says no more runway capacity in the South East of England. I can't cope with that. Surely if we want to stay in the premier league of the world economy, if we are going to access export markets of the world's emerging economies, we have got to have a world-leading airport.[12]

His preference for expanding Heathrow caused conflict with Birmingham Airport, a CBI member, which was trying to position itself as a London airport when HS2 would put it just 38 minutes from the capital. What everyone within the business community agreed on was the need for more airport capacity. As with the case for road-building, George Osborne listened, and agreed; but he faced several problems. The Liberal Democrats would never agree to changing that element of the Coalition Agreement. A month earlier Osborne had sanctioned the appointment of Greening, a committed opponent of Heathrow expansion, as Transport Secretary. And there was the potential embarrassment for Cameron who had said before the election: 'the third runway is not going ahead: no ifs, no buts'.

Osborne began to work on both Cameron and Greening, while unidentified government sources began briefing the media to apply pressure. In March 2012 the *Observer* reported that 'according to senior sources, both David Cameron and George Osborne have been convinced of the need' to re-examine their policy on Heathrow. The Coalition Agreement restricted their options in the short term, but 'many Tories now want the party to admit the decision was wrong and back the new runway in the manifesto for the next general election'. In the meantime, they were 'examining other options', including a provocative suggestion to transform RAF Northfield, on the edge of London, into a commercial airport.[13]

An adviser remembers 'at least one difficult meeting' between Greening and Osborne. Over the summer of 2012 speculation began to appear in the media that Greening's days at the DfT were numbered. Some of these stories described her as a 'roadblock' to Heathrow expansion – to be removed. Others made unrelated derogatory comments. The *Telegraph* suggested that Cameron had only promoted her to solve 'a women problem in the polls'.[14] An adviser says: 'Clearly at one stage Osborne was briefing against Justine. It didn't last long but there was some hostile media comment about Justine and I'm pretty sure it came from Osborne or his advisers. He was certainly asserting his authority over the Transport Secretary.'

In July 2012 Greening made a public appeal to save her job, telling the *Evening Standard* she was '"uniquely placed" to oversee Britain's airports strategy'. A month later she told the BBC that she would feel unable to continue in her position if the government changed its policy on Heathrow. That determination probably sealed her fate. In September 2012 she was replaced by Patrick McLoughlin and effectively demoted. Theresa Villiers was also moved, though in her case it was a promotion. Baker remembered Greening leaving the DfT 'her face strained and taut, staring ahead, I think trying not to cry'.[15] He says of the reshuffle: 'It was not based on merit. Who got sacked? [Effective Conservative ministers like] Tim Long and Charles Hendry. And who got promoted? Idiots who were going to do what Osborne wanted.'

McLoughlin was not one of the 'idiots' (his was a sideways move) but he was prepared to support Osborne's preferred solution. The day after his appointment the government announced that an 'independent commission' would be held into airport capacity in the southeast. They allowed McLoughlin to tell parliament that it would be headed by Sir Howard Davies, a former head of the CBI, and that it would report in 2015, after the next election. Both points had already appeared in the press, suggesting that McLoughlin had little or no influence on the decision. In principle, the Commission would be able to consider all options, but an adviser explains:

> I am sure Sir Howard would never go into something where he was behaving improperly but I have no doubt that those who set up the Airports Commission had a strong expectation of where it would end up ... [it] was all about trying to find an empirical basis for changing the policy on expanding Heathrow ... The timing was entirely deliberate; we didn't want this to be an issue in the run-up to a general election.

An adviser to the aviation industry agrees with that assessment, and adds:

> In the end, the lobbying didn't matter that much. Once the government had grasped in the early 2000s that they could do it, logistically, I think they bought the argument, even though they accepted that Heathrow is probably the wrong place altogether; you start from where you are rather than where you want to be ... when the Coalition came in and reversed the decision, in reality the government machine [particularly the civil servants] was still in favour of a third runway ...

The government adviser adds: 'Right to the end, David Cameron had reservations about the change of policy. The "no ifs, no buts" line haunted him.'

John Stewart was fully aware of the true purpose of the Airports Commission but after their victory in 2010, the influence of the campaigners began to wane:

> This isn't a criticism of anyone, but the big NGOs felt that's done – they moved on to other things. Direct action stopped ... It left groups like HACAN on our own. We could continue making arguments at a local or regional level but some of the wider arguments against airport expansion generally weren't being made ...

The decision to appoint a commission also helped to defuse opposition. As Stewart says: 'It's very difficult to get local people to campaign against something that's not absolutely definite.'

As Osborne and his supporters had hoped, airport expansion did not feature in the 2015 election campaign as it had five years earlier. The Conservative manifesto said they would 'improve our airports' and 'respond to the Airports Commission's report'. The Liberal Democrats remained opposed to any expansion but lost seats to the Conservatives, who returned to power with an overall majority, freed from the constraints of coalition.

In July 2015 the Airports Commission published its final report, recommending a third runway at Heathrow, as expected. In October 2016, after Cameron and Osborne had left front-line politics, the cabinet finally endorsed that 'preferred option', although the details and the conditions attached to any expansion would take several more years to finalise. Stewart says:

[By 2016] the process had ground people down. Unless there is a clear show-stopper emerging, we are in the final furlong leading to a third runway. There comes a time where you're thinking: it may happen. It's different for the NGOs but for HACAN, if it does happen, we want to ensure the best possible deal for residents.

A New Era of Growth – in Traffic, Aviation and Carbon Emissions

By 2017, when a minority Conservative government took office, UK transport policy had largely returned to where it was at the start of this book in 1989. The environmental concerns, which had constrained road-building since the 1990s, had fallen down the political agenda and the public were now more concerned about congestion and less hostile to road-building than they were during the protests of the 1990s (according to the British Social Attitudes Survey[16]). While demand management remained of interest to transport planners, academics and a few local politicians in major cities, the main thrust of national policy was expansion of capacity to support economic growth.

Emboldened by these trends, national and local authorities were now looking beyond smart motorways and widening schemes, to entirely new roads through countryside or urban areas. Many of these were connected to plans for housing growth, such as a new 'express-way' between Oxford and Cambridge. Several of them threatened environmentally protected areas, such as the South Downs National Park and Kenn Moor Site of Special Scientific Interest (SSSI) south of Bristol. Some of them spawned local protest groups, but there was no sign of any national protest movement.

The most prominent of these schemes was the M4 Relief Road in South Wales. In 2013 the Welsh Government published revised plans to build a new motorway across the Gwent Levels SSSI near Newport. This prompted FoE, the Gwent Wildlife Trust, the Royal Society for the Protection of Birds and several other organisations to join local campaigners in a coalition 'Against the Levels Motorway'. There was no suggestion of direct action although, like Stop HS2, the campaigners assumed that this would begin if the scheme was approved. The campaigners worked on public opinion, political lobbying and preparing for a public inquiry, at which I gave evidence for the objectors in 2017. Welsh government politics were in a state of flux, so the objectors were trying to delay a decision for as long as possible. The inspector was a highway engineer who had approved many road schemes and he made his sympathies very clear. By the end of the inquiry it seemed that only seismic political change at the Welsh Government would stop the new motorway. Some of the people I had worked with remained optimistic that this might happen.

Of all the protest movements described in the earlier chapters, the fuel tax protests and the campaigns against road pricing had achieved the most enduring impacts. Many cities had talked about congestion charging but none had followed London's example, while national road pricing was firmly off the political agenda. Fuel duty, which is fixed in pence per litre, declines in value if it is not uprated with inflation. Since the fuel tax protests, duty has been frozen or cut in almost every year, so that its value fell by over a quarter between 2000 and 2017. The total cost of motoring also fell over those years, while public transport became considerably more expensive.[17]

Partly because of those policies, the downward trends in car mileage observed in the early 2000s came to an end around 2013; since then traffic volumes have been increasing, while rail patronage has recently begun to fall.

The trends in aviation were even more pronounced. Passenger numbers dipped during the recession, reaching a low point in 2010. Over the next seven years they increased by over a third, encouraging the owners of airports across the UK to plan for expansion. After the government decision to approve a third runway at Heathrow, Gatwick, Stansted and many regional airports also published plans to expand. Bristol Airport declared an intention to more than double in size by 2040.

These positive trends for airport owners and road-building companies were worrying the Climate Change Committee. By 2017 transport carbon emissions had increased to over a third of the national total – much larger than any other sector. The Climate Change Act had proved more effective than many had expected. Since it became law total UK carbon emissions had fallen faster than the national carbon budgets required. Most of that progress was due to changes in electricity generation, with wind, solar and gas power replacing coal and oil. Other sectors were flatlining or declining more slowly; only one was increasing: transport. To make matters worse, the climate scientists were now advising governments that deeper and faster cuts were needed.

Each year the Climate Change Committee submits a report to parliament on progress and policies for reducing carbon emissions. Over the years, their careful measured language had been growing stronger. Their 2017 report began: 'The UK urgently needs new policies to cut greenhouse gas emissions.' Although the early budgets had been met, progress was stalling; without urgent action the later budgets would be missed. Among the different sectors they reviewed, transport was now their biggest concern.

A few weeks after the publication of that report I interviewed Lord Deben (ex-Environment Secretary John Gummer), the Chairman of the Committee, who said:

> The first, second and third carbon budgets were dealing with low-hanging fruit, doing the things you had to do to prepare for the future, like decarbonising electricity … As you move along that trajectory, in order to reach the 80 per cent reduction, which we are required to do by law, other things become more urgent. Transport has now become more urgent.

13

The Climate Rebellion Begins

By 2018 I had been giving lectures on transport and climate change for eight years, drawing on the Climate Change Committee's reports, explaining the growing gap between the science and the actions of governments and the transport professions. At the end of one lecture a student came up to me with a look of puzzlement and pity and said: 'it must be really frustrating, teaching this stuff', and she was right. Most of my research was about making urban transport more sustainable. I was sometimes invited to give advice to government departments or local authorities, but it all seemed rather futile when the big decisions were moving away from sustainability. Rational analysis seemed to be getting us nowhere; I began planning to retire as soon as I could.

Studying climate change had other, more personal consequences. I gave up flying in 2005 and driving (when I moved from Devon to Bristol) in 2010. I lost count of the number of marches I went on before international climate conferences, which all failed to stop rising emissions, rising temperatures, melting ice and worsening storms. The scientific literature was beginning to talk of 'existential threats to the majority of the population',[1] but everyone was carrying on as normal or tinkering with minor changes. Even the green movement was avoiding any talk of threats to human existence, because it might frighten people. Were the world and people around me going mad, or was it just me?

To unwind, I often go walking. As I noticed changes in the land-scape – daffodils flowering in January, coastal paths diverted away from erosion – I was afflicted by a sense of loss and foreboding. I had no idea how many other people felt the same way.

Rising Up! and the Origins of Extinction Rebellion

Unknown to me, or many of the usual suspects involved in Bristol's environmental groups, a small group of people had identified climate change as the key issue to ignite a new social movement. In May 2018 they met in a cafe in Bristol to launch what would become Extinction Rebellion (XR). One way or another, most of XR's actions would target transport systems, because of their ecological impacts, or simply to create disruption. Their actions would also cause shock waves across academia and the transport planning profession.

The origins of XR stretch back through several years of failed campaigns, and a few which had seemed to work, including the anti-roads protests and Plane Stupid. In 2016 two veteran activists, Gail Bradbrook and Roger Hallam, were separately exploring some similar ideas about civil disobedience and social change. They made contact online and agreed to meet up. With a few others they agreed to set up a network called Rising Up! to seed and support environmental and social campaigns. The original members would start some campaigns themselves, work with others and invite activists everywhere to join the network. Autonomous groups were welcome to join, providing they supported ten 'principles and values'. Two years later these would become the guiding principles for XR:

1. We have a shared vision of change.
2. We set our mission on what is necessary.
3. We need a regenerative culture.
4. We openly challenge ourselves and our toxic system.
5. We value reflecting and learning.
6. We welcome everyone and every part of everyone.
7. We actively mitigate for power.
8. We avoid blaming and shaming.
9. We are a non-violent network.
10. We are based on autonomy and decentralisation.[2]

One of Rising Up!'s principles aimed to mobilise 3.5 per cent of the population to achieve system change. Hallam proposed this following American academic Erica Chenoweth, who said that 3.5 per cent was a threshold, above which no campaign was likely to fail.[3] Chapter 15 will discuss the evidence behind that statement, but relevant or not, it provided a motivational target for a 'theory of change' that would drive Rising Up! and later XR.

Over the next couple of years Rising Up! supported several campaigns, including Grow Heathrow (squatting on land earmarked for the third runway), Stop Killing Londoners (against air pollution), and campaigns to make London's universities divest from fossil fuels and pay living wages to cleaning staff.

In December 2017 Hallam wrote a short strategy paper entitled 'Pivoting to the Real Issue', drawing on Rising Up!'s recent experience and on his reading of research evidence. It defined climate change as 'the greatest mobilisation story of all time'. Unlike other threats this one was existential – it threatened the elites as well as the people, but campaigners, politicians and the wider public were stuck in a 'death spiral of pragmatism'. The conventional wisdom said that 'if you tell people the truth about climate change, they will switch off', which might be true for most people, but '1 to 5 per cent will be shitting themselves over it and this will drive them to action'.

One of Hallam's sources was *Rules for Revolutionaries*, a book about Bernie Sanders's 2016 presidential election campaign.[4] A key conclusion of that book was that if the cause is big enough people may be more willing to make big sacrifices than small ones. For this new campaign Rising Up! should ask people to commit to break the law and, if necessary, go to prison. However, Chenoweth's study also found that successful campaigns were more likely to encourage defections among the security forces. So, this new movement would try a new approach: breaking the law without antagonising the police.

Hallam's paper was discussed for the first time at a meeting in January 2018. There was much support for the plan, but Bradbrook and some others felt more preparatory work was needed before embarking on anything so ambitious.

Robin Boardman was a student at Bristol University in 2017 when he joined Rising Up! after hearing Hallam speak at a student gathering. He remembers Hallam's paper being re-tabled at a meeting in Bradbrook's house in April 2018:

> It caused a lot of debate in Rising Up! As a decentralised movement with different campaigns all across the country, the suggestion was that we stop all of that and just focus on this one thing. I remember reading it over and over again that night because at the same time, in my university life, I was booking my year abroad for my third

year of studies ... Reading that paper, knowing in my heart that this theory of change was working, that we had a responsibility in the UK to act on it ... So, I decided to drop out of university, cancel my year abroad and put everything towards this new campaign.

Despite the misgivings of some members, and an argument over the name, they decided to go ahead with XR as a campaign – not an organisation. XR would have three demands, mainly for governments but also for other organisations such as the media: *tell the truth*, by declaring a climate emergency, *act now* to halt biodiversity loss and reduce emissions to net zero by 2025, and move *beyond politics* by convening a citizens' assembly, representative of the UK population, to decide how all this was to be done.

Annie Randall was another early recruit to Rising Up! She spent a year living at Grow Heathrow and other camps across Europe, alternating between enthusiasm and disillusion. She was taking a break, cat-sitting for a friend in Amsterdam, when she started to reconnect with friends in Rising Up!

I'd seen some of the debates going on between the different activist networks in the UK. A lot of people were saying: should we support this? Or is it another grandiose plan for change, using Roger's wacky intellectual theories that we've listened to before? All the way through the summer [of 2018] he was saying: there's this thing called Extinction Rebellion, Annie, it's going to be absolutely massive! Come back to England and help us.

XR Goes Viral and Occupies London

Bradbrook remembers the core membership of Rising Up! was about 30 people with about 2,000 more registered on their website. Some of those people were involved in related campaigns but many were simply names on a mailing list. Clearly, XR would need many more activists before the plan could be put into practice.

Over the summer of 2018 some of the founder members toured the country giving talks, based on Hallam's original pitch, aiming to make emotional connections. Boardman remembers that they were not very well attended – the biggest had 40 people. They would attract a few anarchists, vegan activists or anti-capitalists, but most of them were 'ordinary people from the local area, maybe on the radical environmental scene already, who were excited and keen to be engaged in something that was actually moving. Many of these people would cry and have a shoulder for them afterwards to share that grief.'

The date for the launch event was set as 31 October 2018. A Declaration of Rebellion would be read out in Parliament Square in London. The organisers listed it as an event on Facebook; Boardman says they were expecting about 50 people. The writer and veteran campaigner George Monbiot accepted an invitation to speak. So did a little-known Swedish teenager called Greta Thunberg, who came from Stockholm in an electric car to explain why she had stopped going to school and started sitting outside the Swedish parliament.

On 19 October Monbiot wrote an impassioned article in *The Guardian* about how the leaders of many countries, including Britain, were conspiring with fossil fuel companies to destroy the climate for short-term financial gain.[5] In two paragraphs at the end he mentioned that he would be talking at XR's launch event 12 days later. Boardman remembers this as the moment when XR went viral:

> The day afterwards Bernie Sanders shared it on his Facebook page, reaching a massive audience. I woke up at 5 a.m. I looked at my Facebook feed and I couldn't believe it. I remember that feeling of: 'Oh my God, this is actually happening!' From that, we had several hundred people saying they were going on the Facebook event and had over a thousand people on the day. We didn't have the logistics prepared for it, but we did have Greta who had come from Sweden … the bluntness of her communication about the emergency [was very effective.] The line that moved me was 'adults are shitting on my future'!

Central London was also the target for XR's first action a couple of weeks later. Sympathisers within Transport for London helped the organisers identify key points on London's road network, which would maximise traffic disruption if they were blocked. Breaking with radical protest tradition, the organisers discussed their plans with the police. Bradbrook says:

That can be controversial, but we think it's for the best ... They have this duty to facilitate the right to protest as well as facilitating the public to go about its business ... so if you say what you are going to do, and you've got active people managing the crowd and supporting de-escalation, it's more likely to go well. It's a lot of paperwork and headaches for them to clear you off the street.

The action began on 17 November. To everyone's surprise around 6,000 people turned out – enough to block or disrupt five of the bridges across the Thames in central London. Many of them were determined to be arrested. Some of the bridges were blocked; on others the protestors used 'swarming' – moving into the road for a few minutes at a time. A delay of around seven minutes is usually enough to cause tailbacks across the road network. This tactic provoked the ire of Richard Littlejohn in the *Daily Mail*, who branded XR 'anti-car fanatics', but unlike Reclaim the Streets 20 years earlier, the traffic was not the target, it was simply a means to cause economic disruption. To defuse the tension, protestors handed out cakes and carried placards saying 'sorry for the disruption'.

An avalanche of media coverage, hostile and sympathetic, helped to spread the protests, on a smaller scale, to other parts of the country. Some of these actions were transport-focussed. In Oxford, XR supporters blocked Botley Road to protest against road-building plans around the city. A few days later XR members occupied the HS2 site in the Colne Valley (see page 160) and members in Norwich occupied council buildings to protest at plans for a new ring road.

The London action was planned to finish with a tree-planting ceremony in Parliament Square, but some people were still occupying Lambeth Bridge. Someone told Bradbrook afterwards:

They just weren't going to move, and the police were saying: '*Please* can you move, because we just wanna go home? What would it take to get you to move?' They couldn't arrest them because they didn't have [enough] vans, so one of them said: 'I'd love a gin and tonic', so they took him to the pub and bought him a gin and tonic!

The story may be apocryphal but the message, that police resources were overstretched, would have a strong influence on XR's future actions. As the protests encouraged more people to sign up on XR's website, the organisers began planning another, bigger, occupation of central London the following spring.

The London actions caught the attention of the media across the world. Annie Randall was now working in a small international team, helping to grow XR around the world. She remembers:

> People abroad had expressed interest in XR. We started setting up international calls and it gathered momentum so quickly. We were doing calls with 50 or 60 people in them from different parts of Europe, three or four nights a week … I hadn't seen people pick up on a movement like this in ages. It was mind-blowing.

Some people who had been campaigning on local issues in Britain with modest support saw this upsurge of direct action as an opportunity. One of these people was Hilary Burn, Chair of the Parish Councils Airport Association in North and Northeast Somerset. In December 2018 Bristol Airport submitted a planning application to North Somerset Council to expand passenger numbers and car parking as the first step towards doubling in size. When she heard XR was active in Bristol, she began attending their meetings, where she met Tarisha Finnegan-Clarke, and then her husband, Steve Clarke, who is a Green Councillor in South Bristol, and Mark Smalley, a former BBC producer. They agreed that this issue should be a priority for XR in Bristol. As the first aim was to influence Conservative councillors in North Somerset, the group decided not to campaign under the XR name but to create a new organisation, the Bristol Airport Action Network (BAAN) with Tarisha as the coordinator. This alliance between XR members and affected villagers in north and east Somerset would re-energise the campaign against expanding Bristol Airport and give me my first experience of illegal direct action.

My Introduction to XR – and Police Custody

A few months after XR's London actions I was invited to a pre-Christmas party by Jo Flanagan, a Quaker and stalwart of many progressive campaigns in Bristol. She and several others I met that night had joined XR; some of them had taken part in the London actions. I was encouraged to hear that people were finally taking direct action over climate change and were challenging the conventional consensus that we must downplay what the science was telling us. But I was unsure about some of XR's tactics. It was a decentralised movement with small affinity groups, free to organise their own actions. What was the point of a handful – or a few hundred – people blocking a few roads in Bristol?

Then in February 2019 Jo forwarded a video of an XR 'Heading for Extinction' talk she had organised. I was struck by the audacity of their next plan, to close down central London for as long as it took to force the government to negotiate. In a desperate situation that had to be worth a try. A few days later I went to an XR meeting near where I live in central Bristol.

During an induction session I discovered the man next to me was another academic from my university. He was surprised when I ticked 'yes' to the questions 'Are you willing to be arrested?' and 'Are you willing to go to prison?' There was no pressure on that point; to support the people willing to be arrested we needed logistics, welfare officers, legal observers and many others.

Details of the London 'Spring Rebellion' were sketchy at that stage, but I discovered some people were planning to cycle there, starting in Cornwall and picking people up along the way. I agreed to lead a small group from Bristol.

We met the rest of the 'Rebel Riders' in Frome in Somerset two days before the Spring Rebellion was due to start. In total around 20 people joined the ride at different points, including some veterans of the anti-roads protests of the 1990s. We stopped to take courage from their memory before passing underneath the Newbury Bypass.

The light was fading as we arrived at the impromptu camp site in Hyde Park. My heart sank as I saw just a few hundred tents. I didn't know how many others were staying elsewhere, but closing down central London was starting to look rather optimistic.

Shortly before 11 o'clock the following morning XR groups from around the country gathered at five strategic locations. The Bristol groups were allocated to Oxford Circus. As a handful of people gathered on each corner of the road junction surrounded by police my fears seemed confirmed. Who would make the first move? Then, to loud cheers, a van towing a trailer covered with a tarpaulin drove into the centre of the junction, released the trailer and drove away. More people came from the side roads to surround it. Some of them removed the tarpaulin to reveal a pink boat with the words 'Tell the Truth'. The police made no attempt to stop any of this. They redirected the traffic away from Oxford Circus, where a carnival atmosphere now reigned.

I had heard that campaigners against Bristol Airport's expansion were planning an action against the Ontario Teachers' Pension Plan, the main shareholders of the airport. We gathered outside their London office on nearby Baker Street, a major route into central London. Their officials refused to come down to meet us, so Tarisha politely delivered a letter before we unfurled a banner, swarming across Baker Street to block the traffic for several minutes at a time. Standing in front of angry motorists, a few minutes seems a long time. To my surprise, Tarisha told me, swarming was not considered arrestable (obstructing the highway is an offence, but the police do not normally regard swarming as obstruction).

For most of that day the police seemed content to manage the protest. Then late that night an announcement went around the camp site that reinforcements were arriving to clear Waterloo Bridge. Anyone 'arrestable' was called to join them.

We sat on the bridge for several hours in falling temperatures before the police made their move. I watched with trepidation as they surrounded, handcuffed and carried or marched the people sitting in front of me to the waiting vans. I can still hear young female voices singing protest songs around me as the police finally came for me; I will remember those moments for the rest of my life.

I was held for 13 hours, then, like most others, 'released under investigation'. As I made my way to Parliament Square, to give a talk following the Vice-Chancellor of Winchester University, I was delighted to hear the blockade of Waterloo Bridge had held; the police had arrested over 200 people and then paused. Had they reached a capacity or were they playing the politicians for more resources?

I was determined to continue being arrested until they charged me. My chance came on day 3, sitting in front of the pink boat on Oxford Circus. In the back of a police van I found myself face to face with a transport consultant from one of the top international consultancies. He had come on his own without telling his employer or colleagues.

'They are all educated people,' he said. 'Why are they not drawing the same conclusions?'

A sergeant taking down my details told me about the problems they faced; fewer officers and police stations closing down while cuts in mental health and social services were pushing more sick people into custody. Then he leaned forward, looked me straight in the eye and said: 'You do realise we're all with you on climate change?'

This time I was charged with two public order offences and released more quickly (they needed the cells). I felt I had done enough, for now, and decided to go home.

On a short break with my wife a few days later I picked up a message from XR's media team. Was I the Steve Melia described by the *Daily Telegraph* as a 'government adviser'? The personal consequences were just beginning.

Controversy as XR Targets Public Transport and Heathrow Airport

While I was being arrested and re-arrested, heated discussions were raging within XR's Rapid Response Team about plans to disrupt the tube network across central London. Bradbrook recalls the arguments:

> When the press is not focussing properly on this issue mass disruption is the way you get them to pay attention to it ... but we really didn't want people to be held up in tunnels... Londoners had been traumatised by terrorist actions and we didn't want to retrigger that trauma.

In the end, a compromise was agreed. There would be a single action targeting a Docklands Light Rail station above ground in the financial district of Canary Wharf. One of the activists waiting to hear the outcome of that debate was Mark Ovland. He had already been arrested several times, most famously for gluing his buttocks to the glass pane overlooking the House of Commons with ten others. Like Bradbrook, he came to XR through a spiritual route, training to teach in the Buddhist tradition. Like Boardman, he abandoned his plans to devote himself to XR full-time. He recalls:

I got a phone call, last thing [on day 2], saying: 'Yes we're going ahead but we'll just do this one step. It will be symbolic, not in the rush-hour, in a really open station, just as a warning ...'

It was about 11 o'clock in the morning and there weren't a lot of people on the trains. We got off [at Canary Wharf]. Someone pressed the emergency alarm and stayed in the way of the doors while Cathy and Luke climbed on top of the train. I stuck myself to the side and half an hour later we were arrested ...

We assumed that on the following day, if government hadn't engaged, everyone would shut down six or seven stations and seriously disrupt things ... When we were in prison, watching the news, and seeing that it hadn't happened, we thought: 'Ah! they must have decided not to go ahead.'

Another factor which weighed in that decision, according to Boardman, was 'we were getting so much media attention. April had taken off in a way we hadn't imagined. Why do something controversial to draw attention when you're already on the front page?'

A member of XR UK says 'If that action had gone ahead, and likely trapped many people underground, I think it would have self-strangled XR at birth.'

As XR grew partly from campaigns against Heathrow expansion, several members of national XR wanted to target Heathrow. Boardman says:

For the Easter holiday weekend, we put a message out that said we were going to disrupt Heathrow on the Friday [Day 5], which caused a lot of controversy again in the movement. Why block people going on their holidays? These aren't the kind of people we want to target. It went out on a WhatsApp broadcast group ... The media picked it up and they loved it because they thought it was a leak: 'Leaked paper from XR says they're going to block Heathrow!' That sort of mentality in the media spreads like wildfire.

Boardman explains what happened next as a tactic drawn from the academic literature (specifically advocated by Gene Sharp): 'political jiu-jitsu', turning an attack against your opponents:[6]

Let's not throw all our resources at blocking Heathrow; it's obviously controversial. It's not the right time … Instead, let's get all this media that are so boiled up … and let's put a group of young people, all under the age of 20, in front of the airport with a banner saying: 'We are the last generation.'

The climate rebellion had already activated many young people. Following Greta Thunberg's example, school strikes for the climate started in Australia and spread to Britain in February 2019. In March 2019 a handful of young XR members formed XR Youth. Talia Woodin was a student in London at the time. She says: 'My involvement in activism pre-dated my birth. Both my parents were involved in environmental activism … I was brought up in those circles and I wanted to go down that route when I was older.'

She became a photographer for XR and then decided to leave university to work full-time for XR. She remembers a group of them going to an office at around 11 p.m. on day 4 to hear how the plan had changed. She went along to photograph and provide support but 'in an arrestable capacity':

It didn't go as planned. We didn't want to block a road; we just wanted to do some swarming on one of the roads into Heathrow … we were followed to Heathrow by about ten police officers. As soon as we got there, they completely surrounded us. There were huge amounts of press. There were five or six kids holding the banner, all under the age of 16, and they were all determined to stay there until they were arrested, but there was no way the police were going to arrest a bunch of kids in front of the international media … We stayed for about two hours. It was great; we got all over the press and it made the police look really stupid!

On day 4 the national television news showed police officers dancing and skateboarding with the protestors, embarrassing the Metropolitan Commissioner and provoking calls for a crackdown. The following day the police surrounded the pink boat on Oxford Circus, as actress Emma Thomson was reading poetry, and towed it away. On day 7 they cleared Parliament Square, but the protests continued for four more days. By the time of the closing ceremony on 25 April there had been 1,130 arrests.

Bradbrook reminisces:

> April felt like a miracle. It was sunny; all these people came; we did what we said we would do. The police left us alone – well they did stuff but not very effectively. There was all this togetherness, there was a spirit of beauty and mischief. People will talk about it like they did about Woodstock.[7] I had the time of my life.

The Spring Rebellion had certainly exceeded my expectations. It propelled climate change up the national political agenda, it was bringing thousands of new members to XR, but it also exposed a few tensions, which would recur, particularly around Heathrow and public transport.

14

The Climate Emergency Changes the Transport World

The Government and Parliament Respond to XR's Demands

On 30 April 2019, five days after the end of the Spring Rebellion, Environment Minister Michael Gove met five members of XR in his office. The tone of the meeting was surprisingly cordial. Gove complimented XR on its rapid growth and collective decision-making. He expressed interest in the idea of a citizens' assembly and promised to take the issues raised to a cabinet meeting.

Some Conservative MPs had publicly supported XR's actions, infuriating many right-wing commentators. Policy Exchange, a right-wing think tank partly funded by fossil fuel companies,[1] would later publish a report entitled 'Extremism Rebellion', pointing out the radical aims of XR's founders and calling for a tougher response from the police. What was going on? Paul Harrison was Press Secretary to Prime Minister Theresa May:

> Over several years, pre-dating Theresa May's time in government, the environment was becoming an increasing concern … particularly among younger demographics of voters … A lot of people saw [David Attenborough's programme] *Blue Planet* and it genuinely made a difference in raising the salience of those issues. If you look at successive climate agreements, Kyoto and Paris, people are worried about the prospect of global warming and the sustainability impacts as humans we have on the planet. It's reflected in a lot of public polling and it's reflected in a lot of the private polling we did …

Ipsos Mori's tracker of public opinion on climate change showed public concern falling in the late 2000s then rebounding after 2010 with a sharp rise to its highest recorded level in the summer of 2019. Harrison adds: 'Politicians reflect the society that surrounds them, probably more than most people realise. We know that people are worried about environmental impact. So what you see is a political class that reflects that importance.'

In the 1990s some influential Conservative MPs publicly questioned whether human beings were causing climate change, but Harrison cannot remember hearing such arguments within government in recent years. Privately, people I knew who worked within government were telling me how climate change was moving up the political agenda, but would this lead to different policies and decisions?

In October 2018, the government had asked the Climate Change Committee to reconsider the national carbon targets in the light of the Paris Agreement and the latest scientific assessments. On 2 May the Committee published their advice, recommending a target of net zero emissions by 2050. That would mean reducing emissions to minimal levels, which could be offset by planting trees or capturing carbon from the air in other ways (not fully identified). Their advice would have radical implications for transport, the largest emitting sector. Sale of petrol and diesel cars and vans would have to end by 2035 at the latest and aviation would need to be constrained.

The international scientific report following the Paris Agreement had called for net zero emissions by 2050 worldwide. Developing and newly industrialising countries (such as China and India) would not be expected to cut so quickly, so developed countries would need to go faster than 2050, as XR was quick to point out. But the principle of net zero was a big step for a government pre-occupied with other issues, particularly Brexit. How would they react?

By May 2019 Theresa May's attempts to break the parliamentary deadlock over Brexit had failed. On 24 May she announced her resignation, remaining in post until the Conservative Party chose a new leader. The Treasury was concerned about the potential costs and economic consequences of the net zero target. The DfT were predictably worried about the consequences for aviation. Treasury Minister Liz Truss called for the decision to be deferred until a new Prime Minister was in place. The Chancellor Philip Hammond wrote to May arguing for a review clause in any legislation, so the target might be changed or scrapped if other countries did not follow suit.[2]

A spokesman for Theresa May repudiated the letter, arguing that the figures it quoted 'don't factor in the benefits [of net zero or] the costs of not doing anything'.

Harrison says:

Theresa May saw it as a priority. We were pushing quite hard to announce it promptly because legislation was going through the French parliament, and there were other countries looking to put it on the statute books and we thought there would be international leadership in being the first … that came directly from Theresa.

On 26 June parliament approved an amendment to the Climate Change Act, making the net zero target a legal requirement. As before, the Act did not refer to international aviation, but the Prime Minister's office said: 'This is a whole economy target … and we intend for it to apply to international aviation.' Harrison adds: 'There is some evidence that the net zero announcement was the single most popular thing the government did in 2019 while I was there. It got instant public recognition' (which government announcements rarely do).

The government did not respond directly to XR's calls for a declaration of climate emergency and a citizens' assembly, but parliament did. On 1 May, parliament declared a climate emergency, then on 20 June six parliamentary committees, including the transport committee, announced that they would convene a citizens' assembly on 'combatting climate change and achieving the pathway to net zero emissions'. The assembly would only be advisory, so it did not satisfy XR's third demand, but it was a sign of progress.

Earlier in June the new Welsh First Minister Mark Drakeford rejected the recommendation of the inquiry inspector to approve a new M4 south of Newport (see page 164). This was the best news I had heard in a long time. I cycled across to the Gwent Levels for a celebration party three weeks before the date set for my trial.

My Trial and Its Consequences

In the spring of 2019 XR organised several support and training sessions for the people facing trial. There was lots of discussion about tactics and lots of legal advice. Travelling home from one of these sessions I suddenly realised that what happened inside the court was not really important. My 'justification' defence was never going to convince a judge to acquit me. There wasn't much point in trying to persuade him and the court clerk of the need to act on climate change; my real audience was the wider public, particularly people who might be persuaded to join XR. That realisation made things much easier. My one worry was my emotional state; I can talk dispassionately about climate change in a lecture but explaining what drove me, and so many others, to break the law over climate change unleashes emotions I find difficult to control.

A small group of supporters, including my wife, gathered outside Westminster Magistrates Court with a banner for the press photographs before I went inside. Professor Paul Ekins, who had advised the Climate Change Committee, appeared as an expert witness, clearly explaining how UK governments were failing to comply with the Climate Change Act.[3] I was explaining how studying transport brought me face to face with that failure when the tears took over.

I had regained my composure when the judge came to pass sentence. XR's actions have divided opinion in the legal profession. Some judges and magistrates have expressed understanding and regret at having to convict XR's activists. I was not so lucky. I have noticed in planning inquiries the gestures, the tones of voice, the throwaway comments which betray the true feelings of even the most professional people sitting in judgement. The judge in my case was obviously not on our side. Most people were given conditional discharges, even for gluing themselves to trains; I was fined £500 plus £330 costs just for sitting down in the road.

In my 2015 book *Urban Transport Without the Hot Air* I described how the *Daily Mail* distorts and misrepresents stories about transport. I did not realise that one day they would apply the same tactics to me. 'Government Transport Adviser Cries as he is Fined £500' was how they headlined the story online. It took two attempts and a threat to refer the case to the Independent Press Standards Office before they changed 'as' to 'before'. They refused to correct another false statement, which you can still read online today,[4] but I thought: a *Daily Mail* article with just one false statement – that must count as a minor victory!

That story had several consequences, good and bad. It provoked online trolling, email abuse and a personal attack in the *Daily Tele-*

graph by a commentator who assumed that what she had read in the Mail must be true.[5] Someone I know in a high-profile position said: 'Yeah, that's normal. Get used to it.' *The Guardian* also noticed the story and asked me to write an article, which gave me the opportunity I had hoped for, to explain my reasons and appeal to readers to join XR.

The story also prompted Dr Jenny Vaughan, a leading member of the Doctors Association UK, to email me, offering to help raise money for the fine. I said I wanted to pay some of the costs myself, but with Jenny's help we raised the £500 in four days.

The media coverage in April had caught my university by surprise. I was shown, but not sent, an email from a senior manager threatening me with unspecified consequences after I emailed my students explaining why I had been arrested. In the meantime, many staff had joined XR and a groundswell of concern about climate change was sweeping across all universities. When I returned to work in July another senior manager came to check that I was all right. Colleagues and students were very supportive and external organisations started asking me to talk about transport and climate change.

The only negative consequences came from a predictable source. Some colleagues were working on a project for the DfT. One of them passed on a message that I was now blacklisted. Did this apply to all of their projects, to all government work? In classic Whitehall style the message was verbal, third-hand, unspecific and presumably deniable.

Roger Hallam and a Plan to Fly Drones at Heathrow Divide XR

In December 2018, shortly after XR's first action in London, flights at Gatwick Airport were cancelled or delayed over several days following sightings of drones flying near the runways. XR denied any involvement, pointing out that all its actions were conducted openly. The cause of the incident was never established but the disruption it caused suggested a new tactic to some of XR's most radical activists.

Over the summer of 2019 national XR floated plans to close down Heathrow by flying drones in the exclusion zone around Heathrow (where drones are banned). This prompted a backlash from members on online forums. Many felt (as I did) that threatening the safety of aircraft, even if the risk was very small, was inconsistent with XR's principle of non-violence. The plans were promoted by Hallam and some others within national XR. The strongest opposition came from the rapidly growing XR regions and, when news travelled overseas, from XR in other countries. A member of XR's International Support Team says:

> At this point, the UK is still larger than any other national group, but the UK still has a tricky relation with International … The Heathrow drones were incredibly divisive. A lot of people were saying if you execute this action as XR then politicians in vulnerable and politically troubled countries … may then label XR as a terrorist organisation, which will really put the XR activists in danger.

The promoters of the idea responded by curtailing the action; the drones would be flown in the exclusion zone, up to head height and a safe distance from the runways. But if there was no threat to aircraft, would the authorities really ground flights for box-ticking procedural reasons? (I didn't think so.)

The compromise did not satisfy the internal critics, including XR Youth. Talia Woodin recalls: 'We crashed a strategy meeting, that we hadn't been invited to because those that were wanting to push forward with the action knew that we were opposing it. We gave an ultimatum and said if this action went ahead, we would condemn it.' This action tipped the balance in the meeting; the result was another compromise. The supporters would create a new group, Heathrow Pause, to carry out the action. XR would neither support nor condemn it. About 40 XR members joined the group while remaining XR members.

The action went ahead on 13 September. Hallam and one other were pre-emptively arrested. One drone did leave the ground, but most of them were disabled by signal-jamming devices. In total 19 people were arrested. A member of XR UK says:

> The compromise was not very satisfactory; it is hard to paint Heathrow Pause as a separate group when its figurehead was Roger Hallam, co-founder of XR, and when Heathrow Pause continually referred to him in this way! There is a strong case … for Roger and those closest to him to split off and form a small radical outrider group doing unpopular actions if they want to.

Hallam continued to work (paid) for XR UK until 2020, when he left to form a political party. His actions, and his statements to the media, continued to divide internal opinion. In November 2019 he infuriated XR Germany and XR Jews by calling the Holocaust 'just another fuckery in human history' and saying that the legacy of the Holocaust was holding Germany back.[6] A member of XR's International Support Team says: 'Again this has been really divisive, really polarising internationally … There was distrust by XR Germany in terms of: "How can XR UK have let this happen?"'

Michael Lomotey is a member of XR Jews, who volunteered to join a 'restorative justice' process which brought Hallam face to face with the XR groups who felt wronged by his statements:

> It was not right for him to use the Holocaust in the way he did. There was some discussion about why he said it but … what was worrying was that [it could be] weaponised by groups that … want to use it to attack Jews. We were thankful to XR for calling a restorative justice process. We didn't want it to be an XR Jews versus Roger Hallam. We wanted him to understand the harm, apologise and not do it again in the future.

Hallam did apologise, but continued to make statements offending other groups, including XR Switzerland, where he made a throwaway comment about XR members causing environmental damage as those members, who denied causing any damage, were awaiting trial.

The people who know Hallam talk about him with a mixture of respect, loyalty and frustration. Bradbrook says he is 'our greatest asset and our greatest liability.' She also points out how the right-wing media have demonised him and misrepresented some of his statements: 'Roger is under attack. This is what you do to social movements – you attack the leadership.'

Her choice of words is interesting. In theory, XR is a leaderless movement, a 'holacracy' of self-organising teams, which overlap at the local, regional, national and international levels. But in reality there are de facto leaders and there have been many heated internal debates about holding those leaders to account. XR is no different from more traditional organisations in that respect.

Pigs Fly Over Bristol Airport

During the summer of 2019 I became more involved in the campaign against the expansion of Bristol Airport. For many years North Somerset, where the airport lies, was run by a Conservative group which supported airport expansion and road-building, although they also voted to declare a climate emergency in February 2019. Following local elections in May they were replaced by a loose coalition of Greens, Liberal Democrats and independents, who attached more importance to environmental protection. This gave renewed hope to the campaigners against the airport's latest application to expand.

Some XR members were keen to start direct action against the airport, but we all agreed to campaign within the law and avoid any serious disruption until the vote on the planning application. The campaign concentrated on raising awareness, to encourage as many people as possible to object to the application. Bristol Airport Action Network (BAAN) raised money for legal advice, leafleted homes, collected objections, organised marches, stunts and 'aviation learn-ins' in village and community halls. I spoke at some of these, pointing out how the DfT's own forecasts showed aviation emissions exceeding the Climate Change Committee's budgets, even with Bristol Airport capped at its current level. There were a few timid signs of change at national level, so as with the M4 campaign, delay might work in our favour.

BAAN included many creative people, who devised some impressive, theatrical ways to publicise the cause. Some members dressed as an airport landing crew, marching in formation at our on-street events or posing for photographs, which the media loved. During an XR action in July 2019 several of us held giant letters over a motorway bridge saying 'No Airport Expansion' for a couple of hours in foul weather, watching the gestures of support or rebuke from the motorists below. There were more supporters than opponents. A woman two letters away from me said: 'That was good, I've just had three waves and a wank!'

In 2018 the airport had declared its intention to become 'carbon neutral by 2030' (not including planes or passenger car journeys). As the planning application progressed slowly through the system, with objections growing, they began to flesh out these intentions, including a 'demanding target' to reduce the proportion of passengers arriving by car from 88 to 82.5 per cent. They also hired an independent market research company ComRes to ask the residents of Weston-super-Mare the following independently worded question:

> To increase its capacity from 10 million to 12 million passengers a year Bristol Airport plans to increase its capacity without requiring an additional runway, a runway extension, or a new terminal. Instead, they will improve existing facilities. To what extent do you support or oppose Bristol Airport increasing its passenger capacity in this way?

The airport announced, based on this 'survey', that 'those supporting the Airport's plans outnumbered those opposing them by nearly four to one'.

Ben Moss, one of the 'Rebel Riders' who rode to London with us in April discussed how to respond to all this with his XR affinity group:

> The idea was we would do something that would get into the public eye. I looked at the roundabout by the entrance to the airport, which has got a bizarre sculpture on it, a metal swirling structure, maybe 40 feet high. I saw that it would be easy to scale and that it would be a brilliant place to do a stunt. And so, we created a big banner saying 'tell the truth' … the message was: Bristol Airport, carbon neutral? Pigs might fly … Locals support the airport expansion? Pigs might fly. I scaled the sculpture [dressed as a pig] dropped the banner … and stayed there all night.

Members of his affinity group stayed below him on the grass, putting out press releases and sharing the story on social media. The stunt was a modest success, although Ben says he would stay more tightly 'on message' when dealing with the media in future. I have noticed in the past that cleverly choreographed messages may be too clever for the media to pick up, unless they are spelt out in simple sound bites.

By late summer 2019 over 2000 objections were registered on the council's website, easily outnumbering the postcards of support distributed by the airport to its customer database. But how would all this weigh against the influence of the airport and its allies in the council's planning department when it came to the vote? 'It could go either way' I heard many times from people who knew the set-up in North Somerset.

XR Strikes the Department for Transport and the London Underground

In October 2019 XR targeted central London again. Groups from different parts of the country were allocated to different streets and specific targets. The Bristol groups were directed towards Marsham Street, which hosts the Home Office and the DfT. I had to work most of that week so I missed the action that friends in the airport campaign were planning. Two retired members, James and Mary Collett, volunteered to be 'arrestable', spraying 'Fly Today – Die Tomorrow' in chalk-based paint on the front pillars of the DfT, while the others sang, performed or tried to distract the security guards. James and Mary were spraying the final pillar when a young policeman snatched the can from Mary's hands and told them that they were protesting in an unauthorised area and must move to the authorised protest site on Trafalgar Square. They were still arguing the point when:

> a senior officer marched up and demanded loudly of the constables: 'What the hell is going on?' He pointed out that Mary and I had committed criminal damage and that they must arrest us – which they promptly did. We were held for about ten minutes outside the building when another officer came to ask us where the stencil had gone, but by then it had mysteriously disappeared.

Stung by the criticism in April, the police were better prepared and more aggressive this time. Marsham Street was cleared of protestors by the time I arrived on Day 5. I decided to keep out of trouble, acting as a cycle courier, towing food and materials between kitchens and camp sites.

On the second Monday (day 8) as I went back to work in Bristol I heard that the police had imposed a London-wide ban on all XR protests. This was an unprecedented move, which the courts eventually ruled unlawful, but in the meantime the police began to clear the 'authorised' camp on Trafalgar Square. On day 9, Gail Bradbrook and a few others returned to Marsham Street:

I found out the woodland of my childhood, Howell Wood, was on the [HS2 route between Sheffield and Leeds]. I was utterly devastated ... Oakervee was about to report the next day. The combination of that department's relationship to HS2 and [Heathrow] and all the transport things, it felt like the most symbolic place to do an action and I feel as somebody visible in this movement I need to be doing some civil disobedience ...

A small group of supporters helped her climb onto one of the revolving doors at the entrance to the DfT. She intended to break a window, but as the glass was bullet-proof, she found it rather difficult: 'I hadn't really planned it in great detail ... Twitter was funny about it. They were saying: "someone needs to teach her how to use a hammer and chisel" – it was actually a bradawl!' She eventually succeeded in breaking the window and was charged with causing criminal damage costing £27,500. That means she will face a jury trial (scheduled for late 2020) and a potential prison sentence.

I was back at work in the second week when I read online of plans to target London Underground stations. I remember writing: 'This is a stupid idea. Who do we need to write to say: don't do it?' As with the Heathrow drone action, a groundswell of XR members seemed to agree. I didn't know that Mark Ovland, who I knew and liked by then, was part of the group planning the action. He says:

There wasn't a discussion centrally like there had been in April because it was an affinity group action. We were forwarded a huge amount of comments from WhatsApp and Facebook and a poll where 80% of [XR] people on Telegram had said: 'don't go ahead' ... In XR we don't work by polls ... We said: 'Let's sit with this for a few hours, separately.' That was one of the hardest, loneliest experiences ... On the one hand my deepest inner voice is saying: 'this is the right thing to do' and then there's all these people I know and love and respect, saying: please don't go ahead ... When we got together, we found that all of us were still thinking: 'this is the right thing to do'.

Why?

There had been very little engagement [from the government] with XR during the rebellion ... It hadn't had anywhere near the engagement that April brought. It was just: here's these guys on the street again. Let's do a blanket ban and get them out. So, the idea of closing tubes was to cause a crisis …

The group agreed to target four London Underground stations early on the morning of day 11. They would climb on top of trains with banners. The stations chosen were open to the surface, to avoid the risk of people being trapped underground. None of the activists knew those parts of London. There had been relatively little planning, but everyone knew it was important to start early. The first thing to go wrong was that some of the activists arrived late. By the time the group entered Canning Town station the rush hour had begun. Ovland and James Mee from Bristol agreed to climb on top of a train. Ovland continues:

> We had no idea it was a working-class area. We thought it was a financial district, next to City Airport … there were hundreds of people wanting to get to jobs that were probably zero-hour contracts that they just won't get paid, so there were a lot of angry people and the police didn't show up for about 25 minutes … People were throwing things and shouting, and we couldn't make our voices heard … People were [shouting] how desperate they were to get to work. I thought: 'should we just call it off?' But we didn't know what was happening in the other stations.

In a moment which would go viral shortly afterwards, a camera caught the image of Mee kicking the head of a man who was trying to pull his legs down from the train among a hail of missiles. The man persisted and dragged Mee down into the crowd, who forced him to the ground and started kicking him. An XR photographer was also pushed to the ground and kicked in the head. Ovland says:

> My one regret was that when he kicked out, in fear, we didn't just call the action off then … A little while later someone got on top of the train to try and get me down. I was thinking: 'What's the safest, most non-violent thing to do here?' So I tried to walk away and see if he followed me, which he did … I sat down and was pulled off [the train] and then I managed to cover my head … there were

people shouting: 'Don't hit him, don't beat him, get off him' so I managed to get up quite quickly, walk through the crowd and wait for the police to arrest me.

One of the videos which captured the chaos on the platform shows a man calling in exasperation: 'but it's an electric train!'

The action provoked an avalanche of criticism in the media and internally. A member of XR UK says:

We – nearly everyone in XR – begged and begged for the October tube action not to proceed. It still did, with the awful consequences that many of us had envisioned. We are now working on how to make it much less likely that in future a small affinity group is able to hijack the national infrastructure of XR in pursuit of something which virtually no one in XR wants. If small affinity groups have the autonomy to undertake such actions, then the rest of XR deserves the autonomy to disavow them.

The national XR response did not go as far as disavowal, but did acknowledge that 'obviously we did not get that right' and promised to learn lessons. An internal agreement was circulated online afterwards that we would not target public transport in future.

The impact of the October Rebellion was not as great, or as positive, as the Spring Rebellion; the number of people joining XR online spiked during the actions but then fell to a much lower level than post-April.[7] Was this influenced by the negative publicity around the Canning Town action? An XR press release acknowledged 'the second album was never going to be easy'. In a movement with many different views, everyone seemed to agree on one thing: for future actions, new tactics would be needed.

The Climate Emergency Puts 'Transport Planning on Speed'

During 2019 the climate emergency refocussed and reinvigorated the small world of transport planning professionals and academics. Demand management and environmental protection were always important to transport planners (if not always to highway engineers) but the net zero legislation and councils declaring climate emergencies were giving the profession a new purpose. One consultant described it as 'transport planning on speed'.[8]

At the annual conference of the Universities Transport Study Group I was due to speak about the academic study I did (alongside this book) about road-building[9] (discussed further in the next chapter). Professor Jillian Anable from Leeds University was due to speak later. She asked me if I would mind her mentioning me in her talk; I agreed, but wasn't quite sure what she would say. As the conference drew to a close, she delivered a hard-hitting appeal: what was the transport research community doing to address the climate emergency? Why weren't we all out on the streets (with me) in April? A succession of delegates, including Glenn Lyons and Phil Goodwin, took the microphone to say: 'Yes, we get it.'

Local Transport Today, the main publication for the profession, which has often given favourable coverage to climate change deniers, noted with concern how climate change was 'starting to dominate the UK transport policy debate'. Conferences, research programmes and speaking invitations were all influenced by this trend. XR's third demand for a citizens' assembly was also catching on, though the assemblies were always advisory; no authorities were committing to implement their findings.

I had my first experience of advising a citizens' assembly organised by the Greater Cambridge Partnership in October 2019. I was impressed with the good sense and capacity for understanding of that cross-section of the public – so different from the puerile abuse which characterises so much 'debate' online.

The UK Climate Assembly organised by the parliamentary committees chose Anable to organise the expert advice on surface transport, one of several themes the citizen members would consider (including aviation), in Birmingham on 8 February 2020. She invited me and four others to speak for ten minutes and then go around each table answering questions from the members,. The presentations were live streamed and put on the parliamentary YouTube channel afterwards.

One of the other presenters was Jason Torrance, who had spent many years working for respectable organisations such as the Campaign for Better Transport and Sustrans, but somebody watching online found an account of his past as a protest leader and cried conspiracy – just as well he didn't check what I had been doing recently!

Some of the speakers were 'informants', asked to stick to purely factual information. I was an 'advocate', invited to make a personal argument. I said that there are only two ways to decarbonise surface transport: change the vehicles to run without fossil fuels and/or cut the volume of traffic. By 2050 all petrol and diesel vehicles will have to come off the road, by law. The faster we do that, the less we will have to rely on cutting traffic, but even on the most optimistic assumptions about electrification, some cuts in traffic will be necessary to meet the carbon budgets between now and 2050. Any measures to cut traffic will be controversial but it is generally easier to do that in cities, where we will need to house more of our growing population from now on. In the meantime, we must stop making the problem worse through big road-building.

That pitch provoked the range of expectations you might expect from a cross-section of the UK population. Some were critical of electric vehicles. Others argued that we must carry on building roads. On a couple of the tables we talked through the options and agreed: there's no easy way to do this – but do it we must.

We also spoke to a group of observers. I didn't know at the time but these included people from national XR, who were considering how to respond to the Assembly. Our brief did not allow us to challenge the 2050 target, but I learned through XR that some of the assembly members were doing that. How will they resolve all these conflicts? I look forward to reading what they recommend.

A Ray of Hope in the Year of the Floods

After the Climate Assembly I travelled to the Centre for Alternative Technology (CAT) in Machynlleth in mid-Wales to give a lecture on sustainable transport and the challenge facing the Climate Assembly. That night Storm Ciara hit the west coast of Britain. As Australians sifted through the remains of their worst ever bush fires Britain was about to experience several waves of unprecedented flooding. The Bridge between the CAT and Machynlleth flooded; trains and buses stopped running. For a day and a night a few of us were trapped there. The power was cut, then restored, but without hot water.

One of the people marooned with me was Michael Lomotey of XR Jews. We met over breakfast and talked for hours about climate change and why the environmental movement attracts so few people from ethnic minorities. Michael is black; his friend and mentor Christopher Alder was 'unlawfully killed' in horrific circumstances in police custody,[10] which has made him (like many others) particularly wary of 'arrestable actions'. He also raised another issue of contention within XR: should we add a fourth demand about social and racial justice?

> We have been living an existential crisis for years, for hundreds of years, through empire and exploitation indigenous people around the world have been colonised, brutalised. This thing, climate change, is just one more difficult thing to deal with. That's one reason why traditionally, there's not been that much involvement of black people in green campaigning, we are too busy fighting for liberation. If you look at what the environmental movement has traditionally been about, it's 'Let's save the polar bears or trees.' You can't 'take' people out of 'the environment', so accepting anything over 1.5°C is racist. Every fraction of a decimal point over one degree means more black or brown people dying somewhere in the world. Therefore, justice has to be in every aspect of climate campaigning.

XR has often been criticised for its overwhelmingly white and middle-class membership. Working groups and online discussions have agreed on the need to broaden its appeal, but not on the means. All XR movements around the world share the three founding demands, but some have added to them. In 2019 XR USA added a fourth demand for 'a just transition that prioritizes the most vulnerable people and indigenous sovereignty; establishes reparations and remediation led by and for Black people, Indigenous people, people of color and poor communities'. That decision provoked internal dissension and in March 2020, a breakaway group, calling itself XR America, was formed, with the support of Roger Hallam.[11] Its leaders argued that 'we don't have time to argue about social justice' and aimed to reach out to more conservative groups in Middle America.[12] That split has intensified the ongoing debate in the UK. Rajith Perera, a retired physics lecturer from Haringey, London, has argued for a fourth demand in the UK. He says:

our current theories of change and of oppression are devoid of any understanding of race and class (social and climate justice was removed out of our demands so as 'not to alienate white people')... This 'neither left nor right' but 'beyond politics' is a false position to adopt, it invites only the dominance of middle class elements in the movement ... 'social justice' and 'climate justice' are inseparable.

Several XR groups, have debated or adopted different versions of a fourth demand. Rajith's own group in Haringey consulted members on the following: 'For a just transition that prioritises and protects the most vulnerable and those most impacted by climate breakdown.' However, at a national level the issue remains unresolved.

Back in mid-Wales, the trains re-started just in time for me to leave on the afternoon of 10 February. While I was away my friends in BAAN had been mounting a vigil outside the offices of North Somerset District Council, where the vote on the airport expansion would take place that evening. Over 6,000 people had objected to the application. Many had lobbied their councillors, but the council's planning officers had written an astonishingly one-sided report almost instructing councillors to approve the application. The media, encouraged by the airport, were saying the application was 'expected to be approved'. Councillors do not have to follow the officers' recommendations but they need strong planning reasons for any decision. A few days before, Uttlesford District councillors had rejected a recommendation from their officers to approve the expansion of Stansted Airport. Their declaration of a climate emergency was critical to that decision. How much weight would North Somerset's councillors attach to their own declaration?

I watched the debate intermittently on my phone, on the trains heading home from Wales. Independent councillor Nick Hodge, who represents a village under the flight path, brilliantly rebutted the officers' recommendations (I was told he had help from a planning lawyer). Others spoke in support of him. Could it really be swinging our way?

I was back home when I saw my friends on the late regional news dancing for joy after the vote: 18–7 to reject. At the celebration party the following night I thought we would spend more time discussing tactics for the airport's inevitable appeal, but on that night, people just wanted to celebrate. Someone said Greta Thunberg had retweeted the news of our victory (she celebrated it in front of over 10,000 people in Bristol a few weeks later). Maybe humanity was finally waking up to the threat and its leaders were finally rising to the challenge. That expansion plan, and Heathrow's third runway and the road-building programme, were all heading for the dustbin of history where they belonged, and XR members in the seventy-odd other countries would spread this wave of change worldwide. Maybe.

As we reminisced about the highlights of the campaign I was reminded of something written by Rupert Read, a spokesperson for XR UK: 'I believe history will judge us very kindly. Either we succeed, we are "glorious failures" (paving the way for something better after us), or we fail completely, in which case there won't be very many more history books ...'[13]

15

Protest and the Limits to Growth of Transport – and Other Things

This book has told the story of six protest movements (plus the Big Ask, which was not really a protest movement), and the politics that provoked and responded to them. Four of these movements opposed environmental damage; two of them opposed taxes or charges designed, at least in part, to reduce environmental damage. That tension in transport is part of a broader conflict between growth in human activities and a desire for protection from the consequences of that growth. Over the three decades of this story the seriousness of those consequences has escalated. One of them, climate change, has emerged as the most serious and the most urgent to address. But even if we succeed in solving that one, there are many others escalating behind it such as: biodiversity loss, pollution of different kinds and depletion of finite resources including undeveloped land.

The final sections of this chapter will consider whether it is possible, and what might be done, to reconcile humanity's desire for movement with the need to avert its most disastrous consequences. But, as some of the characters in this story have found, rational arguments on their own don't change very much. If they did, there would be no need for protest movements.

What Difference Did the Protest Movements Make?

Whatever was said in public, policy-makers privately acknowledged that the protest movements described in this book did have at least some influence on policy and practice. Five of them influenced specific decisions: to slash the road-building programme, cut tax on petrol, abandon plans for road pricing, legislate to reduce carbon emissions and abandon expansion of London's airports – at least for a while. The protests against HS2 seem unlikely to cancel the project altogether but they did destabilise it and helped to produce some design changes. It is still too early to assess the impact of XR, but there is no doubt that it was a major factor in the radical change in public, professional and political opinion around climate change, which occurred during 2019.

So, it seems that protest can make a difference, but is it possible to disentangle its influence from other factors and other influences on decision-makers? Alongside this book I wrote a research article, which may help to answer that question. Its title was 'Why Did UK Governments Cut Road Building in the 1990s and Expand it after 2010?'

The circumstances facing the Coalition government after 2010 were similar to the mid-1990s in several ways. In both cases, a Conservative (or Conservative-led) government was grappling with the aftermath of a recession; the public finances were in deficit, the national debt was increasing and both governments declared a priority to cut public spending. Ministers in 1996 attributed their decision to slash the road-building budget to those financial pressures. Why then did the Coalition government decide to treble their road-building budget in 2013? Chapter 12 explains some of the factors, including the strong personal influence of George Osborne, who changed his mind after lobbying from business interests. But the same business interests tried and failed to persuade the Major government to maintain its road-building programme. Clearly deeper forces were at work.

My research article used a critical realist framework to explore those deeper forces. Critical realism is a philosophy of science, originally developed by the British philosopher Roy Bhaskar. Much critical realist writing is complicated and difficult to read (deliberately so, it often seems), but at its heart is a simple idea, which is useful for answering questions like this. Human beings have free will; they can choose to make different decisions, but their choices are influenced by social structures and material circumstances. The challenge for social researchers is to identify the structures, the circumstances and the causal mechanisms which link them to the actions of individuals. None of us can directly see the structures or mechanisms, but people who are involved – including the people I interviewed for this book – will often be able to provide their own explanations for why things happened. These are like the parable of the blind men describing an elephant; they give a partial picture. The researcher starts with no greater vision, but from their explanations, and some other sources, he may piece together a picture of what the elephant looks like.

Using these methods, my case study identified three causal mechanisms, which explain the difference between the decisions of those two governments. The first of these was a *rational response* explanation based on Phil Goodwin's 'Transport: The New Realism'. During the 1990s governments came to recognise that without demand management the best hope that road-building could offer was, in Goodwin's words 'to make things worse more slowly'. By the mid-1990s politicians of all parties recognised that 'we cannot build our way out of congestion' and transport ministers began to act on that recognition. If the road network could not expand to meet demand, then demand would have to be managed by traffic-reducing measures, such as fuel tax rises or road pricing. The Labour government elected in 1997 set out with intentions to manage transport demand but its attempts were short-lived and not very successful, partly because of the fuel tax protests and campaigns against road pricing. So politicians and civil servants began to lower their expectations. Privately their analyses confirmed that building or widening roads would not solve congestion, but it might help to 'make things worse more slowly'. By 2012 most politicians were willing to accept that outcome as the least-worst option.

The second mechanism concerned a change in *economic ideology*. In the words of Steven Norris quoted in Chapter 4, in the late 1990s infrastructure spending was viewed as 'a big lump of money that either had to be borrowed or taxed', whereas by 2012 governments came to believe that new infrastructure was essential to economic recovery. The evidence for or against that view did not really change over those years – it remains uncertain to this day[1] – but after the recession of 2007–9 the economic orthodoxy changed. Politicians stopped listening to the sceptics and preferred to believe that building roads and high-speed rail would boost the economy.

The third mechanism concerned *public opinion*. The British Social Attitudes Survey showed some dramatic swings in public opinion concerning motoring, road-building and the environment over those years. One of the questions in that survey asked whether the government should build more motorways to reduce congestion. After 1993, when protestors first appeared at Twyford Down, the answers turned more negative and they continued to fall, reaching an all-time low in 1996, the year of the Newbury Bypass evictions. During those years, media coverage became more critical of the benefits claimed for road-building, often mentioning evidence that building or widening roads would generate more traffic. From around 2000 onwards public opinion began to move in the opposite direction. Newspapers began to run more stories about rising congestion. They were less likely to mention that building roads generates more traffic. By 2010 many more people believed that building more motorways might help to reduce congestion, although the evidence for or against that belief had not changed.

There was a two-way relationship between the protest movement and wider public opinion during the 1990s. The radical protestors drew much of their support from sympathetic local communities and their actions clearly influenced public opinion, directly in some places and indirectly via the media. They also interacted with the experts who were promoting the 'new realism'; Goodwin and some of his peers worked alongside protestors giving evidence at public inquiries. Media interest, heightened by the protest actions, helped to publicise their arguments. Thus, the different causal mechanisms reinforced each other.

The absence of any coordinated protest movement after 2013 changed the dynamics of media coverage and public opinion. Academics continued to publish studies casting doubt on the effectiveness of road-building. In 2013, 32 transport professors, including Goodwin, wrote to Transport Secretary Grayling expressing concern about the new direction of transport policy and calling for a return to demand management. He ignored their pleas, as did most of the media. That might seem unremarkable were it not for the contrast with the 'new realism' – during the 1990s illegal direct action was a key factor, which made the media and politicians take notice of rational arguments based on research. The actions of XR and the youth climate strikers provoked a similar response during 2019.

So, if protest movements (or their absence) are one element in a complex causal network, can we say *how much* difference they make, or what might have happened if they had never occurred? And can we explain why some protest movements succeed, some partially succeed, or succeed for a while, and others fail altogether? Those are more difficult questions to answer, though many previous writers have tried.

Why Do Some Protest Movements Make More Difference than Others?

There is a vast academic literature about protest, particularly where it is carried out by 'social movements'.[2] A social movement is a particular type of protest movement, which has a strong shared identity and deliberately challenges the structures of power.[3] Two of the six movements reviewed in this book, the anti-roads movement and XR, could be described as social movements; the others were more focussed on specific issues. The literature has less to say about single-issue campaigns, although some research findings may apply to both types.

The most influential research on social movements has come from American writers, drawing on American and transnational examples. These writers draw bold, straightforward conclusions in books, articles or TED talks aimed at a wider audience. By contrast, British researchers are more likely to emphasise the complexity of the problems they are studying and the difficulties of drawing sweeping conclusions from messy real-world situations.[4] Their findings are mainly confined to academic books and journals, so their work is not so widely known. For people, like the founders of XR, looking for practical guidance the American studies have generally proved more useable.

One of the most useful sources that influenced XR, is *This is an Uprising* by Mark and Paul Engler.[5] This very readable book draws on a diverse range of studies concerning: the American civil rights movement and campaign for gay marriage, Occupy Wall Street, Gandhi's civil disobedience, the campaign for democracy in Serbia and EarthFirst!'s campaign against logging in ancient forests, among others. They differentiate between momentum-driven movements, which grow rapidly but often fizzle out, structure-driven movements, which grow more slowly but last longer, and hybrid movements which combine elements of both. Successful protest movements will start with a broad transformational agenda (instead of single issues), they will build a decentralised network, use disruption, symbolic actions, personal sacrifice and escalation, provoking the authorities and opponents to hit back, raising the profile of the issues at stake.

All the movements in *This is an Uprising* were committed to princi-ples of non-violence. Activists put themselves at risk and try to avoid or minimise harm to others. Their sacrifice stimulates public sympathy and attracts new recruits. How to maintain that sympathy while also escalating the conflict is not easy. Actions which alienate the public, particularly if opponents can portray them as violent, can rapidly erode support for a movement. EarthFirst! discovered this when a steel bar, which they (or possibly another group) had driven into a tree, damaged a saw mill and seriously injured the operator. Flying drones near Heathrow could have backfired in a similar way against XR. The action at Canning Town tube station may also have reduced support for XR, at least in the short term.

Erica Chenoweth and Maria Stephans, whose work has influenced XR, drew some similar conclusions about the greater effectiveness of non-violence, based on a statistical study of international resistance movements.[6] The movements they studied were seeking to overthrow governments, expel foreign invaders or gain independence for new nations; social and economic campaigns in democratic countries were specifically excluded.

Their finding that 'no campaigns failed once they'd achieved the active and sustained participation of just 3.5 per cent of the popu-lation' was not part of the original study; that appeared later in the notes accompanying a TED talk.[7] Any finding of that nature raises an obvious question: what caused what? Was that mass participation a *cause* of success or an *effect* of a campaign that was succeeding for other reasons? The critical element missing from the dataset used by Chenoweth and Stephans was any measure of public opinion before, during or after the campaigns. Their study does not answer the obvious question: what happens when a campaign recruits many active members but alienates most of the population? To be fair to Che-noweth and Stephans, their study was not designed for that purpose.

Public opinion was crucial to the growth and successes of the protest movements in this book. Several of them tried to achieve their goals more directly but none of them succeeded. Obstructive direct action did not stop the building of any roads or the expansion of any airports once construction had begun. It is unlikely to stop the con-struction of HS2. An upswell of public concern about climate change propelled XR's rapid growth but the disruption created by XR has not compelled the government to negotiate, although some members still hope that it will. The fuel tax protestors came closest to achieving that aim but their short-lived action achieved only modest gains at the time and their movement rapidly disintegrated as public concern over their tactics began to grow.

Instead, all of the protest movements and campaigns covered in this book owed their medium-term successes to public opinion. This was reflected through the media and on politicians who responded to widespread public concern, as well as some other factors in each case. The protest movements helped to increase that concern and shift public opinion. Their impact on public opinion was measurable for road-building in the 1990s and climate change in 2019. Opinion polls also suggested strong public opposition to road pricing and strong initial support for the fuel tax protestors, although that began to wane as the movement split over tactics later in 2000. Protest activity does not necessarily increase public support; it may have the opposite effect. One reassuring example of this occurred in American states where the Ku Klux Klan began throwing their support behind election candidates, who lost votes as a result.[8]

Some studies have examined the contexts which make it easier or harder to influence political outcomes in democratic countries.[9] It is harder for protest movements to influence issues where big political or financial resources are at stake, where public opinion is very strong or where it is sharply divided along a national political cleavage (like Brexit in the UK or gun laws in the USA). The national political cleavage has posed a challenge to XR; many on the right of British politics have worked hard, with some success, to portray climate change as a left-wing metropolitan issue. Big political and financial resources are clearly involved in HS2, road-building and airport expansion. This story has shown how protestors can make progress, even against those most difficult issues, although counter-pressures are likely to return once the movements recede.

It has also revealed how the most successful protest movements are not necessarily the ones people remember. The most successful of all the campaigns in this book, the Big Ask, has been largely forgotten today, while some of the others, particularly the anti-roads protests, endure in the collective memory of activists and much of the British public. The Big Ask was quickly forgotten because it broke no laws, caused no damage and achieved widespread consensus, enabling politicians to claim its ideas as their own. Success, for that type of campaign, is self-effacing.

Although some tactics tend to work better than others, and some contexts may be easier or harder to change, most surveys of social movements have concluded that there is no common formula for success. Despite some sophisticated attempts, researchers cannot really tell how much difference protest movements have made compared to other factors.[10] Perhaps they never will. All we can say with confidence is that protest movements can make a difference where they benefit from, and are able to influence, public opinion. They may also provoke backlashes or counter-movements with unpredictable outcomes.

Counter-movements and Money as a Motivator

Backlashes and counter-movements are often mentioned in this literature, although the few studies specifically about them have mainly concerned race or gender issues. The fuel tax protests and campaigns against road pricing could both be described as counter-movements.

In considering how they relate to the rest of this story, two issues are notable. Firstly, there was no direct opposition between movements and counter-movements. A line may be traced from the success of the anti-roads movement through New Labour's attempts at demand management, to those counter-movements a few years later. But the specific issues were different in each case and there was a time gap between them. There was no popular pro-roads movement during the 1990s (though there was industry-led lobbying) and there was no popular movement in favour of higher fuel taxes or road pricing during the 2000s. It is difficult to imagine any such movement gaining traction (so Charles Secrett's decision not to confront the fuel protestors might not have been such a big mistake as he describes on page 97). The counter-movements did not immediately reverse the gains of the anti-roads movement, but their legacy helped to create the conditions for a return to large-scale road-building several years later.

Secondly, both these counter-movements were reacting to measures which imposed, or would have imposed, monetary costs on drivers. As a method of achieving social or environmental aims monetary measures suffer from two serious problems. The most obvious problem is unfairness. The people who consume most or travel most are people on higher incomes, whereas cost-raising measures generally impose the greatest constraints on people with low incomes (there are exceptions such as a frequent flyer tax).

Measures involving money also invoke unhelpful psychological responses. Experiments have shown how even a brief mention of money makes people act in a more selfish way.[11] Monetary measures are likely to make people feel less social, less willing to make sacrifices for a greater good. It is not surprising, therefore, that the demand management measures which triggered the strongest counter-movements were measures related to money. These experiments also help to explain why proposals to take money off people, then give it back to them in a different form generally fail to assuage opposition. A 'revenue-neutral' road pricing scheme will invoke the same psychological responses as a scheme designed to raise tax revenues.

These disadvantages have hampered most attempts at transport demand management and led government back towards a default position of unconstrained growth, which is fuelling climate change and many other threats to humanity.

Decarbonising Transport – the Path of Least Resistance

Shortly after my trial and all the publicity surrounding it an academic from another university asked me why I felt it necessary to go to such lengths. He said that in Britain, unlike some other countries, most people accepted that climate change was real and that we needed to do something about it. Wouldn't I be better working with others to find the right solutions?

It was a reasonable question, but moving around the country, talking to local authorities, other academics and the organisers of the parliamentary climate assembly has strengthened my view that we don't lack expertise or potential solutions. If we fail, it will be through lack of political will or possibly a backlash against carbon-cutting measures.

The contrast between acknowledgement of the crisis and denial of the consequences was particularly stark among local authorities. Unlike national government they can do little to accelerate the electrification of the vehicle fleet, but they do have powers to reduce the volume of traffic, if they are willing to use them. In one authority that had declared a climate emergency, a working group had prepared a list of potential measures, such as building a cycle path along two major roads when they were widened into dual carriageways. My comment that 'zero carbon' might entail narrowing or closing the dual carriageway instead provoked incredulity from some of the officers.

Although the implementation may be difficult, the main options for decarbonising surface transport are straightforward: replace fossil fuels with electricity or hydrogen from renewable sources and/or reduce the movements of vehicles powered by fossil fuels. Improving the efficiency of conventional vehicles can make a marginal contribution in the short term but it is easy to be overoptimistic on that score. In recent years efficiency improvements in cars and planes have been outweighed by growth in travel and rising sales of gas-guzzling SUVs. Biofuels can also make a minor contribution, providing they don't replace food crops or uncultivated land, which they will do if governments or industry decide to escalate their use.

My most important messages to people contemplating this challenge were the ones they least wanted to hear. Better, cheaper, more frequent public transport may be desirable for lots of reasons but on its own it will make little difference to volumes of traffic or carbon emissions. The distances currently covered by car dwarf the distances covered by public transport and only a minority of additional journeys by public transport replace car journeys in any case.

A simple calculation in *Urban Transport Without the Hot Air* illustrated how doubling bus use in England could reduce car travel by 1.3 per cent. However, if the road network was left unchanged even that 1.3 per cent would be a big over-estimate, for the following reason: every vehicle taken off a road frees space for another vehicle to take its place.

That principle identified by the 'new realists' in the 1990s (see page 61) applies to public transport improvements as it does to road widening. In congested urban areas or on congested inter-urban roads any free space will fill up very quickly. When new rail or tram lines open researchers have struggled to find any clear evidence of traffic reductions.[12]

Road pricing could reduce traffic volumes, but only if it increased the cost of driving. If the road user charges were fully compensated by cuts in fuel tax this would do nothing to reduce carbon emissions.

So what should be done?

Two factors are paramount: speed of change and public acceptance, or at least acquiescence. Citizens' assemblies do not guarantee public acceptance, but I have been impressed by what I have seen of them so far. Ordinary people, armed with information, are more likely than politicians or professionals to identify solutions acceptable to a wider public.

My personal view is that we have run out of time for ideal solutions. Given the urgency of the situation we must now look for paths of least public resistance and limited technical risk. For most road transport that means much more rapid electrification and scrappage of vehicles powered by fossil fuels. In rural and suburban areas where most car drivers can park near their own houses electric vehicles will usually be charged overnight. In denser urban areas, where we need to house more people in future, home charging will not always be possible. That is where the greatest efforts to reduce the number of vehicles, and change the patterns of travel should be focussed.

Improving public transport does not make much difference on its own. Instead, the most successful cities have combined better public transport and joined-up segregated networks for cyclists with measures to restrain general traffic, parking and vehicle ownership. It is easier to do this when urban populations are rising, because planning policies are concentrating new housing in cities instead of spreading it into the countryside. At high population densities widespread car ownership for most people becomes physically impossible, because there is insufficient space. Car-free developments, which I have visited and researched across Europe, can turn that constraint into an advantage, offering a better quality of urban life, particularly for families with young children. Limited parking for car clubs can provide an alternative for journeys which cannot be done by public transport, cycling or walking.

Progress on decarbonising larger vehicles has been slower than for cars and must now be accelerated. Electric power is now becoming available for a wider range of vans and some buses, but for HGVs and buses covering longer distances hydrogen power seems likely to offer the best option.

HS2 is an unwelcome distraction to these efforts. It will be powered by electricity, but its high speeds will use more energy and generate more travel. By the government's own estimates, it will do little to reduce emissions from driving or flying and the carbon emitted during its construction will outweigh those small gains over the medium term. The straight lines needed to support high speeds will cause unnecessary damage to the countryside and the project will divert over £80 billion, which could be used to decarbonise transport or other sectors of the economy.

Aviation poses the most intractable problem. The Climate Change Committee expects aviation to become the largest emitting sector by 2050, pumping out over 40 per cent of UK carbon emissions. Their projections include some optimistic assumptions about efficiency improvements and technological progress. Battery powered planes may fill some niche markets but there is no prospect of them, or any other technology, replacing fossil fuels for most passenger flights. We may be able to offset some of the carbon emitted by planes but not a business-as-usual scale. For aviation, constraint will be unavoidable.

One study concluded that to achieve the net zero target the UK will have to gradually close all its airports.[13] If we act quickly enough on everything else (a big 'if') that might be avoidable but expanding airport capacity is clearly incompatible with any serious attempt to achieve net zero. And yet, that is what the owners of airports across the UK, aided and abetted by the DfT, have been planning to do. (As I write these lines the Court of Appeal has just upheld a challenge against Heathrow's third runway and the owners of Heathrow have said they will appeal to the Supreme Court.)

Transport and the Limits to Growth

Transport protests and politics reflect a wider tension between the growth of human activities and resistance to their most damaging impacts. Nearly 40 years ago the Club of Rome published a comprehensive survey of human environmental impacts leading to their conclusion that there are limits to growth.[14] Since then economic (and population) growth have continued unabated and so has the erosion of the environmental assets which make planet Earth habitable for human beings. The optimistic view that economic growth might generate the resources to halt or reverse that process is contradicted by a wealth of evidence documenting continuing declines in biodiversity, loss of habitats and depletion of finite resources.

The 2019 State of Nature report from a network of conservation charities shows how rapidly that decline is affecting the UK.[15] It, and many other studies, point to causes such as: farming and forestry methods, climate change, pollution and urbanisation. The common cause behind all of these factors is continuing human expansion on land which is fixed in size.

I have written elsewhere about the relationship between urbanisation and loss of countryside, which is happening at a much faster rate than politicians, developers and media commentators would like people to believe.[16] Fragmented housing development is part of the problem, but the biggest cause is expansion of the road network. Apart from the erosion of countryside valued by people, roads sever habitats isolating other species into small unviable populations. If biodiversity is ever to recover, we will need to reduce that severance. Gimmicks such as 'green bridges' across roads have made little difference;[17] the only long-term solution (if humanity has a long-term future) is to remove or possibly bury roads. In the short term we need to stop making the problem worse.

The impact of road and airport expansion on the climate emergency is greater than the direct contribution of each additional runway or lane of traffic. When governments allow the expansion of carbon-hungry infrastructure they send a strong signal that business as usual can continue for now; if the consequences of decarbonisation are too unpalatable the government remains open to lobbying.

We now have a government legally committed to decarbonisation, albeit too slowly. The commitment was reiterated in the 2019 Conservative manifesto but the government shows little sign of action to make this happen. Many of its biggest decisions continue to make the problem worse. Only public pressure will make them, or any governments, recognise the emergency and act to avert it.

The main message of this book for XR or any other protest groups is that your actions will only work if you bring public opinion with you. XR's demands are on a different scale from the other groups in this book but that principle still applies. It does not mean staying within the law; it does not mean avoiding conflict. As the clock ticks down towards catastrophe that conflict must escalate, but it must be clearly targeted at the decision-makers. The public must understand that we are on their side. Disruption may be necessary to recruit, but there is no reason – and no research evidence to show – that it must directly target the public (as I have often heard people in XR claim).

Tactics such as road blocking are now producing diminishing returns for XR. Their failure to seriously disrupt the economies of cities suggests a very different conclusion – that authorities can and should close roads in cities to reduce traffic, pollution and carbon emissions. I believe XR should now specifically target the government and government-sanctioned activities that are damaging the climate, such as road-building and airport expansion (to cite the two that are most relevant to this book). That will inevitably cause some disruption to the public, but indirectly and as little as possible.[18]

The fate of Reclaim the Streets highlights another wrong turn for social movements, through broadening their remit (see Roger Geffen's comments on page 53). This poses a dilemma for XR. Many XR members are calling for the movement to pay more attention to social and racial injustice. Listening to black and Asian members has changed my view as I have been writing this book; I now accept the arguments for a fourth demand. The wording proposed by the Haringey group (page 209) is appropriate because it applies the principles of social justice to XR's main purpose of combatting climate change. We must also stop or disown our public figures making repeated comments that offend ethnic or national groups (page 210).

However, in recognising social and racial justice in the fight against climate change, we must resist the many calls to broaden XR's objectives. Campaigning success attracts many people with different agendas, some of which may be entirely justified but are not achievable by one social movement. Apart from social and racial demands, members have called online for XR to campaign on issues from veganism to opposing 5G mobile networks. Some members want XR to position itself as an anti-capitalist movement. Regardless of one's views on capitalism (and I am not a fan) that would mean taking one side of a national political cleavage, which is a route to failure. Instead, XR, or any groups campaigning on climate change, should reach across national political cleavages. The anti-roads protestors did that by appealing to Middle England's deep-seated love of the countryside. Road-building (and airport expansion and high-speed rail) is damaging the British countryside directly and indirectly through climate change. Many Conservative voters will respond to a message that says: we must act now to prevent its destruction.

There is a consensus among climate scientists that the next few years will be critical for the future of the planet. Thanks to the Big Ask, the UK has the laws, it has the mechanisms to address that emergency and lead the way for other countries, but its leaders still lack the political will and one sector, transport, threatens to frustrate the law and make all other efforts inadequate. Although the small world of transport planning has woken up to the climate emergency, the big decisions at national level are still moving us in the wrong direction. Road-building and airport expansion remain key battlegrounds where the fight against climate change and destruction of nature will be won or lost. Expert analysis, rational arguments and conventional politics have all failed to halt that race towards self-destruction. The need for disruptive protest action has never been greater.

I did not expect to spend my late middle age protesting and getting arrested, but the contrast between the looming international catastrophe and the pathetic response of governments compelled me to act. And you?

Afterword

I finished the first draft of this book, just before COVID-19 shut down economies and transport systems around the world. I am writing this afterword in late June 2020, as the lockdown (or should I say 'the first lockdown') is beginning to ease across the UK. As the virus began to spread XR decided to pause active campaigning and encourage its members to concentrate on supporting their local communities. The UK Climate Assembly initially stopped its work, then reconvened using online methods becoming more familiar to most of the population. For several months, the virus and its implications dominated the news, eclipsing climate change for people uninvolved in campaigning or direct work to combat it. So wildfires in the Arctic Circle with a record temperature of 38 degrees and accelerated melting of sea ice[1] passed largely unnoticed.

The virus and lockdown had several conflicting implications for transport. Initially, road traffic levels across the UK fell by 70 per cent; cycling nearly doubled and use of different public transport modes fell by between 80 and 95 per cent. Many organisations talked of working from home becoming the 'new normal', leading some commentators to predict lower traffic volumes in future years.[2] Predicting the future is a risky business, particularly at a time of change, but I will hazard one prediction: those hopes will prove over-optimistic. Commuting only accounts for one journey in six.[3] Remote working may reduce the number of commuting journeys but it also encourages people to live further from their place of work and to compensate by travelling more for other purposes.[4] So, although more home working will change patterns of travel (such as times and destinations), I would not expect it to reduce traffic or transport emissions very much. A big rise in unemployment could restrain the rebound in traffic to some extent; how quickly the labour market might recover from the current crisis is, of course, uncertain.

The future of public transport is another uncertainty with wide-ranging implications. Although motor traffic is returning towards pre-lockdown levels, public transport remains severely constrained by social distancing and the reluctance of the public to put themselves at risk. If the virus and social distancing fade into history public transport may recover and begin to grow, but if COVID-19 recurs or new pandemics cause similar reactions then public transport as we know it may become unviable. Greater separation of passengers may be possible in the longer term, but at higher cost and lower capacity.

If that happens, big cities may be unable to support their current population densities. The decarbonisation strategy I outlined on page 207, which depends on housing more people in cities and reducing their travel by car may become impossible. More cycling, walking and use of car clubs might help but will not solve the problem on their own. Spreading the population more widely, connected by roads, would accelerate ecological breakdown. If that scenario does occur, the taboo subject (even for many in the environmental movement[5]) of the limits to population growth may have to be addressed sooner rather than later.

The uncertainty around public transport also applies to aviation. The lockdown has hit the aviation industry hard, pushing some airlines to bankruptcy and others to shed staff, but has not changed its attitude towards airport expansion. On 27 February 2020 the Court of Appeal upheld a challenge from FoE and Plan B Earth to the Airports National Policy Statement with its plans for a third runway at Heathrow. The challenge was based on several grounds, all relating to climate change. Heathrow's owners are appealing to the Supreme Court without the support of the government. Meanwhile, the owners of Bristol Airport have announced that they intend to appeal against North Somerset Council's rejection of their planning application.[6]

In its early weeks, the lockdown reduced carbon global carbon emissions by about 6 per cent, but its effect is likely to be short-lived.[7] The fundamental challenge has not changed, but more time has passed with very little action taken. The Climate Change Committee has just published another report to parliament, documenting that inactivity. The government is consulting on phasing out the sale of new petrol and diesel cars and vans, but the mooted deadlines, 2035 or 2032 would be too late. A recent study estimates that the UK would have to reach net zero emissions between 2035 and 2040 to comply with the Paris climate Agreement, which the government has signed;[8] so if a future government decides to abide by its agreements, it might have to scrap millions of new cars!

COVID-19 and the lockdown created a dilemma for XR. In the early days of the pandemic some in XR saw an opportunity to draw parallels with the threat of climate breakdown; others argued that it would be inappropriate to say so, and it might be used against us. As the pandemic worsened the latter view prevailed, but the feared consequences occurred anyway when an internal report reached David Rose, a 'climate sceptic' who usually writes for the *Mail on Sunday*. The memo, now published in a book by Rupert Read,[9] argued that 'COVID-19 has done XR's job better than XR itself could have hoped for' by revealing the vulnerability of a 'just-in-time food system' to natural or man-made disasters.[10] Rose selectively quoted from the report to argue that: 'XR thinks the pandemic is Gaia's punishment for our profligate, consumerist lifestyles.'[11]

When to re-start protest actions, and in what ways, remained issues of debate within XR during the lockdown. The Black Lives Matters protests, triggered by the asphyxiation of George Floyd by police in the USA, tipped the balance. Several XR members were in the crowd that toppled the statue of slave trader Edward Colston, spreading images from Bristol's harbourside across the world.

While XR UK worked on plans for another rebellion at a later date, local groups were formulating 'intermediate demands', local or regional issues where XR might achieve tangible progress. Air pollution, exceeding legal limits, offered an obvious target for XR Bristol. In June 2020, air quality near the toppled statue, which had improved during the lockdown, returned to illegal levels, while the Council and the government argued over the form and timing of an action plan and who would pay for it.[12]

XR planned its campaign around the slogan 'Let Bristol Breathe' until someone pointed out the unfortunate parallel with the last words of George Floyd; the name was changed to 'Our Air Our City'. Its aim was simple: a plan for legal air quality by April 2021. In the small hours of 25 June five XR rebels climbed onto the roof of County Hall. I joined several speakers in support of their actions on the green in front of the hall (filmed and available on YouTube.[13]) The police decided that their presence was a civil matter and declined to intervene. They stayed there for a week, attracting some personal abuse from the city's mayor,[14] and forcing air pollution back up the local political agenda.

At national level, the easing of the lockdown has intensified XR's internal debate over the most effective tactics. Should we organise another rebellion in central London (and if so, how would we all get there if public transport remains socially distanced) or should we plan simultaneous actions in different places? Is road blocking still an effective tactic or can we target elites and decision-makers without disrupting the general public? No decisions have been made yet, but as a leading member of XR UK told me: 'We've got to organise another rebellion before things go back to normal – whatever that means.'

The pandemic has delayed the next round of international climate talks, COP26 in Glasgow, until November 2021. The repetition of 'last chance' warnings has become unhelpful, so I will not repeat that cliché here. We have already passed the point of safety; bad consequences are coming our way whatever we do, but until we reach a point where human extinction is certain it will never be 'too late'. That said, COP26 will offer the UK a once-only opportunity to influence the global choice between decarbonisation or annihilation. You can expect to hear a lot more about XR between now and then. If you are reading these lines after that conference you may have a clearer view of how history will judge our efforts – if history has a future.

Notes

Preface

1. Steve Melia (2019) Why Did UK Governments Cut Road Building in the 1990s and Expand it after 2010? *Transport Policy* 81, pp. 242–53.

1 The Biggest Road-Building Programme Since the Romans (1989–92)

1. Hansard, House of Commons, 18 May 1989, vol 153, cc485.
2. British Road Federation (1988) Council Minutes, 14 December, Agenda Item 5 – Public Affairs Committee. Unpublished document held in the archives of the Institute of Civil Engineers, London.
3. These statements and some others in this section are drawn from Mick Hamer (1987) *Wheels Within Wheels: A Study of the Roads Lobby*. Routledge & Kegan Paul.
4. Cecil Parkinson (1992) *Right at the Centre, an Autobiography*. Weidenfeld & Nicholson.
5. See for example *The Great Global Warming Swindle*, broadcast 8 March 2007 on Channel 4. Retrieved from www.youtube.com/watch?v=0Yh CQv5tNsQ
6. Margaret Thatcher (2002) *Statecraft: Strategies for a Changing World*. HarperCollins.
7. Michael Dynes (1989) Parkinson Denies Transport Neglected. *The Times*, 9 December, p. 5.
8. Michael McCarthy (1989) Patten Issues Environmental 'Challenge' to Transport Policy. *The Times*, 21 November.
9. *The Times* (1990) Motorway Madness [editorial]. *The Times*, 28 February.
10. Parkinson, *Right at the Centre*.
11. British Road Federation (1989) Local Campaigning Minute 58/89. Unpublished document held in the archives of the Institute of Civil Engineers, London.
12. British Road Federation (1988) Minutes of Public Affairs Committee, 24 May, item 2. Unpublished document held in the archives of the Institute of Civil Engineers, London.
13. Barbara Bryant (1996) *Twyford Down: Roads, Campaigning and Environmental Law*. Routledge.
14. Geoff Meade (1991) New War of Words in Euro Environment Row. Press Association in Brussels, 25 October.
15. Bryant, *Twyford Down*.

2 Direct Action, Arrests and Unexplained Violence

1. Malcolm MacAlister Hall (1992) The Unmaking of the English Landscape. *The Times*, 30 May.
2. Derek Wall (1999) *Earth First! and the Anti-Roads Movement*. Routledge.
3. Peter Kunzlik (1996) The Lawyer's Assessment. In Bryant, *Twyford Down*.
4. Bryant, *Twyford Down*.
5. Ibid.
6. BBC (2007) *The Secret Life of the Motorway. Part 3: The End of the Affair*. TV documentary, BBC4, 5 April. Retrieved from www.youtube.com/watch?v=Rs89onnjI5Y
7. Mayyasa Al-malazi and Neil Goodwin (1995) *Life in the Fast Lane – The No M11 Story*. TV documentary. Retrieved from www.youtube.com/watch?v=49wKgtOooqs
8. Christian Wolmar (1994) Two Men Paid to Burn M11 Protesters' Camp Are Jailed; Mystery Still Surrounds the Identity of Ringleaders. *The Independent*, 6 September.
9. There have been many studies of the protests and activists. See for example Wall, *Earth First! and the Anti-Roads Movement*; Benjamin Seel, Matthew Paterson and Brian Doherty (eds) (2000) *Direct Action in British Environmentalism*. Routledge; and Alex Plows (2002) Praxis and Practice: The 'What, How and Why' of the UK Environmental Direct Action (EDA) Movement in the 1990's. PhD thesis (unpublished), University of Bangor.

3 The Newbury Bypass, Reclaim the Streets and 'Swampy'

1. Interview quoted in G. Dudley (2007) Individuals and The Dynamics of Policy Learning: The Case of The Third Battle of Newbury. *Public Administration*, 85(2), pp. 405–28.
2. Major Projects Association (2000) The Newbury Bypass. Unpublished notes held at the Library of the Institution of Civil Engineers, from a conference held at the Royal Academy of Engineering, London, 13 March.
3. See for example Jim Hindle (2006) *Nine Miles: Two Winters of Anti-Road Protest*. Underhill Books.
4. John Vidal (1996) Newbury Guards Urged to Attack Protesters. *The Guardian*, 25 January, p. 1.
5. John Vidal (1996) Petrol Bomb 'Prankster' is Cleared. *The Guardian*, 16 August, p. 10.
6. Jim Perrin (1996) High Treason in the Treetops; *The Guardian*, 13 March, p. 4.
7. John Vidal (1996) Climbers in Hand to Hand Battles 50ft Up. *The Guardian*, 13 March, p. 3.

8. BBC (1997) U-Turn. *Panorama*, BBC 1, 17 March.

9. Major Projects Association, The Newbury Bypass.

10. David Taylor (1995) The Road Warrior: M11 Protesters Wage a New Campaign to Rid London of Cars. *Evening Standard*, 13 June, p. 18.

11. History is Made at Night (2018) Reclaim the Streets Brixton Street Party, June 1998. Retrieved from https://history-is-made-at-night.blogspot.com/2018/06/. The author is not entirely sure, but see the evidence below.

12. Alexis Petridis (2017) 'A Lost Freedom': When New Age Travellers Found Acid House – in Pictures. *The Guardian*, 10 May. Retrieved from www.theguardian.com/artanddesign/2017/may/10/a-lost-freedom-when-new-age-travellers-found-acid-house-in-pictures

13. Rob Evans and Paul Lewis (2013) *Undercover: The True Story of Britain's Secret Police*. London: Guardian Books. This paragraph also draws on several more recent newspaper articles.

14. Stephen Farrell (1996) Human Moles Lead Bailiffs Deeper into Treacherous Tunnels. *The Times*, 28 January.

15. M. Paterson (2000) Swampy Fever: Media Constructions and Direct Action Politics. In Seel et al., *Direct Action in British Environmentalism*, pp. 151–66.

4 The Biggest Hit on the Road Programme Since the Romans Left (1992–7)

1. Kevin Eason (1992) MacGregor Angers Environmentalists. *The Times*, 30 May.

2. The *Independent* (1994) The Cabinet Reshuffle: Ministers Make Their Last Farewells. Full text of letters to Prime Minister from the outgoing ministers. *The Independent*, 21 July, p. 2.

3. Brian Mawhinney (1999) *In the Firing Line*. HarperCollins.

4. Steven Norris and Tony Austin (1996) *Changing Trains*. Hutcheson.

5. Mawhinney, *In the Firing Line*.

6. Ibid.

7. Melia, Why Did UK Governments Cut Road Building in the 1990s and Expand it after 2010?

8. Christian Wolmar (1996) Ministers Axe Plan to Cut Pollution; Road Lobby Kills Green Agenda for Traffic. *The Independent*, 3 April, p. 1.

9. Christian Wolmar (1996) Transport Paper Opts for the Easy Route. *The Independent*, 26 April.

10. Paul Brown (1996) Eco-Soundings. *The Guardian*, 27 November.

11. Norris and Austin, *Changing Trains*.

12. BBC, U-Turn.

13. Sian Clare and Peter Woodman (1996) Budget Day 'Disguise' For Road Programme Cuts. Press Association, 26 November.

5 Integrated Transport, the New Labour Ideal (1997–2000)

1. John Prescott with Hunter Davies (2008) *Prezza, My Story: Pulling No Punches*. Headline Review.
2. Prescott with Davies, *Prezza*.
3. Andrew Rawnsley (2001) *Servants of the People, the Inside Story of New Labour*. Penguin.
4. *The Scotsman* (2010) Gavin Strang to Bow Out as MP after 40 Years. *The Scotsman*, 5 April.
5. Prescott with Davies, *Prezza*.
6. Christian Wolmar (2005) *On the Wrong Line*. Aurum Press.

6 The Fuel Protests and their Aftermath

1. Mary Ann Sieghart (2000) Why the French are Always up in Arms. *The Times*, 1 September.
2. P. Salini (2002) Fuel Taxation and an Account of the Fuel Tax Protests in France. In Glenn Lyons and Kiron Chatterjee (eds), *Transport Lessons from the Fuel Tax Protests of 2000*. Ashgate, pp. 47–61.
3. B. Doherty, M. Paterson, A. Plows and D. Wall (2003) Explaining the Fuel Protests. *The British Journal of Politics & International Relations* 5(1), pp. 1–23.
4. Ibid.
5. Peter Hetherington and David Ward (2000) Fuel Crisis Looms as Pickets Hit Depots: Britain: Queues at Pumps as Campaigners for Lower Prices Block Refineries. *The Guardian*, 11 September.
6. G. Marsden and M. Beecroft (2002) Crisis or Drama? – A Summary of the Response to the Fuel Crisis in the UK. In Lyons and Chatterjee, *Transport Lessons from the Fuel Tax Protests of 2000*.
7. Tony Blair (2010) *A Journey: My Political Life*. London: Hutchison.
8. Patrick Wintour (2000) Fuel Crisis: How Blair Misread the Momentum. *The Guardian*, 13 September.
9. Andrew Buncombe, Andrew Grice and Marie Woolf (2000) Fuel Crisis: The Siege Is Lifted. The Misery Goes On. *The Independent*, 15 September. The private assurances that fuel duty would be cut were also mentioned by two interviewees.
10. Jason Burke, Kamal Ahmed, Paul Harris and Nick Walsh (2000) Investigation: Labour's Secret War to Crush Fuel Protest. *The Observer*, 5 November.
11. *The People* (2000) Demo Leader Was A Four-Star Loser Long Before Crisis. *The People*, 5 November.
12. Steve Melia, Kiron Chatterjee and Gordon Stokes (2018) Is the Urbanisation of Young Adults Reducing Their Driving? *Transportation Research Part A: Policy and Practice* 118, pp. 444–56.

7 How Road Pricing Came to London – and Nowhere Else

1. Steve Melia (2015) *Urban Transport Without the Hot Air, Volume 1: Sustainable Solutions for UK Cities.* UIT Cambridge. Chapter 14, about London, is available from www.stevemelia.co.uk.
2. Ken Livingstone (2011) *You Can't Say That: Memoirs.* Faber & Faber.
3. Paul Waugh (1999) Millbank: 'We Want to See Ken's Blood on the Carpet'. *The Independent*, 13 October.
4. Philip Webster (2000) Defeated Livingstone Cries Foul. *The Times*, 21 February.
5. Livingstone, *You Can't Say That.*
6. Ibid.
7. C. Buckingham, A. Doherty, D. Hawkett and S. Vitouladiti (2010) Central London Congestion Charging: Understanding its Impacts. *Proceedings of the ICE-Transport* 163(2), pp. 73–83.
8. T. Rye, M. Gaunt and S. Ison (2008) Edinburgh's Congestion Charging Plans: An Analysis of Reasons for Non-Implementation. *Transportation Planning and Technology* 31(6), pp. 641–61.
9. S. Braunholtz and R. Cumming (2006) *Evaluation of Edinburgh Residents' Attitudes to the Proposed Road User Charging Scheme.* Mori Scotland for the Scottish Executive Social Research.
10. Rye et al., Edinburgh's Congestion Charging Plans.
11. Confirmed in email correspondence with Andrew Burns, Edinburgh's Transport Convenor at the time.
12. Braunholtz and Cumming, *Evaluation of Edinburgh Residents' Attitudes.*
13. Raymond Duncan (2005) Councillors who went too fast, too soon on scheme. *Glasgow Herald*, 23 February, p. 10.
14. David Millward and Brendan Carlin (2007) Blair Defiant over Road Pricing Row. *Daily Telegraph*, 11 January, p. 1.
15. BBC News (2007) Blair's Statement in Full. Retrieved from http://news.bbc.co.uk/1/hi/uk/6381279.stm
16. See www.trafficremoval.uk.
17. Kiron Chatterjee, Phil Goodwin, Tim Schwanen, Ben Clark, Juliet Jain, Steve Melia, Jennie Middleton, Anna Plyushteva, Miriam Ricci, Georgina Santos and Gordon Stokes (2018) Young People's Travel – What's Changed and Why? Review and Analysis. Project Report. Department for Transport, Bristol. Available from: http://eprints.uwe.ac.uk/34640 '

8 Airport Expansion and Climate Change

1. Sam Greenhill (2003) The Record that Put the Heat in Heathrow. *Daily Mail*, 11 August. Page 6.
2. Tim Radford (2004) Freak Summers Will Become Regular Event. *The Guardian*, 12 January, p. 6.

3. Friends of the Earth (2005) What the Government Should Do to Tackle Climate Change. Friends of the Earth's response to the Climate Change Programme review. Retrieved from https://friendsoftheearth.uk.

4. N. Carter and M. Childs (2017) Friends of the Earth as a Policy Entrepreneur: 'The Big Ask' Campaign for a UK Climate Change Act. *Environmental Politics* 27(6), pp. 994–1013.

5. Institute for Government (IfG) (2013) *Policy Reunion: The Climate Change Act, 2008*. IfG. Retrieved from www.instituteforgovernment.org.uk

6. Nicholas Davies (2018) The Big Ask: The Story Behind the Climate Change Act. Retrieved from www.linkedin.com/pulse/big-ask-story-behind-climate-change-act-nicholas-davies

7. John Vidal (2009) Aviation Lobbyists Enlisted to Tackle Rebel Climate MPs, Leaked Papers Show. *The Guardian*, 18 February.

8. N. Carter and M. Childs (2017).

9. J. Church (2015) Enforcing the Climate Change Act. *UCL Journal of Law and Jurisprudence* 4(1), pp. 109–34.

10. The official statistic is based on bunker fuels used at UK airports. The higher figure, from www.airportwatch.org.uk, is adjusted to reflect two factors: the composition of the passengers (more UK residents flying out than foreign residents flying in) and the fact that emissions in the upper atmosphere have a greater impact than emissions closer to the ground.

11. This section draws on an interview with Stewart, and also John Stewart (2011) *Victory Against All the Odds: The Story of How the Campaign to Stop a Third Runway at Heathrow Was Won*. Spokesman Books.

9 The Campaign Against a Heathrow Third Runway

1. George Monbiot (2007) Beneath Heathrow's Pall of Misery, a New Political Movement is Born: It Was Not Flawless, but the Climate Camp Was Still the Most Democratic and Best Organised Protest I've Witnessed. *The Guardian*, 21 August.

2. Jon Ungoed-Thomas and Marie Woolf (2008) Revealed: The Plot to Expand Heathrow. *The Sunday Times*, 9 March, p. 1.

3. Jason Beattie (2007) Airport's Third Runway is Set to Win Go-Ahead. *Evening Standard*, 21 November.

4. See Melia, *Urban Transport Without the Hot Air*, for more about the economic impacts of expanding aviation.

5. Martyn Gregory (2000) *Dirty Tricks: British Airways' Secret War Against Virgin Atlantic*, revised edition. Virgin Books.

6. Francis Elliott and Lewis Smith (2008) Cameron Comes Down against Third Heathrow Runway. *The Times*, 17 June, p. 19.

7. Anthony Bevins (1996) Rallying the Troops for the Ultimate Test. *The Independent*, 23 September, p. 4.

8. Stewart, *Victory Against All the Odds*.

10 High-Speed Rail: False Starts and Big Decisions

1. Steve Melia (2018). Does Transport Investment Really Boost Economic Growth? *World Transport Policy and Practice* 23(3–4), pp. 118–28.
2. Stop HS2 (2010) John Bercow's Speech in Quainton, 23 March. Retrieved from http://stophs2.org/news/81-john-bercows-speech-in-quainton
3. Department for Transport (2010) New High Speed Rail Proposals Unveiled. 20 December. Retrieved from www.gov.uk/government/news/new-high-speed-rail-proposals-unveiled
4. Penny Gaines (2011) 'Scathing Transport Select Committee Report Tells Government to Do High Speed Rail Properly, Not Quickly' Says Stop Hs2. Press release from Stop HS2. Retrieved from http://stophs2.org/news/3688-tsc-report-properly-not-quickly

11 HS2: 'On Time and On Budget'

1. *HS2 Action Alliance Limited, Buckinghamshire County Council & Others, Heathrow Hub Limited & Another versus Secretary of State for Transport.* Court of Appeal (Civil Division), EWCA Civ 920, 24 July 2013. Retrieved from www.judiciary.uk/wp-content/uploads/JCO/Documents/Judgments/hs2-approved-judgment.pdf
2. Andrew Gilligan (2018) HS2 Covered up Petrifying Overspends. *The Sunday Times*, 17 June.
3. See for example B. Flyvbjerg (2014) What You Should Know about Megaprojects and Why: An Overview. *Project Management Journal* 45(2), pp. 6–19.
4. Roger Hargreaves (2016) Letter to Cooke, Mike. High-Speed Rail (London to West Midlands) Bill. 23 February. Retrieved from http://news.camden.gov.uk/download/148683/160223londonboroughofcamden-mainpetitionassuranceletter23-02-2016.pdf?10000
5. Glassdoor (2017) High-Speed 2. Retrieved from www.glassdoor.co.uk/Reviews/Employee-Review-High-Speed-Two-RVW14334598.htm
6. Mark Leftly (2016) HS2 in Danger of Coming off the Rails as Problems Multiply; Exclusive: National Audit Office probe and Cabinet Office Review Add to Uncertainty over the Project. *The Independent*, 5 March. Retrieved from www.independent.co.uk/news/uk/home-news/hs2-national-audit-office-and-cabinet-review-poor-scorn-on-railway-plans-a6914261.html
7. Gilligan, HS2 Covered up Petrifying Overspends.
8. Tim Clark (2019) HS2 Issues Legal Threat to Whistleblowers. *New Civil Engineer*, 18 September.
9. Edward Malnick (2019) HS2 Papers that 'Could Lead to Ministers Scrapping the Rail Line' to Be Released. *Daily Telegraph*, 18 October.
10. *Daily Mail* (2019) HS2 Whitewash. *Daily Mail*, 13 November.

11. Lord Berkeley (2020) A Review of High Speed 2 Dissenting Report. 5 January. Retrieved from https://documentcloud.adobe. com/link/review?uri=urn%3Aaaid%3Ascds%3AUS%3A8e9c8f87-2650-4aa0-8e0f-0eaf6e709640#pageNum=1

12. Gwyn Topham (2020) Oakervee Report Gives Boris Johnson Cover for HS2 Decision. *The Guardian*, 11 February.

12 Return to Road-building and Airport Expansion (2010–17)

1. Janan Ganesh (2012) *George Osborne: The Austerity Chancellor*. Biteback Publishing.

2. Chatterjee et al., Young People's Travel.

3. Norman Baker (2015) *Against the Grain*. Biteback Publishing. This supplemented the interview I did with Norman Baker.

4. Ganesh, *George Osborne*.

5. B. Clift (2018) *The IMF and the Politics of Austerity in the Wake of the Global Financial Crisis*. Oxford University Press; and IMF (2012) *Country Report No. 12/190*. Retrieved from www.imf.org.

6. Baker, *Against the Grain*.

7. George Eaton (2012) No. 10 Refuses to Deny Cameron Call to 'Get Rid of All the Green Crap'. *New Statesman*, 21 November.

8. N. Carter and B. Clements (2015) From 'Greenest Government Ever' to 'Get Rid of All the Green Crap': David Cameron, the Conservatives and the Environment. *British Politics* 10(2), pp. 204–25.

9. For a summary see R. Behrens, and L. A. Kane (2004) Road Capacity Change and its Impact on Traffic in Congested Networks: Evidence and Implications. *Development Southern Africa* 21(4), pp. 587–602.

10. Melia, Why Did UK Governments Cut Road Building in the 1990s and Expand it after 2010?

11. S. Griggs and D. Howarth (2013) 'Between a Rock and a Hard Place': The Coalition, the Davies Commission and the Wicked Issue of Airport Expansion. *The Political Quarterly* 84(4), pp. 515–26.

12. Robert Lea (2011) You're Getting it All Wrong on Airports, CBI Tells Cameron. *The Times*, 18 November, p. 31.

13. Toby Helm and Jamie Doward (2012) Top Tories Admit: We Got it Wrong on Heathrow: Ministers to Rethink Runway Pledge. *The Observer*, 25 March, p. 1.

14. Donata Huggins (2012) There's No Way Out of this Ugly Reshuffle for David Cameron. *Daily Telegraph*, 3 May.

15. Baker, *Against the Grain*.

16. Melia, Why Did UK Governments Cut Road Building in the 1990s and Expand it after 2010?

17. Rail fares grew by 20% more than inflation bus fares by inflation plus 42%. DfT (2019) Table TSGB1308 Retail and Consumer Prices Indices, Transport Components: From 1997. Retrieved from https://assets.

publishing.service.gov.uk/government/uploads/system/uploads/attach-ment_data/file/852493/tsgb1308.ods

13 The Climate Rebellion Begins

1. Y. Xu and V. Ramanathan (2017) Well Below 2°C: Mitigation Strategies for Avoiding Dangerous to Catastrophic Climate Changes. *Proceedings of the National Academy of Sciences* 114(39), pp. 10,315–23.
2. Retrieved from https://extinctionrebellion.uk/the-truth/about-us.
3. See Erica Chenoweth (2013) The Success of Nonviolent Civil Resistance: Erica Chenoweth at TEDxBoulder. Retrieved from www.youtube.com/watch?v=YJSehRlU34w
4. B. Bond and Z. Exley (2016) *Rules for Revolutionaries: How Big Organizing Can Change Everything.* Chelsea Green Publishing.
5. George Monbiot (2018) As the Fracking Protesters Show, a People's Rebellion is the Only Way to Fight Climate Change. *The Guardian,* 18 October.
6. See Gene Sharp (1973) *The Politics of Nonviolent Action.* P. Sargent.
7. Referring to the music festival that took place there in 1969.

14 The Climate Emergency Changes the Transport World

1. Solomon Hughes (2019) Group That Called Extinction Rebellion 'Extremist' is Funded by Big Energy. *Vice,* 19 August. Retrieved from www.vice.com/en_uk/article/ywagdx/policy-exchange-extinction-rebellion-funding
2. Jim Pickard (2019) UK Net Zero Emissions Target Will 'Cost More than £1tn'. *Financial Times,* 5 June.
3. His evidence can be downloaded from www.stevemelia.co.uk/pe.pdf
4. The false statement is: 'For 22 years I have been acting, in my diet, in my work, and in all aspects of my life to combat climate change.' I did not mention diet; I was referring to my written statement to the court which explained my decisions to stop flying and driving. If you read the *Daily Mail's* coverage of flying by XR's supporters, you will realise why they chose not to correct this apparently trivial error.
5. M. Grant (2019) Eco-zealots and Hardline Remainers Are Driven by Their Feelings, Not Facts. *Daily Telegraph,* 7 August.
6. Katrin Scheib (2019) Roger Hallam Calls Holocaust 'Just Another Fuckery in Human History'. *Die Zeit,* 20 November.
7. Internal analysis by XR's Feedback and Learning Culture Circle.
8. Annette Smith, technical director of Mott McDonald.
9. Melia, Why Did UK Governments Cut Road Building in the 1990s and Expand it after 2010?
10. The case was mentioned in parliament and widely reported in the media, describing events such as police officers apparently making monkey

chants as Alder lay dying, the body swap after his death and how the police spied on his family as they campaigned for justice. See e.g. James Campbell (2019) Death in Custody, Bodies in Wrong Graves and a Sister Fighting for Justice: The Full Christopher Alder Story. *Hull Daily Mail*, 3 March; and Vikram Dodd (2002) Monkey Chants as Black Man Died 'Not Racist'. *The Guardian*, 23 July.

11. Roger Hallam (2020) Extinction Rebellion America Mobilization #01: Our Plan for Success – Mass Civil Disobedience. Retrieved from www.youtube.com/watch?v=mBTyo-uxhrg

12. Geoff Dembicki (2020) A Debate Over Racism Has Split One of the World's Most Famous Climate Groups. *Vice*, 28 April. Retrieved from www.vice.com/en_uk/article/jgey8k/a-debate-over-racism-has-split-one-of-the-worlds-most-famous-climate-groups

13. Rupert Read and Samuel Alexander (2020) *Extinction Rebellion: Insights from the Inside*. Simplicity Institute.

15 Protest and the Limits to Growth of Transport

1. Melia, Does Transport Investment Really Boost Economic Growth?

2. This section draws on many different sources, some of which have already been cited, some of which are listed below.

3. Brian Doherty (2005) *Ideas and Actions in the Green Movement*. Routledge.

4. See Doherty, *Ideas and Actions in the Green Movement*; Wall, *Earth First! and the Anti-Roads Movement*; and Graeme A Hayes, Brian Doherty, Christopher Rootes (2016) Social Movement Studies in Britain: No Longer the Poor Relation? In Guya Accornero and Olivier Fillieuleeds (eds), *Social Movement Studies in Europe: The State of the Art*. Berghahn Books, pp. 191–213.

5. Mark Engler and Paul Engler (2016) *This is an Uprising: How Nonviolent Revolt is Shaping the Twenty-First Century*. Bold Type Books.

6. Maria J. Stephan and Erica Chenoweth (2008) Why Civil Resistance Works: The Strategic Logic of Nonviolent Conflict. *International Security* 33(1), pp. 7–44.

7. Erica Chenoweth (2013) My Talk at TEDx Boulder: Civil Resistance and the '3.5% Rule'. Retrieved from https://rationalinsurgent.com/2013/11/04/my-talk-at-tedxboulder-civil-resistance-and-the-3-5-rule.

8. Edwin Amenta, Neal Caren, Elizabeth Chiarello and Yang Su (2010) The Political Consequences of Social Movements. *Annual Review of Sociology* 36, pp. 287–307.

9. Ibid.

10. Ibid.

11. Kathleen D. Vohs, Nicole L. Mead and Miranda R. Goode (2006) The Psychological Consequences of Money. *Science* 314(5802), pp. 1154–6.

12. Genevieve Giuliano and Sandip Chakrabarti. Download as PDF. (2018) Does Light Rail Reduce Traffic? The Case of the LA Expo Line. Trans-

fers Magazine, Fall. Retrieved from https://transfersmagazine.org/magazine-article/does-light-rail-reduce-traffic; Richard D. Knowles (1996) Transport Impacts of Greater Manchester's Metrolink Light Rail System. *Journal of Transport Geography* 4(1), pp. 1–14.

13. Julia Allwood et al. (2019) Absolute Zero. Retrieved from https://doi.org/10.17863/CAM.46075

14. Donella H. Meadows, Dennis L. Meadows, Jørgen Randers and William W. Behrens III (1972) *The Limits to Growth: A Report for the Club of Rome's Project on the Predicament of Mankind.* Pan Books.

15. National Biodiversity Network (2019) *State of Nature 2019.* National Biodiversity Network. Retrieved from https://nbn.org.uk.

16. Steve Melia (in press) Road Building, Urbanisation and Loss of Countryside. *World Transport Policy and Practice.*

17. J. E. Underhill and P. G. Angold (1999) Effects of Roads on Wildlife in an Intensively Modified Landscape. *Environmental Reviews* 8(1), pp. 21–39.

18. Rupert Read and Samuel Alexander's *Extinction Rebellion* comes to some similar conclusions.

Afterword

1. @UNFCC (2020) A Dataviz by @ZLabe Showing Diminishing Arctic Sea Ice along the Siberian Coast, Based on Data from the National Snow and Ice Data Center. 25 June. Retrieved from https://twitter.com/UNFCCC

2. Roger Harrabin (2020) Coronavirus Will Transform UK Work and Travel, says AA. BBC, 3 April. Retrieved from www.bbc.co.uk/news/science-environment-52137968

3. DfT (2019) Table NTS0409a. Average Number of Trips (Trip Rates) by Purpose and Main Mode: England, from 2002. Retrieved from https://assets.publishing.service.gov.uk/government/uploads/system/uploads/attachment_data/file/905956/nts0409.ods

4. P. Zhu (2012) Are Telecommuting and Personal Travel Complements or Substitutes? *The Annals of Regional Science* 48(2), pp. 619–39.

5. This article is a good example of how to use valid arguments in support of invalid conclusions: George Monbiot (2009) Stop Blaming the Poor: It's the Wally Yachters Who Are Burning the Planet. *The Guardian*, 28 September.

6. BBC Somerset (2020) Bristol Airport to Appeal against Rejected Expansion Plans. 6 August. Retrieved from www.bbc.co.uk/news/uk-england-somerset-53682129

7. UN News (2020) Fall in COVID-Linked Carbon Emissions Won't Halt Climate Change – UN Weather Agency Chief. UN News, 22 April. Retrieved from https://news.un.org/en/story/2020/04/1062332

8. Kevin Anderson, John F. Broderick and Isak Stoddard (2020) A Factor of Two: How the Mitigation Plans of 'Climate Progressive' Nations Fall Far Short of Paris-Compliant Pathways. *Climate Policy*, online first. Retrieved from https://doi.org/10.1080/14693062.2020.1728209

9. Read, Rupert and Alexander, Samuel (2020) *Extinction Rebellion: Insights from the Inside.* Simplicity Institute.

10. Read and Alexander, *Extinction Rebellion.*

11. David Rose (2020) Revealed: Extinction Rebellion's Plan to Exploit the Covid Crisis. *The Spectator*, 4 April.

12. Andrew Forster (2020) Economic Damage of Covid-19 Means CAZ Must Be Delayed, Says Bristol. *Local Transport Today* 797 (1 May), p. 4.

13. Steve Melia (2020) College Green Air Quality Talk. Retrieved from www.youtube.com/watch?v=idt7Hhkl630

14. Amanda Cameron (2020) 'It's Privilege Activism' – Mayor Marvin Rees Slams XR Protesters Over City Hall 'Stunt'. *Bristol Post*, 2 July.

Index

Thanks to our Patreon Subscribers:

Abdul Alkalimat
Andrew Perry

Who have shown their generosity and comradeship in difficult times.

Printed and bound by CPI Group (UK) Ltd, Croydon, CR0 4YY